Incidents in the Life
of a Slave Girl

THE SCHOMBURG LIBRARY OF
NINETEENTH-CENTURY BLACK WOMEN WRITERS

General Editor, Henry Louis Gates, Jr.

Titles are listed chronologically; collections that include works published over a span of years are listed according to the publication date of their initial work.

Phillis Wheatley, *The Collected Works of Phillis Wheatley*

Six Women's Slave Narratives: M. Prince; Old Elizabeth; M. J. Jackson; L. A. Delaney; K. Drumgoold; A. L. Burton

Spiritual Narratives: M. W. Stewart; J. Lee; J. A. J. Foote; V. W. Broughton

Ann Plato, *Essays*

Collected Black Women's Narratives: N. Prince; L. Picquet; B. Veney; S. K. Taylor

Frances E. W. Harper, *Complete Poems of Frances E. W. Harper*

Charlotte Forten Grimké, *The Journals of Charlotte Forten Grimké*

Mary Seacole, *Wonderful Adventures of Mrs. Seacole in Many Lands*

Harriet Jacobs, *Incidents in the Life of a Slave Girl*

Collected Black Women's Poetry, Volumes 1–4: M. E. Tucker; A. I. Menken; M. W. Fordham; P. J. Thompson; C. A. Thompson; H. C. Ray; L. A. J. Moorer; J. D. Heard; E. Bibb; M. P. Johnson; Mrs. H. Linden

Elizabeth Keckley, *Behind the Scenes. Or, Thirty Years a Slave, and Four Years in the White House*

C. W. Larison, M.D., *Silvia Dubois, A Biografy of the Slav Who Whipt Her Mistres and Gand Her Fredom*

Mrs. A. E. Johnson, *Clarence and Corinne; or, God's Way*

Octavia V. Rogers Albert, *The House of Bondage: or Charlotte Brooks and Other Slaves*

Emma Dunham Kelley, *Megda*

Anna Julia Cooper, *A Voice From the South*

Frances E. W. Harper, *Iola Leroy, or Shadows Uplifted*

Amanda Smith, *An Autobiography: The Story of the Lord's Dealings with Mrs. Amanda Smith the Colored Evangelist*

Mrs. A. E. Johnson, *The Hazeley Family*

Mrs. N. F. Mossell, *The Work of the Afro-American Woman*

Alice Dunbar-Nelson, *The Works of Alice Dunbar-Nelson*, Volumes 1–3

Emma D. Kelley-Hawkins, *Four Girls at Cottage City*

Pauline E. Hopkins, *Contending Forces: A Romance Illustrative of Negro Life North and South*

Pauline Hopkins, *The Magazine Novels of Pauline Hopkins*

Hallie Q. Brown, *Homespun Heroines and Other Women of Distinction*

Incidents in the Life of a Slave Girl

HARRIET JACOBS

With an Introduction by
VALERIE SMITH

❧ ❧ ❧

❧ ❧ ❧

OXFORD UNIVERSITY PRESS
New York   Oxford

Oxford University Press

Oxford   New York   Toronto
Delhi   Bombay   Calcutta   Madras   Karachi
Petaling Jaya   Singapore   Hong Kong   Tokyo
Nairobi   Dar es Salaam   Cape Town
Melbourne   Auckland

and associated companies in
Berlin   Ibadan

Library of Congress Cataloging-in-Publication Data

Jacobs, Harriet A. (Harriet Ann), 1813–1897
Incidents in the life of a slave girl.
(The Schomburg library of nineteenth-century black
women writers)
1. Jacobs, Harriet A. (Harriet Ann), 1813–1897.
2. Slaves—United States—Biography.   3. Women
slaves—United States—Biography.   I. Title.
II. Series.
E444.J17A3   1988   973′.0496024 [B]   87-28261
ISBN 0-19-505243-9
ISBN 0-19-505267-6 (set)
ISBN 0-19-506670-7 (PBK.)

17 19 20 18 16

Printed in the United States of America
on acid-free paper

The
Schomburg Library
of
Nineteenth-Century
Black Women Writers
is
Dedicated
in Memory
of
PAULINE AUGUSTA COLEMAN GATES

1916–1987

PUBLISHER'S NOTE

FOREWORD
In Her Own Write

Henry Louis Gates, Jr.

> One muffled strain in the Silent South, a jarring chord and a
> vague and uncomprehended cadenza has been and still is the
> Negro. And of that muffled chord, the one mute and voice-
> less note has been the sadly expectant Black Woman, ...
>
> The "other side" has not been represented by one who "lives
> there." And not many can more sensibly realize and more
> accurately tell the weight and the fret of the "long dull pain"
> than the open-eyed but hitherto voiceless Black Woman of
> America.
>
> . . . as our Caucasian barristers are not to blame if they
> cannot *quite* put themselves in the dark man's place, neither
> should the dark man be wholly expected fully and adequately
> to reproduce the exact Voice of the Black Woman.
>
> —ANNA JULIA COOPER, *A Voice From the South* (1892)

The birth of the Afro-American literary tradition occurred
in 1773, when Phillis Wheatley published a book of poetry.
Despite the fact that her book garnered for her a remarkable
amount of attention, Wheatley's journey to the printer had
been a most arduous one. Sometime in 1772, a young African girl walked demurely into a room in Boston to undergo
an oral examination, the results of which would determine
the direction of her life and work. Perhaps she was shocked
upon entering the appointed room. For there, perhaps gath-

ered in a semicircle, sat eighteen of Boston's most notable citizens. Among them were John Erving, a prominent Boston merchant; the Reverend Charles Chauncy, pastor of the Tenth Congregational Church; and John Hancock, who would later gain fame for his signature on the Declaration of Independence. At the center of this group was His Excellency, Thomas Hutchinson, governor of Massachusetts, with Andrew Oliver, his lieutenant governor, close by his side.

Why had this august group been assembled? Why had it seen fit to summon this young African girl, scarcely eighteen years old, before it? This group of "the most respectable Characters in *Boston*," as it would later define itself, had assembled to question closely the African adolescent on the slender sheaf of poems that she claimed to have "written by herself." We can only speculate on the nature of the questions posed to the fledgling poet. Perhaps they asked her to identify and explain—for all to hear—exactly who were the Greek and Latin gods and poets alluded to so frequently in her work. Perhaps they asked her to conjugate a verb in Latin or even to translate randomly selected passages from the Latin, which she and her master, John Wheatley, claimed that she "had made some Progress in." Or perhaps they asked her to recite from memory key passages from the texts of John Milton and Alexander Pope, the two poets by whom the African claimed to be most directly influenced. We do not know.

We do know, however, that the African poet's responses were more than sufficient to prompt the eighteen august gentlemen to compose, sign, and publish a two-paragraph "Attestation," an open letter "To the Publick" that prefaces Phillis Wheatley's book and that reads in part:

> We whose Names are under-written, do assure the World, that the Poems specified in the following Page, were (as we

verily believe) written by Phillis, a young Negro Girl, who
was but a few Years since, brought an uncultivated Barbarian
from *Africa,* and has ever since been, and now is, under the
Disadvantage of serving as a Slave in a Family in this Town.
She has been examined by some of the best Judges, and is
thought qualified to write them.

So important was this document in securing a publisher for
Wheatley's poems that it forms the signal element in the
prefatory matter preceding her *Poems on Various Subjects, Religious and Moral,* published in London in 1773.

Without the published "Attestation," Wheatley's publisher
claimed, few would believe that an African could possibly
have written poetry all by herself. As the eighteen put the
matter clearly in their letter, "Numbers would be ready to
suspect they were not really the Writings of Phillis." Wheatley and her master, John Wheatley, had attempted to publish
a similar volume in 1772 in Boston, but Boston publishers
had been incredulous. One year later, "Attestation" in hand,
Phillis Wheatley and her master's son, Nathaniel Wheatley,
sailed for England, where they completed arrangements for
the publication of a volume of her poems with the aid of the
Countess of Huntington and the Earl of Dartmouth.

This curious anecdote, surely one of the oddest oral ex-
aminations on record, is only a tiny part of a larger, and
even more curious, episode in the Enlightenment. Since the
beginning of the sixteenth century, Europeans had wondered aloud whether or not the African "species of men," as
they were most commonly called, *could* ever create formal
literature, could ever master "the arts and sciences." If they
could, the argument ran, then the African variety of humanity was fundamentally related to the European variety. If not,
then it seemed clear that the African was destined by nature

to be a slave. This was the burden shouldered by Phillis
Wheatley when she successfully defended herself and the au-
thorship of her book against counterclaims and doubts.

Indeed, with her successful defense, Wheatley launched
two traditions at once—the black American literary tradition
and the black woman's literary tradition. If it is extraordinary
that not just one but both of these traditions were founded
simultaneously by a black woman—certainly an event unique
in the history of literature—it is also ironic that this important fact of common, coterminous literary origins seems to
have escaped most scholars.

That the progenitor of the black literary tradition was a
woman means, in the most strictly literal sense, that all subsequent black writers have evolved in a matrilinear line of
descent, and that each, consciously or unconsciously, has extended and revised a canon whose foundation was the poetry
of a black woman. Early black writers seem to have been
keenly aware of Wheatley's founding role, even if most of
her white reviewers were more concerned with the implica-
tions of her race than her gender. Jupiter Hammon, for example, whose 1760 broadside "An Evening Thought. Sal-
vation by Christ, With Penitential Cries" was the first
individual poem published by a black American, acknowledged Wheatley's influence by selecting her as the subject of
his second broadside, "An Address to Miss Phillis Wheatly
[*sic*], Ethiopian Poetess, in Boston," which was published at
Hartford in 1778. And George Moses Horton, the second
Afro-American to publish a book of poetry in English (1829),
brought out in 1838 an edition of his *Poems By A Slave*
bound together with Wheatley's work. Indeed, for fifty-six
years, between 1773 and 1829, when Horton published *The
Hope of Liberty*, Wheatley was the *only* black person to have
published a book of imaginative literature in English. So

central was this black woman's role in the shaping of the
Afro-American literary tradition that, as one historian has
maintained, the history of the reception of Phillis Wheatley's
poetry *is* the history of Afro-American literary criticism. Well
into the nineteenth century, Wheatley and the black literary
tradition were the same entity.

But Wheatley is not the only black woman writer who
stands as a pioneering figure in Afro-American literature.
Just as Wheatley gave birth to the genre of black poetry, Ann
Plato was the first Afro-American to publish a book of essays
(1841) and Harriet E. Wilson was the first black person to
publish a novel in the United States (1859).

Despite this pioneering role of black women in the tradition, however, many of their contributions before this century have been all but lost or unrecognized. As Hortense
Spillers observed as recently as 1983,

> With the exception of a handful of autobiographical narratives
> from the nineteenth century, the black woman's realities are
> virtually suppressed until the period of the Harlem Renais-
> sance and later. Essentially the black woman as artist, as
> intellectual spokesperson for her own cultural apprenticeship,
> has not existed before, for anyone. At the source of [their]
> own symbol-making task, [the community of black women
> writers] confronts, therefore, a tradition of work that is quite
> recent, its continuities, broken and sporadic.

Until now, it has been extraordinarily difficult to establish
the formal connections between early black women's writing
and that of the present, precisely because our knowledge of
their work has been broken and sporadic. Phillis Wheatley,
for example, while certainly the most reprinted and discussed
poet in the tradition, is also one of the least understood. Ann
Plato's seminal work, *Essays* (which includes biographies and
poems), has not been reprinted since it was published a cen-

tury and a half ago. And Harriet Wilson's *Our Nig,* her
compelling novel of a black woman's expanding consciousness in a racist Northern antebellum environment, never received even *one* review or comment at a time when virtually
all works written by black people were heralded by abolitionists as salient arguments against the existence of human slavery. Many of the books reprinted in this set experienced a
similar fate, the most dreadful fate for an author: that of
being ignored then relegated to the obscurity of the rare book
section of a university library. We can only wonder how
many other texts in the black woman's tradition have been
lost to this generation of readers or remain unclassified or
uncatalogued and, hence, unread.

This was not always so, however. Black women writers
dominated the final decade of the nineteenth century, perhaps
spurred to publish by an 1886 essay entitled "The Coming
American Novelist," which was published in *Lippincott's
Monthly Magazine* and written by "A Lady From Philadelphia." This pseudonymous essay argued that the "Great
American Novel" would be written by a black person. Her
argument is so curious that it deserves to be repeated:

> When we come to formulate our demands of the Coming
> American Novelist, we will agree that he must be native-
> born. His ancestors may come from where they will, but we
> must give him a birthplace and have the raising of him. Still,
> the longer his family has been here the better he will represent
> us. Suppose he should have no country but ours, no traditions
> but those he has learned here, no longings apart from us, no
> future except in our future—the orphan of the world, he
> finds with us his home. And with all this, suppose he refuses
> to be fused into that grand conglomerate we call the "Amer-
> ican type." With us, he is not of us. He is original, he has
> humor, he is tender, he is passive and fiery, he has been

taught what we call justice, and he has his own opinion about it. He has suffered everything a poet, a dramatist, a novelist need suffer before he comes to have his lips anointed. And with it all he is in one sense a spectator, a little out of the race. How would these conditions go towards forming an original development? In a word, suppose the coming novelist is of African origin? When one comes to consider the subject, there is no improbability in it. One thing is certain,—our great novel will not be written by the typical American.

An atypical American, indeed. Not only would the great American novel be written by an African-American, it would be written by an African-American *woman:*

Yet farther: I have used the generic masculine pronoun because it is convenient; but Fate keeps revenge in store. It was a woman who, taking the wrongs of the African as her theme, wrote the novel that awakened the world to their reality, and why should not the coming novelist be a woman as well as an African? She—the woman of that race—has some claims on Fate which are not yet paid up.

It is these claims on fate that we seek to pay by publishing The Schomburg Library of Nineteenth-Century Black Women Writers.

This theme would be repeated by several black women authors, most notably by Anna Julia Cooper, a prototypical black feminist whose 1892 *A Voice From the South* can be considered to be one of the original texts of the black feminist movement. It was Cooper who first analyzed the fallacy of referring to "the Black man" when speaking of black people and who argued that just as white men cannot speak through the consciousness of black men, neither can black *men* "fully and adequately . . . reproduce the exact Voice of the Black Woman." Gender and race, she argues, cannot be conflated, except in the instance of a black woman's voice, and it is this voice which must be uttered and to which we must listen. As Cooper puts the matter so compellingly:

> It is not the intelligent woman vs. the ignorant woman; nor the white woman vs. the black, the brown, and the red,—it is not even the cause of woman vs. man. Nay, 'tis woman's strongest vindication for speaking that *the world needs to hear her voice*. It would be subversive of every human interest that the cry of one-half the human family be stifled. Woman in stepping from the pedestal of statue-like inactivity in the domestic shrine, and daring to think and move and speak,— to undertake to help shape, mold, and direct the thought of her age, is merely completing the circle of the world's vision. Hers is every interest that has lacked an interpreter and a defender. Her cause is linked with that of every agony that has been dumb—every wrong that needs a voice.
>
> It is no fault of man's that he has not been able to see truth from her standpoint. It does credit both to his head and heart that no greater mistakes have been committed or even wrongs perpetrated while she sat making tatting and snipping paper flowers. Man's own innate chivalry and the mutual interdependence of their interests have insured his treating her cause, in the main at least, as his own. And he is pardonably surprised and even a little chagrined, perhaps, to find his legislation not considered "perfectly lovely" in every respect. But in any case his work is only impoverished by her remaining dumb. The world has had to limp along with the wobbling gait and one-sided hesitancy of a man with one eye. Suddenly the bandage is removed from the other eye and the whole body is filled with light. It sees a circle where before it saw a segment. The darkened eye restored, every member rejoices with it.

The myopic sight of the darkened eye can only be restored when the full range of the black woman's voice, with its own special timbres and shadings, remains mute no longer.

Similarly, Victoria Earle Matthews, an author of short stories and essays, and a cofounder in 1896 of the National Association of Colored Women, wrote in her stunning essay, "The Value of Race Literature" (1895), that "when the literature of our race is developed, it will of necessity be different in all essential points of greatness, true heroism and real Christianity from what we may at the present time, for convenience, call American literature." Matthews argued that this great tradition of Afro-American literature would be the textual outlet "for the unnaturally suppressed inner lives which our people have been compelled to lead." Once these "unnaturally suppressed inner lives" of black people are unveiled, no "grander diffusion of mental light" will shine more brightly, she concludes, than that of the articulate Afro-American woman:

> And now comes the question, What part shall we women play in the Race Literature of the future? . . . within the compass of one small journal ["Woman's Era"] we have struck out a new line of departure—a journal, a record of Race interests gathered from all parts of the United States, carefully selected, moistened, winnowed and garnered by the ablest intellects of educated colored women, shrinking at no lofty theme, shirking no serious duty, aiming at every possible excellence, and determined to do their part in the future uplifting of the race.
>
> If twenty women, by their concentrated efforts in one literary movement, can meet with such success as has engendered, planned out, and so successfully consummated this convention, what much more glorious results, what wider spread success, what grander diffusion of mental light will not come forth at the bidding of the enlarged hosts of women writers, already called into being by the stimulus of your efforts?
>
> And here let me speak one word for my journalistic sisters

who have already entered the broad arena of journalism. Before the "Woman's Era" had come into existence, no one except themselves can appreciate the bitter experience and sore disappointments under which they have at all times been compelled to pursue their chosen vocations.

If their brothers of the press have had their difficulties to contend with, I am here as a sister journalist to state, from the fullness of knowledge, that their task has been an easy one compared with that of the colored woman in journalism.

Woman's part in Race Literature, as in Race building, is the most important part and has been so in all ages. . . . All through the most remote epochs she has done her share in literature. . . .

One of the most important aspects of this set is the republication of the salient texts from 1890 to 1910, which literary historians could well call "The Black Woman's Era." In addition to Mary Helen Washington's definitive edition of Cooper's *A Voice From the South*, we have reprinted two novels by Amelia Johnson, Frances Harper's *Iola Leroy*, two novels by Emma Dunham Kelley, Alice Dunbar-Nelson's two impressive collections of short stories, and Pauline Hopkins's three serialized novels as well as her monumental novel, *Contending Forces*—all published between 1890 and 1910. Indeed, black women published more works of fiction in these two decades than black men had published in the previous half century. Nevertheless, this great achievement has been ignored.

Moreover, the writings of nineteenth-century Afro-American women in general have remained buried in obscurity, accessible only in research libraries or in overpriced and poorly edited reprints. Many of these books have never been reprinted at all; in some instances only one or two copies are extant. In these works of fiction, poetry, autobiography, biography, essays, and journalism resides the mind of the nineteenth-century Afro-American woman. Until these works are made readily available to teachers and their students, a significant segment of the black tradition will remain silent.

Oxford University Press, in collaboration with the Schomburg Center for Research in Black Culture, is publishing thirty volumes of these compelling works, each of which contains an introduction by an expert in the field. The set includes such rare texts as Johnson's *The Hazeley Family* and *Clarence and Corinne*, Plato's *Essays*, the most complete edition of Phillis Wheatley's poems and letters, Emma Dunham Kelley's pioneering novel *Megda*, several previously unpublished stories and a novel by Alice Dunbar-Nelson, and the first collected volumes of Pauline Hopkins's three serialized novels and Frances Harper's poetry. We also present four volumes of poetry by such women as Mary Eliza Tucker Lambert, Adah Menken, Josephine Heard, and Maggie Johnson. Numerous slave and spiritual narratives, a newly discovered novel—*Four Girls at Cottage City*—by Emma Dunham Kelley (-Hawkins), and the first American edition of *Wonderful Adventures of Mrs. Seacole in Many Lands* are also among the texts included.

In addition to resurrecting the works of black women authors, it is our hope that this set will facilitate the resurrection of the Afro-American woman's literary tradition itself by unearthing its nineteenth-century roots. In the works of Nella Larsen and Jessie Fauset, Zora Neale Hurston and Ann Petry, Lorraine Hansberry and Gwendolyn Brooks, Paule Marshall and Toni Cade Bambara, Audre Lorde and Rita Dove, Toni Morrison and Alice Walker, Gloria Naylor and Jamaica Kincaid, these roots have branched luxuriantly. The eighteenth- and nineteenth-century authors whose works are presented in this set founded and nurtured the black women's literary tradition, which must be revived, explicated, analyzed, and debated before we can understand more completely the formal shaping of this tradition within a tradition, a coded literary universe through which, regrettably, we are only just beginning to navigate our way. As Anna Cooper said nearly one hundred years ago, we have been blinded by the loss of sight in one eye and have therefore been unable to detect the full *shape* of the Afro-American literary tradition.

Literary works configure into a tradition not because of some mystical collective unconscious determined by the biology of race or gender, but because writers read other writers and *ground* their representations of experience in models of language provided largely by other writers to whom they feel akin. It is through this mode of literary revision, amply evident in the *texts* themselves—in formal echoes, recast metaphors, even in parody—that a "tradition" emerges and defines itself.

This is formal bonding, and it is only through formal bonding that we can know a literary tradition. The collective publication of these works by black women now, for the first time, makes it possible for scholars and critics, male and female, black and white, to *demonstrate* that black women writers read, and revised, other black women writers. To demonstrate this set of formal literary relations is to demonstrate that sexuality, race, and gender are both the condition and the basis of *tradition*—but tradition as found in discrete acts of language use.

A word is in order about the history of this set. For the past decade, I have taught a course, first at Yale and then at Cornell, entitled "Black Women and Their Fictions," a course that I inherited from Toni Morrison, who developed it in

the mid-1970s for Yale's Program in Afro-American Studies. Although the course was inspired by the remarkable ac-
complishments of black women novelists since 1970, I gradually extended its beginning date to the late nineteenth century,
studying Frances Harper's *Iola Leroy* and Anna Julia Cooper's *A Voice From the South*, both published in 1892. With
the discovery of Harriet E. Wilson's seminal novel, *Our Nig*
(1859), and Jean Yellin's authentication of Harriet Jacobs's
brilliant slave narrative, *Incidents in the Life of a Slave Girl*
(1861), a survey course spanning over a century and a quarter
emerged.

But the discovery of *Our Nig*, as well as the interest in
nineteenth-century black women's writing that this discovery
generated, convinced me that even the most curious and
diligent scholars knew very little of the extensive history
of the creative writings of Afro-American women before
1900. Indeed, most scholars of Afro-American literature
had never even read most of the books published by black
women, simply because these books—of poetry, novels, short
stories, essays, and autobiography—were mostly accessible only
in rare book sections of university libraries. For reasons un-
clear to me even today, few of these marvelous renderings of
the Afro-American woman's consciousness were reprinted in
the late 1960s and early 1970s, when so many other texts of
the Afro-American literary tradition were resurrected from
the dark and silent graveyard of the out-of-print and were
reissued in facsimile editions aimed at the hungry readership
for canonical texts in the nascent field of black studies.

So, with the help of several superb research assistants—
including David Curtis, Nicola Shilliam, Wendy Jones, Sam
Otter, Janadas Devan, Suvir Kaul, Cynthia Bond, Elizabeth
Alexander, and Adele Alexander—and with the expert advice

of scholars such as William Robinson, William Andrews, Mary Helen Washington, Maryemma Graham, Jean Yellin, Houston A. Baker, Jr., Richard Yarborough, Hazel Carby, Joan R. Sherman, Frances Foster, and William French, dozens of bibliographies were used to compile a list of books written or narrated by black women mostly before 1910. Without the assistance provided through this shared experience of scholarship, the scholar's true legacy, this project could not have been conceived. As the list grew, I was struck by how very many of these titles that I, for example, had never even heard of, let alone read, such as Ann Plato's *Essays*, Louisa Picquet's slave narrative, or Amelia Johnson's two novels, *Clarence and Corinne* and *The Hazeley Family*. Through our research with the Black Periodical Fiction and Poetry Project (funded by NEH and the Ford Foundation), I also realized that several novels by black women, including three works of fiction by Pauline Hopkins, had been serialized in black periodicals, but had never been collected and published as books. Nor had the several books of poetry published by black women, such as the prolific Frances E. W. Harper, been collected and edited. When I discovered still another "lost" novel by an Afro-American woman (*Four Girls at Cottage City,* published in 1898 by Emma Dunham Kelley-Hawkins), I decided to attempt to edit a collection of reprints of these works and to publish them as a "library" of black women's writings, in part so that I could read them myself.

Convincing university and trade publishers to undertake this project proved to be a difficult task. Despite the commercial success of *Our Nig* and of the several reprint series of women's works (such as Virago, the Beacon Black Women Writers Series, and Rutgers' American Women Writers Series), several presses rejected the project as "too large," "too limited," or as "commercially unviable." Only two publishers recognized the viability and the import of the project and, of these, Oxford's commitment to publish the titles simultaneously as a set made the press's offer irresistible.

While attempting to locate original copies of these exceedingly rare books, I discovered that most of the texts were housed at the Schomburg Center for Research in Black Culture, a branch of The New York Public Library, under the direction of Howard Dodson. Dodson's infectious enthusiasm for the project and his generous collaboration, as well as that of his stellar staff (especially Diana Lachatanere, Sharon Howard, Ellis Haizip, Richard Newman, and Betty Gubert), led to a joint publishing initiative that produced this set as part of the Schomburg's major fund-raising campaign. Without Dodson's foresight and generosity of spirit, the set would not have materialized. Without William P. Sisler's masterful editorship at Oxford and his staff's careful attention to detail, the set would have remained just another grand idea that tends to languish in a scholar's file cabinet.

I would also like to thank Dr. Michael Winston and Dr. Thomas C. Battle, Vice-President of Academic Affairs and the Director of the Moorland-Spingarn Research Center (respectively) at Howard University, for their unending encouragement, support, and collaboration in this project, and Esme E. Bhan at Howard for her meticulous research and bibliographical skills. In addition, I would like to acknowledge the aid of the staff at the libraries of Duke University, Cornell University (especially Tom Weissinger and Donald Eddy), the Boston Public Library, the Western Reserve Historical Society, the Library of Congress, and Yale University. Linda Robbins, Marion Osmun, Sarah Flanagan, and Gerard Case, all members of the staff at Oxford, were

A NOTE FROM
THE SCHOMBURG CENTER

Howard Dodson

The Schomburg Center for Research in Black Culture, The New York Public Library, is pleased to join with Dr. Henry Louis Gates and Oxford University Press in presenting The Schomburg Library of Nineteenth-Century Black Women Writers. This thirty-volume set includes the work of a generation of black women whose writing has only been available previously in rare book collections. The materials reprinted in twenty-four of the thirty volumes are drawn from the unique holdings of the Schomburg Center.

A research unit of The New York Public Library, the Schomburg Center has been in the forefront of those institutions dedicated to collecting, preserving, and providing access to the records of the black past. In the course of its two generations of acquisition and conservation activity, the Center has amassed collections totaling more than 5 million items. They include over 100,000 bound volumes, 85,000 reels and sets of microforms, 300 manuscript collections containing some 3.5 million items, 300,000 photographs and extensive holdings of prints, sound recordings, film and videotape, newspapers, artworks, artifacts, and other book and nonbook materials. Together they vividly document the history and cultural heritages of people of African descent worldwide.

Though established some sixty-two years ago, the Center's book collections date from the sixteenth century. Its oldest item, an Ethiopian Coptic Tunic, dates from the eighth or ninth century. Rare materials, however, are most available for the nineteenth-century African-American experience. It is from these holdings that the majority of the titles selected for inclusion in this set are drawn.

The nineteenth century was a formative period in African-American literary and cultural history. Prior to the Civil War, the majority of black Americans living in the United States were held in bondage. Law and practice forbade teaching them to read or write. Even after the war, many of the impediments to learning and literary productivity remained. Nevertheless, black men and women of the nineteenth century persevered in both areas. Moreover, more African-Americans than we yet realize turned their observations, feelings, social viewpoints, and creative impulses into published works. In time, this nineteenth-century printed record included poetry, short stories, histories, novels, autobiographies, social criticism, and theology, as well as economic and philosophical treatises. Unfortunately, much of this body of literature remained, until very recently, relatively inaccessible to twentieth-century scholars, teachers, creative artists, and others interested in black life. Prior to the late 1960s, most Americans (black as well as white) had never heard of these nineteenth-century authors, much less read their works.

The civil rights and black power movements created unprecedented interest in the thought, behavior, and achievements of black people. Publishers responded by revising traditional texts, introducing the American public to a new generation of African-American writers, publishing a variety of thematic anthologies, and reprinting a plethora of "classic texts" in African-American history, literature, and art. The reprints usually appeared as individual titles or in a series of bound volumes or microform formats.

The Schomburg Center, which has a long history of supporting publishing that deals with the history and culture of Africans in diaspora, became an active participant in many of the reprint revivals of the 1960s. Since hard copies of original printed works are the preferred formats for producing facsimile reproductions, publishers frequently turned to the Schomburg Center for copies of these original titles. In addition to providing such material, Schomburg Center staff members offered advice and consultation, wrote introductions, and occasionally entered into formal copublishing arrangements in some projects.

Most of the nineteenth-century titles reprinted during the 1960s, however, were by and about black men. A few black women were included in the longer series, but works by lesser known black women were generally overlooked. The Schomburg Library of Nineteenth-Century Black Women Writers is both a corrective to these previous omissions and an important contribution to Afro-American literary history in its own right. Through this collection of volumes, the thoughts, perspectives, and creative abilities of nineteenth-century African-American women, as captured in books and pamphlets published in large part before 1910, are again being made available to the general public. The Schomburg Center is pleased to be a part of this historic endeavor.

I would like to thank Professor Gates for initiating this project. Thanks are due both to him and Mr. William P. Sisler of Oxford University Press for giving the Schomburg Center an opportunity to play such a prominent role in the set. Thanks are also due to my colleagues at The New York Public Library and the Schomburg Center, especially Dr. Vartan Gregorian, Richard De Gennaro, Paul Fasana, Betsy

INTRODUCTION

Valerie Smith

Published in 1861, Harriet Jacobs's *Incidents in the Life of a Slave Girl* is one of the last of over a hundred slave narratives published separately before the Civil War. Although these autobiographical accounts represent the earliest genre in which large numbers of black Americans wrote, the overwhelming majority of the slave narrators were male.[1] As one of the few extant narratives written by a woman, Jacobs's *Incidents* (written under the pseudonym of Linda Brent) provides a unique perspective on the complex position of the black woman as slave and as writer. In her account of her experience and in her search for her own voice, Jacobs confronts the contradictions that inhere in the category "the black woman writer." By engaging these issues and negotiating a course through them, she anticipates the literary and ideological position of subsequent generations of black women writers.

Slave narratives are in general highly formulaic accounts of the journey from slavery to freedom. The plots are predetermined. Most are framed by prefaces, testimonials, and postscripts witten by white abolitionists and editors. Most also contain detailed descriptions of whippings, slave auctions, and other instances of slaveholders' cruelty.[2] Moreover, many of the more prominent male-authored accounts describe the process of self-liberation in similar terms. For narrators such as Frederick Douglass and William Wells Brown, for instance, the path to freedom was marked by the acquisition of literacy, the physical mastery over the slaveholder or overseer, and the solitary journey North.

Deborah Gray White and Hazel Carby argue that historians and literary critics have traditionally assumed that the patterns of the narratives provide reliable representations of slave life. They and other recent feminist scholars, however, have demonstrated that while these patterns might reflect the experience of certain kinds of male slaves, they ignore the unique features of the slave woman's existence.[3]

It is conceivable that the narrators of male-authored accounts were able to represent themselves as solitary figures because the circumstances of their captivity granted them a greater degree of relative autonomy than that allowed to female slaves. As White argues, "the division of labor on most plantations conferred greater mobility on male than on female slaves." She continues:

> Few of the chores performed by bondwomen took them off the plantation. Usually masters chose their male slaves to assist in the transportation of crops to market, and the transport of supplies and other materials to the plantation. More male than female slaves were artisans and craftsmen, and this made it more difficult to hire out a female slave than a male slave.[4]

In addition, women slaves were more likely than men to be tied to the plantation by the demands of child care; moreover, men were more likely than women to be sold separately from their offspring.[5] Factors such as these underscore important differences between the nature of male and female slavery in the American South and suggest why male slave narrators would figure themselves as self-sustaining individuals.[6]

Mary Helen Washington and I have argued that by representing themselves as isolated heroic subjects, male slave narrators also defined their humanity in the terms of prevailing conceptions of American male identity:[7]

> By mythologizing rugged individuality, physical strength, and geographical mobility, the narratives enshrine cultural definitions of masculinity. The plot of the standard narrative may thus be seen as not only the journey from slavery to freedom but also the journey from slavehood to manhood.[8]

William Wells Brown's account turns, for instance, on the moment when a Quaker friend renames him, saying, "Since thee has got out of slavery, thee has become a man."[9] Frederick Douglass describes his transformations in the same way. Learning to read made him a man, but being beaten made him a slave. By overpowering his overseer, he regains the condition of symbolic freedom upon which his physical and geographical liberation are predicated.

By contrast, Harriet Jacobs underscores her reliance on other people and in so doing reveals that the story of slavery and escape might be written differently. In at least one specific place in her narrative she makes obvious her problematic relation to the masculinist rhetoric that characterizes the slave narrative as genre. The title of the fourth chapter, "The Slave who Dared to Feel like a Man," recalls one of the most familiar lines from Douglass's 1845 *Narrative:* "You have seen how a man was made a slave; you shall see how a slave was made a man.[10] Here Jacobs links several anecdotes to illustrate the fact that independence of mind is incompatible with the demands of life as a slave. She begins with a scene in which her grandmother urges her family to content themselves with their lot as slaves; her son Ben and her grandchildren, however, cannot help resenting her admonitions. The chapter then centers on the story of Ben, Linda Brent's uncle. Retaliating when his master tries to beat him and eventually escaping to the North, Ben is the one to whom the chapter title explicitly refers; he is the slave who, by defending himself, dares to feel like a man. And yet the title might also refer to two other stories included in the chapter. In one story, Brent's brother, William, refuses to capitulate to his master's authority. In another, Linda describes her own earliest resolution to resist her master's advances. Although the situation does not yet require her to fight back, she does say that her young arm never felt half so strong. Like her uncle and brother, she determines to remain unvanquished.

The chapter therefore indicates that Linda and William can resist authority as well as their Uncle Ben can. The chapter title's exclusive reference to a male slave, however, indirectly suggests that as long as the rhetoric of the slave narrative identifies freedom and independence of thought with manhood, it lacks a category for describing the achievements of the tenacious black woman.

The conventions of the male-authored narratives thus conflate the experience of slavery and freedom with prevailing definitions of masculinity. The form and rhetoric might broadly suit the outline of the slave woman's quest for liberation, but they inadequately capture the specifics of her experience. They rarely feature protagonists who suffer over the separation from their families or who bring relatives North with them. More importantly, they fail to represent the slave woman's sexual vulnerability, the crucial fact that differentiated her experience from that of her male counterparts.

The value of male slaves was primarily determined by the work they performed for whites. The value of female slaves derived not only from their work, but also from their ability to bear and rear children, the human property upon which the slave system depended. The slave codes drew no distinction between the slave's sexual autonomy and the master's property rights; slave women were thus subject to rape and to forced liaisons that both satisfied their masters' sexual desires and increased their capital accumulation.

As Carby demonstrates, slave women, figures of secondary importance within male-authored narratives, are represented in these contexts as victims of sexual abuse.[11] Rare indeed is the account that provides glimpses of the interior lives or survival strategies of women so victimized. Linda Brent certainly experienced this kind of abuse. She fought off the advances of her master Dr. Flint for many years, ultimately taking another white man, Mr. Sands, as her lover and bearing two of his children in order to protect herself. In order to tell of her sexual vulnerability, a condition that the techniques and conventions of the slave narrative could not adequately represent, Jacobs employed the techniques of the sentimental novel.

Jacobs's use of these techniques makes sense when we consider that the sentimental novel was popular among the white women readers to whom her book was addressed. The form allowed her to identify with both her readers and the protagonists of sentimental fiction. It also provided her with the means by which to cast her story of virtue under siege. Like her readers, she aspired to chastity and piety as consummate feminine virtues and hoped that marriage and family would be her earthly reward. As her account details, her master, though reluctant to force her to submit sexually, still harasses her, pleads with her, and tries to bribe her into capitulating to his desires. As such, he resembles an importunate suitor like Mr. B., the seducer in Samuel Richardson's

Pamela. Dr. Flint tells Brent, for example, that he would be within his rights to kill her or have her imprisoned for resisting his advances, but he wishes to make her happy and thus will be lenient with her. She likens his behavior to that of a jealous lover on one occasion, when he becomes violent with her son. And he repeatedly offers to make a lady of her—even volunteering to set her up in a cottage of her own where she can raise her children—if she will grant him her favors.

By pointing out the similarities between her own story and those plots with which her readers would have been familiar, Jacobs could thus expect her readers to identify with her suffering. Moreover, this technique would enable them to appreciate the ways in which slavery converted into liabilities the very qualities of virtue and beauty that women—or rather elite white women—were taught to cultivate.[12] But by attempting to universalize her circumstances, Jacobs deemphasized the complexity of her situation and the material conditions that differentiated her position from that of her readers and white fictional protagonists.

Like Richardson's Pamela, Linda Brent is her pursuer's servant. But Pamela is free to escape, if she chooses, to the refuge of her parents' home, while as Dr. Flint's property, Brent has severely limited options. Moreover, Mr. B., in the terms that the novel constructs, can redeem his importunities by marrying Pamela and elevating her and their progeny to his position. No such possibility exists for Brent and her master. Indeed, the system of slavery, conflating as it does the categories of property and sexual relationships, ensures that her posterity will become his material possessions.

The sentimental fiction genre seems inappropriate for Jacobs's purposes for other reasons as well. As the book's prefatory documents imply, Jacobs's readers were accustomed to a certain degree of propriety and circumlocution in fiction. In keeping with cultural injunctions against women's assertiveness and directness in speech, the literature they wrote and read tended to be "exercises in euphemism" that excluded certain subjects from the purview of fiction.[13] The tension between the decorousness of the genre and the urgency of the slave woman's situation thus underscores how inadequate the sentimental novel's techniques are in telling Jacobs's story. They fail, like those of the slave narrative, to meet the demands of her situation. If the male context of the slave narrative renders her invisible, then so too do the white middle-class assumptions of the sentimental novel marginalize her.

Still, although Jacobs's account is closely circumscribed by the conventions of these two genres, she is able to negotiate her way around their limitations in a manner similar to the way she negotiates her freedom. By manipulating linguistic spaces—verbal equivalents analogous to the garret in which she hides for several years and from which she orchestrates her freedom—she interrogates the two genres and points out their inadequacy to her story.

One might be tempted to characterize Linda Brent as a victim of her circumstances. But she repeatedly demonstrates her ability to transform the conditions of her oppression into the preconditions of her liberation and that of her loved ones. Her garret, ostensibly a place of confinement, renders her spiritually independent of her master and makes possible her eventual escape to freedom. It is thus hardly surprising that Brent finds her imprisonment, however uncomfortable, an improvement over her "lot as a slave."[14] As her statement implies, she dates her emancipation from the time she enters her hiding place, even though she does not cross into the free states until seven years later. Given the constraints that frame her life, even the act of choosing her own mode of confinement constitutes an exercise of will, an indirect assault against her master's domination.[15]

The plot of Jacobs's narrative, her journey from slavery to freedom, is set in a series of similar structures of confinement, both literal and figurative. Not only does she spend much of her time in tiny rooms (for example, her grandmother's garret), but she seems as well to be penned in by the importunities of Dr. Flint: "My master met me at every turn, reminding me that I belonged to him, and swearing by heaven and earth that he would compel me to submit to him. If I went out for a breath of fresh air, after a day of unwearied toil, his footsteps dogged me. If I knelt by my mother's grave, his dark shadow fell on me even there" (p. 46). Repeatedly she escapes overwhelming persecutions only by choosing her own space of confinement: the stigma of unwed motherhood over sexual submission to her master; the concealment in one friend's home, another friend's closet, and her grandmother's garret over her own and her children's enslavement on a plantation; and Jim Crowism and the threat of the Fugitive Slave Law in the North over institutionalized slavery at home. Yet each moment of apparent enclosure actually empowers her to redirect her own and her children's destiny.

To borrow a formulation from Elaine Showalter, Jacobs inscribes a subversive plot of empowerment beneath the more orthodox, public plot of vulnerability.[16] On the one hand, her helplessness and vulnerability are indicated by the fact that she leaves each of her hiding places only with the aid of someone else. To be sure, when she goes to her second and third hiding places, she is entirely at the mercy of her companion, for she is kept ignorant of her destination. On the other hand, each hiding place, while at one level a prison, is also a station on her journey to freedom and a place of real empowerment. From the garret, she is able to secure Sands's promise to help free her children. In hiding, she prevents her own capture not merely by remaining concealed but, more importantly, by embroiling her master in an elaborate plot that deflects his attention. Fearing that he suspects her whereabouts, she writes him letters that she then has postmarked in Boston and New York to send him off in hot pursuit in the wrong direction. Despite her grandmother's trepidation, Brent clearly delights in exerting some influence over the man who has tried to control her.

Indeed, just as the confining spaces are at once prisons and exits, so too is her relationship to Sands both imprisoning and liberating. When Brent decides to take him as a lover, she is trapped between two untenable options. Forbidden to marry the free black man she loves, she knows that by becoming Sands's mistress she will compromise her virtue and reputation. But, she remarks, since her alternative is to yield to the master she loathes, she has no choice but to have sexual relations with Sands. As she writes: "It seems less degrading to give one's self, than to submit to compulsion. There is something akin to freedom in having a lover who has no control over you, except that which he gains by kindness and attachment" (pp. 84–85).

One might argue that Brent's dilemma encapsulates the slave woman's sexual victimization and vulnerability. Without impugning that reading, I would suggest that her relationship with Sands provides her with a measure of power. Out of his consideration for her, he purchases her children and her brother William from Flint. William eventually escapes from slavery, but Sands frees the children in accordance with their mother's wishes. In a system that allowed the buying and selling of human beings as if they were animals, Brent's influence is clearly minimal, but in her association with Sands at least, she exercises some degree of control.

At the level of narrative, Jacobs negotiates her relationship to confining literary forms in a similar manner. The lacunae of her narrative constitute spaces from which she interrogates and thus controls the genres in which she writes. For example, in an often cited line near the end of her account, she states: "Reader, my story ends with freedom; not in the usual way, with marriage" (p. 302). In this sentence she calls attention to the space between the traditional happy ending of the novel of domestic sentiment and the ending of her story. She acknowledges that, however much her story may resemble superficially the story of the sentimental heroine, as a black woman she plays for different stakes; marriage is not the ultimate reward she seeks.

Another lacuna occurs when she reveals her second pregnancy. She describes her initial involvement with Sands as a conundrum. The brutality of neighboring masters, the indifference of the legal system, and her own master's harassment have forced her to take a white man as her lover. Both in the way she builds to this revelation and in the apostrophes to the reader, she presents the situation as one in which she has no choice. Her explanation for taking Sands as her lover is accompanied by expressions of the appropriate regret and chagrin and then followed by two general chapters about slave religion and the local response to the Nat Turner rebellion. When we return to Jacobs's story, she remarks that Flint's harassment has persisted, and she announces her second pregnancy by saying simply, "When Dr. Flint learned that I was again to be a mother, he was exasperated beyond measure" (p. 118). Her continued relationship with Sands and her own response to this pregnancy are submerged in the subtext of the two previous chapters and in the space between paragraphs. By consigning to the narrative spaces those aspects of her own sexuality for which the genre does not allow, Jacobs points to an inadequacy in the form.

The third such space occurs a bit later, just before she leaves the plantation. Her master's great aunt, Miss Fanny, a kind-hearted elderly woman who is a great favorite with Brent's grandmother, comes to visit. Brent is clearly fond of this woman, but as she tells the story, she admits that she resents Miss Fanny's attempts to sentimentalize her situation. Miss Fanny remarks at one point that she "wished that I and all my grandmother's family were at rest in our graves, for not until then should she feel any peace about us" (p. 136). The narrator then reflects privately that "the good old soul did not dream that I was planning to bestow peace upon her, with regard to myself and my children; not by death, but by securing our freedom." Here she resists becoming the object of pity and calls attention instead to the inappropriateness of Miss Fanny's remark. Although she certainly draws on the conventions of sentimentalism when they suit her purposes, Brent is also capable of replacing the self-indulgent mythification of death with the more practical solution of freedom.

In its relation to form, Jacobs's account demonstrates the limitations of additive representations of the black woman's experience.[17] Her story is not what is yielded up after one superimposes the story of (white) woman's experience over that of black (male) experience. Rather, her unique cultural experience requires her to question the assumptions of literary conventions. Her self-conscious use of the techniques at her disposal anticipates the anomalous relation that exists between subsequent black women writers and their craft.

NOTES

1. Mary Helen Washington writes that black women wrote approximately twelve percent of the total number of extant slave narratives. See *Invented Lives: Narratives of Black Women 1860–1960*, ed. Mary Helen Washington (Garden City, N.Y.: Anchor Press, 1987). Historians such as John Blassingame discredited the authenticity of Jacobs's narrative precisely because as a woman-authored text it was unrepresentative of the genre. Jean Fagan Yellin, a literary historian, critic, and biographer of Jacobs has discovered the external evidence that establishes the veracity of Jacobs's account. See Blassingame, "Critical Essay on Sources," *The Slave Community: Plantation Life in the Antebellum South*, 2nd ed. (New York: Oxford University Press, 1979), pp. 367–82. See also Yellin's essay, "Texts and Contexts of Harriet Jacobs's *Incidents in the Life of a Slave Girl: Written by Herself*" in *The Slave's Narrative*, ed. Charles T. Davis and Henry Louis Gates, Jr. (New York: Oxford University Press, 1985), pp. 262–82; and her "Introduction" to Jacobs's *Incidents in the Life of a Slave Girl*, ed. Jean Fagan Yellin (Cambridge, Mass.: Harvard University Press, 1987).

2. See Robert B. Stepto's discussion of the relationship between the narratives and their authenticating documents in *From Behind the Veil: A Study of Afro-American Narrative* (Urbana: University of Illinois Press, 1979), pp. 3–31. See also James Olney's discussion of the generic properties of the slave narratives, " 'I Was Born': Slave Narratives, Their Status as Autobiography and as Literature," in Davis and Gates, *The Slave's Narrative*, pp. 148–75.

3. See Deborah Gray White, *Ar'n't I a Woman?: Female Slaves in the Plantation South* (New York: Norton, 1985), pp. 17–25; and

Hazel V. Carby, *Reconstructing Womanhood: The Emergence of the Afro-American Novelist* (New York: Oxford University Press, 1987), pp. 45–46.

4. White, *Ar'n't I a Woman?*, p. 76.

5. Ibid., p. 71.

6. For a comprehensive discussion of the nature of black women's work during and after slavery, see Jacqueline Jones, *Labor of Love, Labor of Sorrow: Black Women, Work, and the Family from Slavery to the Present* (New York: Basic Books, 1985). See also Angela Davis, *Women, Race and Class* (New York: Random House, 1981).

7. See Washington, *Invented Lives*, pp. 7–8; and Valerie Smith, *Self-Discovery and Authority in Afro-American Narrative* (Cambridge, Mass.: Harvard University Press, 1987), pp. 9–28.

8. Smith, *Self-Discovery and Authority*, p. 34.

9. William Wells Brown, *Narrative of William W. Brown* (Boston: The Anti-Slavery Office, 1847; rpt. New York: Arno Press, 1968), p. 105.

10. Frederick Douglass, *Narrative of the Life of Frederick Douglass, An American Slave, Written by Himself*, ed. Benjamin Quarles (Cambridge, Mass.: Harvard University Press, 1960), p. 97.

11. Carby, *Reconstructing Womanhood*, p. 35.

12. See Hazel Carby's discussion, in *Reconstructing Womanhood*, pp. 20–39, of ways in which the "cult of true womanhood" denies the black woman's gender identity.

13. See Annette Niemtzow, "The Problematic of Self in Autobiography: The Example of the Slave Narrative," in *The Art of the Slave Narrative: Original Essays in Criticism and Theory*, ed. John Sekora and Darwin T. Turner (Macomb, Ill.: Western Illinois University Press, 1982), pp. 105–6.

14. [Linda Brent/Harriet Jacobs], *Incident in the Life of a Slave Girl* (Boston, 1861), p. 174. Subsequent references will be given in the text.

15. Houston A. Baker, Jr., makes a similar observation in *Blues, Ideology, and Afro-American Literature: A Vernacular Theory* (Chicago: University of Chicago Press, 1984), pp. 50–56.

16. Elaine Showalter, "Review Essay," *Signs* 1 (1975):435.

17. See Elizabeth V. Spelman's provocative discussion of the limits of the additive approach to the black woman's experience in "Theories of Race and Gender: The Erasure of Black Women," *Quest* 5 (1979):36–62. See also Barbara Smith, "Notes for Yet Another Paper on Black Feminism, or Will the Real Enemy Please Stand Up," *Conditions: Five* 3 (October 1978):123–32.

INCIDENTS

IN THE

LIFE OF A SLAVE GIRL.

WRITTEN BY HERSELF.

———————•———————

"Northerners know nothing at all about Slavery. They think it is perpetual bondage only. They have no conception of the depth of *degradation* involved in that word, SLAVERY; if they had, they would never cease their efforts until so horrible a system was overthrown."

A WOMAN OF NORTH CAROLINA.

"Rise up, ye women that are at ease! Hear my voice, ye careless daughters! Give ear unto my speech."

ISAIAH xxxii. 9.

———————

EDITED BY L. MARIA CHILD.

———————

BOSTON:
PUBLISHED FOR THE AUTHOR.
1861..

Preface by the Author.

Reader, be assured this narrative is no fiction. I am aware that some of my adventures may seem incredible; but they are, nevertheless, strictly true. I have not exaggerated the wrongs inflicted by Slavery; on the contrary, my descriptions fall far short of the facts. I have concealed the names of places, and given persons fictitious names. I had no motive for secrecy on my own account, but I deemed it kind and considerate towards others to pursue this course.

I wish I were more competent to the task I have undertaken. But I trust my readers will excuse deficiencies in consideration of circumstances. I was born and reared in Slavery; and I remained in a Slave State twenty-seven years. Since I have been at the North, it has been necessary for me to work diligently for my own support, and the education of my children. This has not left me much leisure to make up for the loss of early opportunities to improve myself; and it has compelled me to write these pages at irregular intervals, whenever I could snatch an hour from household duties.

1*   (5)

When I first arrived in Philadelphia, Bishop Paine advised me to publish a sketch of my life, but I told him I was altogether incompetent to such an undertaking. Though I have improved my mind somewhat since that time, I still remain of the same opinion; but I trust my motives will excuse what might otherwise seem presumptuous. I have not written my experiences in order to attract attention to myself; on the contrary, it would have been more pleasant to me to have been silent about my own history. Neither do I care to excite sympathy for my own sufferings. But I do earnestly desire to arouse the women of the North to a realizing sense of the condition of two millions of women at the South, still in bondage, suffering what I suffered, and most of them far worse. I want to add my testimony to that of abler pens to convince the people of the Free States what Slavery really is. Only by experience can any one realize how deep, and dark, and foul is that pit of abominations. May the blessing of God rest on this imperfect effort in behalf of my persecuted people!

Linda Brent.

INTRODUCTION BY THE EDITOR.

THE author of the following autobiography is personally known to me, and her conversation and manners inspire me with confidence. During the last seventeen years, she has lived the greater part of the time with a distinguished family in New York, and has so deported herself as to be highly esteemed by them. This fact is sufficient, without further credentials of her character. I believe those who know her will not be disposed to doubt her veracity, though some incidents in her story are more romantic than fiction.

At her request, I have revised her manuscript; but such changes as I have made have been mainly for purposes of condensation and orderly arrangement. I have not added any thing to the incidents, or changed the import of her very pertinent remarks. With trifling exceptions, both the ideas and the language are her own. I pruned excrescences a little, but otherwise I had no reason for changing her lively and dramatic way of telling her own story. The names of both persons and places are known to me; but for good reasons I suppress them.

It will naturally excite surprise that a woman reared in Slavery should be able to write so well. But circumstances will explain this. In the first place, nature endowed her with quick perceptions. Secondly, the mistress, with whom she lived till she was twelve years old, was a kind, considerate friend, who taught her to read and spell. Thirdly, she was placed in favorable circumstances after she came to the North; having frequent intercourse with intelligent persons, who felt a friendly interest in her welfare, and were disposed to give her opportunities for self-improvement.

I am well aware that many will accuse me of indecorum for presenting these pages to the public; for the experiences of this intelligent and much-injured woman belong to a class which some call delicate subjects, and others indelicate. This peculiar phase of Slavery has generally been kept veiled; but the public ought to be made acquainted with its monstrous features, and I willingly take the responsibility of presenting them with the veil withdrawn. I do this for the sake of my sisters in bondage, who are suffering wrongs so foul, that our ears are too delicate to listen to them. I do it with the hope of arousing conscientious and reflecting women at the North to a sense of their duty in the exertion of moral influence on the question of Slavery, on all possible occasions. I do it with the hope that every man who reads this narrative will swear solemnly before God that, so far as he has power to prevent it, no fugitive from Slavery shall ever be sent back to suffer in that loathsome den of corruption and cruelty.

L. Maria Child.

CONTENTS.

	PAGE
CHILDHOOD.	11
THE NEW MASTER AND MISTRESS.	17
THE SLAVES' NEW YEAR'S DAY.	25
THE SLAVE WHO DARED TO FEEL LIKE A MAN.	28
THE TRIALS OF GIRLHOOD.	44
THE JEALOUS MISTRESS.	49
THE LOVER.	58
WHAT SLAVES ARE TAUGHT TO THINK OF THE NORTH.	67
SKETCHES OF NEIGHBORING SLAVEHOLDERS.	71
A PERILOUS PASSAGE IN THE SLAVE GIRL'S LIFE.	82
THE NEW TIE TO LIFE.	90
FEAR OF INSURRECTION.	97
THE CHURCH AND SLAVERY.	105
ANOTHER LINK TO LIFE.	117
CONTINUED PERSECUTIONS.	122
SCENES AT THE PLANTATION.	131
THE FLIGHT.	145
MONTHS OF PERIL.	150
THE CHILDREN SOLD.	160
NEW PERILS.	167
THE LOOPHOLE OF RETREAT.	173

CHRISTMAS FESTIVITIES. 179

STILL IN PRISON. 183

THE CANDIDATE FOR CONGRESS. 189

COMPETITION IN CUNNING. 193

IMPORTANT ERA IN MY BROTHER'S LIFE. 201

NEW DESTINATION FOR THE CHILDREN. 207

AUNT NANCY. 217

PREPARATIONS FOR ESCAPE. 224

NORTHWARD BOUND. 237

INCIDENTS IN PHILADELPHIA. 242

THE MEETING OF MOTHER AND DAUGHTER. 249

A HOME FOUND. 254

THE OLD ENEMY AGAIN. 258

PREJUDICE AGAINST COLOR. 264

THE HAIR-BREADTH ESCAPE. 268

A VISIT TO ENGLAND. 275

RENEWED INVITATION TO GO SOUTH. 279

THE CONFESSION. 282

THE FUGITIVE SLAVE LAW. 285

FREE AT LAST. 293

APPENDIX. 304

of merchandise, trusted to them for safe keeping, and liable to be demanded of them at any moment. I had one brother, William, who was two years younger than myself — a bright, affectionate child. I had also a great treasure in my maternal grandmother, who was a remarkable woman in many respects. She was the daughter of a planter in South Carolina, who, at his death, left her mother and his three children free, with money to go to St. Augustine, where they had relatives. It was during the Revolutionary War; and they were captured on their passage, carried back, and sold to different purchasers. Such was the story my grandmother used to tell me; but I do not remember all the particulars. She was a little girl when she was captured and sold to the keeper of a large hotel. I have often heard her tell how hard she fared during childhood. But as she grew older she evinced so much intelligence, and was so faithful, that her master and mistress could not help seeing it was for their interest to take care of such a valuable piece of property. She became an indispensable personage in the household, officiating in all capacities, from cook and wet nurse to seamstress. She was much praised for her cooking; and her nice crackers became so famous in the neighborhood that many people were desirous of obtaining them. In consequence of numerous requests of this kind, she asked permission of her mistress to bake crackers at night, after all the household work was done; and she obtained leave to do it, provided she would clothe herself and her children from the profits. Upon these terms, after working hard all day for her mistress, she began her midnight bakings,

assisted by her two oldest children. The business
proved profitable ; and each year she laid by a little,
which was saved for a fund to purchase her children.
Her master died, and the property was divided among
his heirs. The widow had her dower in the hotel,
which she continued to keep open. My grandmother
remained in her service as a slave ; but her children
were divided among her master's children. As she
had five, Benjamin, the youngest one, was sold, in
order that each heir might have an equal portion of
dollars and cents. There was so little difference in
our ages that he seemed more like my brother than
my uncle. He was a bright, handsome lad, nearly
white ; for he inherited the complexion my grandmother had derived from Anglo-Saxon ancestors.
Though only ten years old, seven hundred and twenty
dollars were paid for him. His sale was a terrible
blow to my grandmother ; but she was naturally hope-
ful, and she went to work with renewed energy, trusting in time to be able to purchase some of her children.
She had laid up three hundred dollars, which her
mistress one day begged as a loan, promising to pay
her soon. The reader probably knows that no promise
or writing given to a slave is legally binding ; for,
according to Southern laws, a slave, *being* property,
can *hold* no property. When my grandmother lent
her hard earnings to her mistress, she trusted solely
to her honor. The honor of a slaveholder to a slave !

To this good grandmother I was indebted for many
comforts. My brother Willie and I often received
portions of the crackers, cakes, and preserves, she
made to sell ; and after we ceased to be children we

were indebted to her for many more important services.

Such were the unusually fortunate circumstances of my early childhood. When I was six years old, my mother died; and then, for the first time, I learned, by the talk around me, that I was a slave. My mother's mistress was the daughter of my grandmother's mistress. She was the foster sister of my mother; they were both nourished at my grandmother's breast. In fact, my mother had been weaned at three months old, that the babe of the mistress might obtain sufficient food. They played together as children; and, when they became women, my mother was a most faithful servant to her whiter foster sister. On her death-bed her mistress promised that her children should never suffer for any thing; and during her lifetime she kept her word. They all spoke kindly of my dead mother, who had been a slave merely in name, but in nature was noble and womanly. I grieved for her, and my young mind was troubled with the thought who would now take care of me and my little brother. I was told that my home was now to be with her mistress; and I found it a happy one. No toilsome or disagreeable duties were imposed upon me. My mistress was so kind to me that I was always glad to do her bidding, and proud to labor for her as much as my young years would permit. I would sit by her side for hours, sewing diligently, with a heart as free from care as that of any free-born white child. When she thought I was tired, she would send me out to run and jump; and away I bounded, to gather berries or flowers to decorate her room. Those were happy days — too happy to last. The slave child had no thought for the morrow ; but there came that blight, which too surely waits on every human being born to be a chattel.

When I was nearly twelve years old, my kind mistress sickened and died. As I saw the cheek grow paler, and the eye more glassy, how earnestly I prayed in my heart that she might live ! I loved her ; for she had been almost like a mother to me. My prayers were not answered. She died, and they buried her in the little churchyard, where, day after day, my tears fell upon her grave.

I was sent to spend a week with my grandmother. I was now old enough to begin to think of the future ; and again and again I asked myself what they would do with me. I felt sure I should never find another mistress so kind as the one who was gone. She had promised my dying mother that her children should never suffer for any thing ; and when I remembered that, and recalled her many proofs of attachment to me, I could not help having some hopes that she had left me free. My friends were almost certain it would be so. They thought she would be sure to do it, on account of my mother's love and faithful service. But, alas ! we all know that the memory of a faithful slave does not avail much to save her children from the auction block.

After a brief period of suspense, the will of my mistress was read, and we learned that she had bequeathed me to her sister's daughter, a child of five years old. So vanished our hopes. My mistress had taught me the precepts of God's Word : " Thou shalt love thy neighbor as thyself." " Whatsoever ye would that men should do unto you, do ye even so unto them." But I was her slave, and I suppose she did not recognize me as her neighbor. I would give much to blot out from my memory that one great wrong. As a child, I loved my mistress ; and, looking back on the happy days I spent with her, I try to think with less bitterness of this act of injustice. While I was with her, she taught me to read and spell ; and for this privilege, which so rarely falls to the lot of a slave, I bless her memory.

She possessed but few slaves ; and at her death those were all distributed among her relatives. Five of them were my grandmother's children, and had shared the same milk that nourished her mother's children. Notwithstanding my grandmother's long and faithful service to her owners, not one of her children escaped the auction block. These God-breathing machines are no more, in the sight of their masters, than the cotton they plant, or the horses they tend.

cold looks, cold words, and cold treatment. We were glad when the night came. On my narrow bed I moaned and wept, I felt so desolate and alone.

I had been there nearly a year, when a dear little friend of mine was buried. I heard her mother sob, as the clods fell on the coffin of her only child, and I turned away from the grave, feeling thankful that I still had something left to love. I met my grandmother, who said, " Come with me, Linda; " and from her tone I knew that something sad had happened. She led me apart from the people, and then said, " My child, your father is dead." Dead! How could I believe it? He had died so suddenly I had not even heard that he was sick. I went home with my grandmother. My heart rebelled against God, who had taken from me mother, father, mistress, and friend. The good grandmother tried to comfort me. " Who knows the ways of God? " said she. " Perhaps they have been kindly taken from the evil days to come." Years afterwards I often thought of this. She promised to be a mother to her grandchildren, so far as she might be permitted to do so; and strengthened by her love, I returned to my master's. I thought I should be allowed to go to my father's house the next morning; but I was ordered to go for flowers, that my mistress's house might be decorated for an evening party. I spent the day gathering flowers and weaving them into festoons, while the dead body of my father was lying within a mile of me. What cared my owners for that? he was merely a piece of property. Moreover, they thought he had spoiled his children, by teaching them to feel that they were human beings.

This was blasphemous doctrine for a slave to teach; presumptuous in him, and dangerous to the masters.

The next day I followed his remains to a humble grave beside that of my dear mother. There were those who knew my father's worth, and respected his memory.

My home now seemed more dreary than ever. The laugh of the little slave-children sounded harsh and cruel. It was selfish to feel so about the joy of others. My brother moved about with a very grave face. I tried to comfort him, by saying, "Take courage, Willie; brighter days will come by and by."

"You don't know any thing about it, Linda," he replied. "We shall have to stay here all our days; we shall never be free."

I argued that we were growing older and stronger, and that perhaps we might, before long, be allowed to hire our own time, and then we could earn money to buy our freedom. William declared this was much easier to say than to do; moreover, he did not intend to *buy* his freedom. We held daily controversies upon this subject.

Little attention was paid to the slaves' meals in Dr. Flint's house. If they could catch a bit of food while it was going, well and good. I gave myself no trouble on that score, for on my various errands I passed my grandmother's house, where there was always something to spare for me. I was frequently threatened with punishment if I stopped there; and my grandmother, to avoid detaining me, often stood at the gate with something for my breakfast or dinner. I was indebted to *her* for all my comforts, spiritual or temporal.

It was *her* labor that supplied my scanty wardrobe. I have a vivid recollection of the linsey-woolsey dress given me every winter by Mrs. Flint. How I hated it! It was one of the badges of slavery.

While my grandmother was thus helping to support me from her hard earnings, the three hundred dollars she had lent her mistress were never repaid. When her mistress died, her son-in-law, Dr. Flint, was appointed executor. When grandmother applied to him for payment, he said the estate was insolvent, and the law prohibited payment. It did not, however, prohibit him from retaining the silver candelabra, which had been purchased with that money. I presume they will be handed down in the family, from generation to generation.

My grandmother's mistress had always promised her that, at her death, she should be free; and it was said that in her will she made good the promise. But when the estate was settled, Dr. Flint told the faithful old servant that, under existing circumstances, it was necessary she should be sold.

On the appointed day, the customary advertisement was posted up, proclaiming that there would be a " public sale of negroes, horses, &c." Dr. Flint called to tell my grandmother that he was unwilling to wound her feelings by putting her up at auction, and that he would prefer to dispose of her at private sale. My grandmother saw through his hypocrisy; she understood very well that he was ashamed of the job. She was a very spirited woman, and if he was base enough to sell her, when her mistress intended she should be free, she was determined the public should know it. She had for a long time supplied many families with crackers and preserves; consequently, "Aunt Marthy," as she was called, was generally known, and every body who knew her respected her intelligence and good character. Her long and faithful service in the family was also well known, and the intention of her mistress to leave her free. When the day of sale came, she took her place among the chattels, and at the first call she sprang upon the auction-block. Many voices called out, "Shame! Shame! Who is going to sell *you*, aunt Marthy? Don't stand there! That is no place for *you*." Without saying a word, she quietly awaited her fate. No one bid for her. At last, a feeble voice said, "Fifty dollars." It came from a maiden lady, seventy years old, the sister of my grandmother's deceased mistress. She had lived forty years under the same roof with my grandmother; she knew how faithfully she had served her owners, and how cruelly she had been defrauded of her rights; and she resolved to protect her. The auctioneer waited for a higher bid; but her wishes were respected; no one bid above her. She could neither read nor write; and when the bill of sale was made out, she signed it with a cross. But what consequence was that, when she had a big heart overflowing with human kindness? She gave the old servant her freedom.

At that time, my grandmother was just fifty years old. Laborious years had passed since then; and now my brother and I were slaves to the man who had defrauded her of her money, and tried to defraud her of her freedom. One of my mother's sisters, called Aunt Nancy, was also a slave in his family. She was a kind, good aunt to me; and supplied the place of both housekeeper and waiting maid to her mistress. She was, in fact, at the beginning and end of every thing.

Mrs. Flint, like many southern women, was totally deficient in energy. She had not strength to super-intend her household affairs; but her nerves were so strong, that she could sit in her easy chair and see a woman whipped, till the blood trickled from every stroke of the lash. She was a member of the church; but partaking of the Lord's supper did not seem to put her in a Christian frame of mind. If dinner was not served at the exact time on that particular Sunday, she would station herself in the kitchen, and wait till it was dished, and then spit in all the kettles and pans that had been used for cooking. She did this to prevent the cook and her children from eking out their meagre fare with the remains of the gravy and other scrapings. The slaves could get nothing to eat except what she chose to give them. Provisions were weighed out by the pound and ounce, three times a day. I can assure you she gave them no chance to eat wheat bread from her flour barrel. She knew how many biscuits a quart of flour would make, and exactly what size they ought to be.

Dr. Flint was an epicure. The cook never sent a dinner to his table without fear and trembling; for if there happened to be a dish not to his liking, he would either order her to be whipped, or compel her to eat every mouthful of it in his presence. The poor, hungry creature might not have objected to eating it; but she did object to having her master cram it down her throat till she choked.

They had a pet dog, that was a nuisance in the house.

The cook was ordered to make some Indian mush for him. He refused to eat, and when his head was held over it, the froth flowed from his mouth into the basin. He died a few minutes after. When Dr. Flint came in, he said the mush had not been well cooked, and that was the reason the animal would not eat it. He sent for the cook, and compelled her to eat it. He thought that the woman's stomach was stronger than the dog's; but her sufferings afterwards proved that he was mistaken. This poor woman endured many cruelties from her master and mistress; sometimes she was locked up, away from her nursing baby, for a whole day and night.

When I had been in the family a few weeks, one of the plantation slaves was brought to town, by order of his master. It was near night when he arrived, and Dr. Flint ordered him to be taken to the work house, and tied up to the joist, so that his feet would just escape the ground. In that situation he was to wait till the doctor had taken his tea. I shall never forget that night. Never before, in my life, had I heard hundreds of blows fall, in succession, on a human being. His piteous groans, and his "O, pray don't, massa," rang in my ear for months afterwards. There were many conjectures as to the cause of this terrible punishment. Some said master accused him of stealing corn; others said the slave had quarrelled with his wife, in presence of the overseer, and had accused his master of being the father of her child. They were both black, and the child was very fair.

I went into the work house next morning, and saw the cowhide still wet with blood, and the boards all covered with gore. The poor man lived, and continued to quarrel with his wife. A few months afterwards Dr. Flint handed them both over to a slave-trader. The guilty man put their value into his pocket, and had the satisfaction of knowing that they were out of sight and hearing. When the mother was delivered into the trader's hands, she said, "You *promised* to treat me well." To which he replied, "You have let your tongue run too far; damn you!" She had forgotten that it was a crime for a slave to tell who was the father of her child.

From others than the master persecution also comes in such cases. I once saw a young slave girl dying soon after the birth of a child nearly white. In her agony she cried out, "O Lord, come and take me!" Her mistress stood by, and mocked at her like an incarnate fiend. "You suffer, do you?" she exclaimed. "I am glad of it. You deserve it all, and more too."

The girl's mother said, "The baby is dead, thank God; and I hope my poor child will soon be in heaven, too."

"Heaven!" retorted the mistress. "There is no such place for the like of her and her bastard."

The poor mother turned away, sobbing. Her dying daughter called her, feebly, and as she bent over her, I heard her say, "Don't grieve so, mother; God knows all about it; and HE will have mercy upon me."

Her sufferings, afterwards, became so intense, that her mistress felt unable to stay; but when she left the room, the scornful smile was still on her lips. Seven children called her mother. The poor black woman had but the one child, whose eyes she saw closing in death, while she thanked God for taking her away from the greater bitterness of life.

III.

THE SLAVES' NEW YEAR'S DAY.

Dr. Flint owned a fine residence in town, several farms, and about fifty slaves, besides hiring a number by the year.

Hiring-day at the south takes place on the 1st of January. On the 2d, the slaves are expected to go to their new masters. On a farm, they work until the corn and cotton are laid. They then have two holidays. Some masters give them a good dinner under the trees. This over, they work until Christmas eve. If no heavy charges are meantime brought against them, they are given four or five holidays, whichever the master or overseer may think proper. Then comes New Year's eve; and they gather together their little alls, or more properly speaking, their little nothings, and wait anxiously for the dawning of day. At the appointed hour the grounds are thronged with men, women, and children, waiting, like criminals, to hear their doom pronounced. The slave is sure to know who is the most humane, or cruel master, within forty miles of him.

It is easy to find out, on that day, who clothes and feeds his slaves well; for he is surrounded by a crowd, begging, "Please, massa, hire me this year. I will work *very* hard, massa."

If a slave is unwilling to go with his new master, he is whipped, or locked up in jail, until he consents to go, and promises not to run away during the year.

Should he chance to change his mind, thinking it justifiable to violate an extorted promise, woe unto him if he is caught! The whip is used till the blood flows at his feet; and his stiffened limbs are put in chains, to be dragged in the field for days and days!

If he lives until the next year, perhaps the same man will hire him again, without even giving him an opportunity of going to the hiring-ground. After those for hire are disposed of, those for sale are called up.

O, you happy free women, contrast *your* New Year's day with that of the poor bond-woman! With you it is a pleasant season, and the light of the day is blessed. Friendly wishes meet you every where, and gifts are showered upon you. Even hearts that have been estranged from you soften at this season, and lips that have been silent echo back, " I wish you a happy New Year." Children bring their little offerings, and raise their rosy lips for a caress. They are your own, and no hand but that of death can take them from you.

But to the slave mother New Year's day comes laden with peculiar sorrows. She sits on her cold cabin floor, watching the children who may all be torn from her the next morning; and often does she wish that she and they might die before the day dawns. She may be an ignorant creature, degraded by the system that has brutalized her from childhood; but she has a mother's instincts, and is capable of feeling a mother's agonies.

On one of these sale days, I saw a mother lead seven children to the auction-block. She knew that *some* of them would be taken from her; but they took *all*. The children were sold to a slave-trader, and their mother was bought by a man in her own town. Before night her children were all far away. She begged the trader to tell her where he intended to take them; this he refused to do. How *could* he, when he knew he would sell them, one by one, wherever he could command the highest price? I met that mother in the street, and her wild, haggard face lives to-day in my mind. She wrung her hands in anguish, and exclaimed, " Gone! All gone! Why *don't* God kill me?" I had no words wherewith to comfort her. Instances of this kind are of daily, yea, of hourly occurrence.

Slaveholders have a method, peculiar to their institution, of getting rid of *old* slaves, whose lives have been worn out in their service. I knew an old woman, who for seventy years faithfully served her master. She had become almost helpless, from hard labor and disease. Her owners moved to Alabama, and the old black woman was left to be sold to any body who would give twenty dollars for her.

IV.

THE SLAVE WHO DARED TO FEEL LIKE A MAN.

Two years had passed since I entered Dr. Flint's family, and those years had brought much of the knowledge that comes from experience, though they had afforded little opportunity for any other kinds of knowledge.

My grandmother had, as much as possible, been a mother to her orphan grandchildren. By perseverance and unwearied industry, she was now mistress of a snug little home, surrounded with the necessaries of life. She would have been happy could her children have shared them with her. There remained but three children and two grandchildren, all slaves. Most earnestly did she strive to make us feel that it was the will of God : that He had seen fit to place us under such circumstances ; and though it seemed hard, we ought to pray for contentment.

It was a beautiful faith, coming from a mother who could not call her children her own. But I, and Benjamin, her youngest boy, condemned it. We reasoned that it was much more the will of God that we should be situated as she was. We longed for a home like hers. There we always found sweet balsam for our troubles. She was so loving, so sympathizing ! She always met us with a smile, and listened with patience to all our sorrows. She spoke so hopefully, that unconsciously the clouds gave place to sunshine. There was a grand big oven there, too, that baked bread and nice things for the town, and we knew there was always a choice bit in store for us.

But, alas! even the charms of the old oven failed to reconcile us to our hard lot. Benjamin was now a tall, handsome lad, strongly and gracefully made, and with a spirit too bold and daring for a slave. My brother William, now twelve years old, had the same aversion to the word master that he had when he was an urchin of seven years. I was his confidant. He came to me with all his troubles. I remember one instance in particular. It was on a lovely spring morning, and when I marked the sunlight dancing here and there, its beauty seemed to mock my sadness. For my master, whose restless, craving, vicious nature roved about day and night, seeking whom to devour, had just left me, with stinging, scorching words; words that scathed ear and brain like fire. O, how I despised him! I thought how glad I should be, if some day when he walked the earth, it would open and swallow him up, and disencumber the world of a plague.

When he told me that I was made for his use, made to obey his command in *every* thing; that I was nothing but a slave, whose will must and should surrender to his, never before had my puny arm felt half so strong.

So deeply was I absorbed in painful reflections afterwards, that I neither saw nor heard the entrance of any one, till the voice of William sounded close beside me. "Linda," said he, "what makes you look so sad?
3 *

I love you. O, Linda, isn't this a bad world? Every body seems so cross and unhappy. I wish I had died when poor father did."

I told him that every body was *not* cross, or unhappy; that those who had pleasant homes, and kind friends, and who were not afraid to love them, were happy. But we, who were slave-children, without father or mother, could not expect to be happy. We must be good; perhaps that would bring us contentment.

"Yes," he said, "I try to be good; but what's the use? They are all the time troubling me." Then he proceeded to relate his afternoon's difficulty with young master Nicholas. It seemed that the brother of master Nicholas had pleased himself with making up stories about William. Master Nicholas said he should be flogged, and he would do it. Whereupon he went to work; but William fought bravely, and the young master, finding he was getting the better of him, undertook to tie his hands behind him. He failed in that likewise. By dint of kicking and fisting, William came out of the skirmish none the worse for a few scratches.

He continued to discourse on his young master's *meanness;* how he whipped the *little* boys, but was a perfect coward when a tussle ensued between him and white boys of his own size. On such occasions he always took to his legs. William had other charges to make against him. One was his rubbing up pennies with quicksilver, and passing them off for quarters of a dollar on an old man who kept a fruit stall. William was often sent to buy fruit, and he earnestly inquired

of me what he ought to do under such circumstances.
I told him it was certainly wrong to deceive the old
man, and that it was his duty to tell him of the imposi-
tions practised by his young master. I assured him the
old man would not be slow to comprehend the whole,
and there the matter would end. William thought it
might with the old man, but not with *him*. He said
he did not mind the smart of the whip, but he did not
like the *idea* of being whipped.

While I advised him to be good and forgiving I was
not unconscious of the beam in my own eye. It was
the very knowledge of my own shortcomings that
urged me to retain, if possible, some sparks of my
brother's God-given nature. I had not lived fourteen
years in slavery for nothing. I had felt, seen, and
heard enough, to read the characters, and question the
motives, of those around me. The war of my life had
begun ; and though one of God's most powerless creatures, I resolved never to be conquered. Alas, for
me !

If there was one pure, sunny spot for me, I believed
it to be in Benjamin's heart, and in another's, whom I
loved with all the ardor of a girl's first love. My
owner knew of it, and sought in every way to render
me miserable. He did not resort to corporal punishment, but to all the petty, tyrannical ways that human
ingenuity could devise.

I remember the first time I was punished. It was
in the month of February. My grandmother had
taken my old shoes, and replaced them with a new
pair. I needed them ; for several inches of snow had
fallen, and it still continued to fall. When I walked

through Mrs. Flint's room, their creaking grated harshly on her refined nerves. She called me to her, and asked what I had about me that made such a horrid noise. I told her it was my new shoes. "Take them off," said she; "and if you put them on again, I'll throw them into the fire."

I took them off, and my stockings also. She then sent me a long distance, on an errand. As I went through the snow, my bare feet tingled. That night I was very hoarse; and I went to bed thinking the next day would find me sick, perhaps dead. What was my grief on waking to find myself quite well!

I had imagined if I died, or was laid up for some time, that my mistress would feel a twinge of remorse that she had so hated "the little imp," as she styled me. It was my ignorance of that mistress that gave rise to such extravagant imaginings.

Dr. Flint occasionally had high prices offered for me; but he always said, "She don't belong to me. She is my daughter's property, and I have no right to sell her." Good, honest man! My young mistress was still a child, and I could look for no protection from her. I loved her, and she returned my affection. I once heard her father allude to her attachment to me; and his wife promptly replied that it proceeded from fear. This put unpleasant doubts into my mind. Did the child feign what she did not feel? or was her mother jealous of the mite of love she bestowed on me? I concluded it must be the latter. I said to myself, "Surely, little children are true."

One afternoon I sat at my sewing, feeling unusual depression of spirits. My mistress had been accusing

me of an offence, of which I assured her I was perfectly innocent; but I saw, by the contemptuous curl
of her lip, that she believed I was telling a lie.

I wondered for what wise purpose God was leading
me through such thorny paths, and whether still
darker days were in store for me. As I sat musing
thus, the door opened softly, and William came in.
" Well, brother," said I, " what is the matter this
time ? "

" O Linda, Ben and his master have had a dreadful time ! " said he.

My first thought was that Benjamin was killed.
" Don't be frightened, Linda," said William ; " I will
tell you all about it."

It appeared that Benjamin's master had sent for
him, and he did not immediately obey the summons.
When he did, his master was angry, and began to
whip him. He resisted. Master and slave fought,
and finally the master was thrown. Benjamin had
cause to tremble ; for he had thrown to the ground his
master — one of the richest men in town. I anxiously
awaited the result.

That night I stole to my grandmother's house, and
Benjamin also stole thither from his master's. My
grandmother had gone to spend a day or two with an
old friend living in the country.

" I have come," said Benjamin, " to tell you good
by. I am going away."

I inquired where.

" To the north," he replied.

I looked at him to see whether he was in earnest. I
saw it all in his firm, set mouth. I implored him not

to go, but he paid no heed to my words. He said he was no longer a boy, and every day made his yoke more galling. He had raised his hand against his master, and was to be publicly whipped for the offence. I reminded him of the poverty and hardships he must encounter among strangers. I told him he might be caught and brought back; and that was terrible to think of.

He grew vexed, and asked if poverty and hardships with freedom, were not preferable to our treatment in slavery. "Linda," he continued, "we are dogs here; foot-balls, cattle, every thing that's mean. No, I will not stay. Let them bring me back. We don't die but once."

He was right; but it was hard to give him up. "Go," said I, "and break your mother's heart."

I repented of my words ere they were out.

"Linda," said he, speaking as I had not heard him speak that evening, "how *could* you say that? Poor mother! be kind to her, Linda; and you, too, cousin Fanny."

Cousin Fanny was a friend who had lived some years with us.

Farewells were exchanged, and the bright, kind boy, endeared to us by so many acts of love, vanished from our sight.

It is not necessary to state how he made his escape. Suffice it to say, he was on his way to New York when a violent storm overtook the vessel. The captain said he must put into the nearest port. This alarmed Benjamin, who was aware that he would be advertised in every port near his own town. His embarrassment was

noticed by the captain. To port they went. There
the advertisement met the captain's eye. Benjamin so
exactly answered its description, that the captain laid
hold on him, and bound him in chains. The storm
passed, and they proceeded to New York. Before
reaching that port Benjamin managed to get off his
chains and throw them overboard. He escaped from
the vessel, but was pursued, captured, and carried back
to his master.

When my grandmother returned home and found
her youngest child had fled,' great was her sorrow;
but, with characteristic piety, she said, " God's will be
done." Each morning, she inquired if any news had
been heard from her boy. Yes, news *was* heard. The
master was rejoicing over a letter, announcing the capture of his human chattel.

That day seems but as yesterday, so well do I remember it. I saw him led through the streets in
chains, to jail. His face was ghastly pale, yet full of
determination. He had begged one of the sailors to
go to his mother's house and ask her not to meet him.
He said the sight of her distress would take from him
all self-control. She yearned to see him, and she went;
but she screened herself in the crowd, that it might be
as her child had said.

We were not allowed to visit him; but we had
known the jailer for years, and he was a kind-hearted
man. At midnight he opened the jail door for my
grandmother and myself to enter, in disguise. When
we entered the cell not a sound broke the stillness.
" Benjamin, Benjamin ! " whispered my grandmother.
No answer. " Benjamin ! " she again faltered. There

was a jingle of chains. The moon had just risen, and cast an uncertain light through the bars of the window. We knelt down and took Benjamin's cold hands in ours. We did not speak. Sobs were heard, and Benjamin's lips were unsealed; for his mother was weeping on his neck. How vividly does memory bring back that sad night! Mother and son talked together. He asked her pardon for the suffering he had caused her. She said she had nothing to forgive; she could not blame his desire for freedom. He told her that when he was captured, he broke away, and was about casting himself into the river, when thoughts of *her* came over him, and he desisted. She asked if he did not also think of God. I fancied I saw his face grow fierce in the moonlight. He answered, "No, I did not think of him. When a man is hunted like a wild beast he forgets there is a God, a heaven. He forgets every thing in his struggle to get beyond the reach of the bloodhounds."

"Don't talk so, Benjamin," said she. "Put your trust in God. Be humble, my child, and your master will forgive you."

"Forgive me for *what*, mother? For not letting him treat me like a dog? No! I will never humble myself to him. I have worked for him for nothing all my life, and I am repaid with stripes and imprisonment. Here I will stay till I die, or till he sells me."

The poor mother shuddered at his words. I think he felt it; for when he next spoke, his voice was calmer. "Don't fret about me, mother. I ain't worth it," said he. "I wish I had some of your goodness. You bear every thing patiently, just as though you thought it was all right. I wish I could."

She told him she had not always been so; once, she was like him; but when sore troubles came upon her, and she had no arm to lean upon, she learned to call on God, and he lightened her burdens. She besought him to do likewise.

We overstaid our time, and were obliged to hurry from the jail.

Benjamin had been imprisoned three weeks, when my grandmother went to intercede for him with his master. He was immovable. He said Benjamin should serve as an example to the rest of his slaves; he should be kept in jail till he was subdued, or be sold if he got but one dollar for him. However, he afterwards relented in some degree. The chains were taken off, and we were allowed to visit him.

As his food was of the coarsest kind, we carried him as often as possible a warm supper, accompanied with some little luxury for the jailer.

Three months elapsed, and there was no prospect of release or of a purchaser. One day he was heard to sing and laugh. This piece of indecorum was told to his master, and the overseer was ordered to re-chain him. He was now confined in an apartment with other prisoners, who were covered with filthy rags. Benjamin was chained near them, and was soon covered with vermin. He worked at his chains till he succeeded in getting out of them. He passed them through the bars of the window, with a request that they should be taken to his master, and he should be informed that he was covered with vermin.

This audacity was punished with heavier chains, and prohibition of our visits.

4

My grandmother continued to send him fresh
changes of clothes. The old ones were burned up.
The last night we saw him in jail his mother still
begged him to send for his master, and beg his pardon.
Neither persuasion nor argument could turn hin from
his purpose. He calmly answered, "I am waiting his
time."

Those chains were mournful to hear.

Another three months passed, and Benjamin left his
prison walls. We that loved him waited to bid him a
long and last farewell. A slave trader had bought
him. You remember, I told you what price he
brought when ten years of age. Now he was more
than twenty years old, and sold for three hundred dollars. The master had been blind to his own interest.
Long confinement had made his face too pale, his
form too thin; moreover, the trader had heard something of his character, and it did not strike him as
suitable for a slave. He said he would give any price
if the handsome lad was a girl. We thanked God
that he was not.

Could you have seen that mother clinging to her
child, when they fastened the irons upon his wrists;
could you have heard her heart-rending groans, and
seen her bloodshot eyes wander wildly from face to
face, vainly pleading for mercy; could you have witnessed that scene as I saw it, you would exclaim,
Slavery is damnable !

Benjamin, her youngest, her pet, was forever gone !
She could not realize it. She had had an interview
with the trader for the purpose of ascertaining if
Benjamin could be purchased. She was told it was

impossible, as he had given bonds not to sell him till
he was out of the state. He promised that he would
not sell him till he reached New Orleans.

With a strong arm and unvaried trust, my grandmother began her work of love. Benjamin must be free.
If she succeeded, she knew they would still be separated; but the sacrifice was not too great. Day and
night she labored. The trader's price would treble
that he gave; but she was not discouraged.

She employed a lawyer to write to a gentleman,
whom she knew, in New Orleans. She begged him to
interest himself for Benjamin, and he willingly favored
her request. When he saw Benjamin, and stated his
business, he thanked him; but said he preferred to
wait a while before making the trader an offer. He
knew he had tried to obtain a high price for him, and
had invariably failed. This encouraged him to make
another effort for freedom. So one morning, long before day, Benjamin was missing. He was riding over
the blue billows, bound for Baltimore.

For once his white face did him a kindly service.
They had no suspicion that it belonged to a slave;
otherwise, the law would have been followed out to
the letter, and the *thing* rendered back to slavery.
The brightest skies are often overshadowed by the darkest clouds. Benjamin was taken sick, and compelled
to remain in Baltimore three weeks. His strength
was slow in returning; and his desire to continue his
journey seemed to retard his recovery. How could he
get strength without air and exercise? He resolved
to venture on a short walk. A by-street was selected,
where he thought himself secure of not being met by

any one that knew him; but a voice called out, "Halloo, Ben, my boy! what are you doing *here?*"

His first impulse was to run; but his legs trembled so that he could not stir. He turned to confront his antagonist, and behold, there stood his old master's next door neighbor! He thought it was all over with him now; but it proved otherwise. That man was a miracle. He possessed a goodly number of slaves, and yet was not quite deaf to that mystic clock, whose ticking is rarely heard in the slaveholder's breast.

"Ben, you are sick," said he. "Why, you look like a ghost. I guess I gave you something of a start. Never mind, Ben, I am not going to touch you. You had a pretty tough time of it, and you may go on your way rejoicing for all me. But I would advise you to get out of this place plaguy quick, for there are several gentlemen here from our town." He described the nearest and safest route to New York, and added, "I shall be glad to tell your mother I have seen you. Good by, Ben."

Benjamin turned away, filled with gratitude, and surprised that the town he hated contained such a gem — a gem worthy of a purer setting.

This gentleman was a Northerner by birth, and had married a southern lady. On his return, he told my grandmother that he had seen her son, and of the service he had rendered him.

Benjamin reached New York safely, and concluded to stop there until he had gained strength enough to proceed further. It happened that my grandmother's only remaining son had sailed for the same city on business for his mistress. Through God's providence, the brothers met. You may be sure it was a happy meeting. "O Phil," exclaimed Benjamin, "I am here at last." Then he told him how near he came to dying, almost in sight of free land, and how he prayed that he might live to get one breath of free air. He said life was worth something now, and it would be hard to die. In the old jail he had not valued it; once, he was tempted to destroy it; but something, he did not know what, had prevented him; perhaps it was fear. He had heard those who profess to be religious declare there was no heaven for self-murderers; and as his life had been pretty hot here, he did not desire a continuation of the same in another world. "If I die now," he exclaimed, "thank God, I shall die a freeman!"

He begged my uncle Phillip not to return south; but stay and work with him, till they earned enough to buy those at home. His brother told him it would kill their mother if he deserted her in her trouble. She had pledged her house, and with difficulty had raised money to buy him. Would he be bought?

"No, never!" he replied. "Do you suppose, Phil, when I have got so far out of their clutches, I will give them one red cent? No! And do you suppose I would turn mother out of her home in her old age? That I would let her pay all those hard-earned dollars for me, and never to see me? For you know she will stay south as long as her other children are slaves. What a good mother! Tell her to buy *you*, Phil. You have been a comfort to her, and I have been a trouble. And Linda, poor Linda; what'll become of her? Phil, you don't know what a life they lead her. She has told

4 *

me something about it, and I wish old Flint was dead, or a better man. When I was in jail, he asked her if she didn't want *him* to ask my master to forgive me, and take me home again. She told him, No; that I didn't want to go back. He got mad, and said we were all alike. I never despised my own master half as much as I do that man. There is many a worse slaveholder than my master; but for all that I would not be his slave."

While Benjamin was sick, he had parted with nearly all his clothes to pay necessary expenses. But he did not part with a little pin I fastened in his bosom when we parted. It was the most valuable thing I owned, and I thought none more worthy to wear it. He had it still.

His brother furnished him with clothes, and gave him what money he had.

They parted with moistened eyes; and as Benjamin turned away, he said, " Phil, I part with all my kindred." And so it proved. We never heard from him again.

Uncle Phillip came home; and the first words he uttered when he entered the house were, " Mother, Ben is free! I have seen him in New York." She stood looking at him with a bewildered air. " Mother, don't you believe it?" he said, laying his hand softly upon her shoulder. She raised her hands, and exclaimed, " God be praised! Let us thank him." She dropped on her knees, and poured forth her heart in prayer. Then Phillip must sit down and repeat to her every word Benjamin had said. He told her all; only he forbore to mention how sick and pale her darling looked. Why should he distress her when she could do him no good ?

The brave old woman still toiled on, hoping to rescue some of her other children. After a while she succeeded in buying Phillip. She paid eight hundred dollars, and came home with the precious document that secured his freedom. The happy mother and son sat together by the old hearthstone that night, telling how proud they were of each other, and how they would prove to the world that they could take care of themselves, as they had long taken care of others. We all concluded by saying, " He that is *willing* to be a slave, let him be a slave."

V.

THE TRIALS OF GIRLHOOD.

DURING the first years of my service in Dr. Flint's family, I was accustomed to share some indulgences with the children of my mistress. Though this seemed to me no more than right, I was grateful for it, and tried to merit the kindness by the faithful discharge of my duties. But I now entered on my fifteenth year — a sad epoch in the life of a slave girl. My master began to whisper foul words in my ear. Young as I was, I could not remain ignorant of their import. I tried to treat them with indifference or contempt. The master's age, my extreme youth, and the fear that his conduct would be reported to my grandmother, made him bear this treatment for many months. He was a crafty man, and resorted to many means to accomplish his purposes. Sometimes he had stormy, terrific ways, that made his victims tremble; sometimes he assumed a gentleness that he thought must surely subdue. Of the two, I preferred his stormy moods, although they left me trembling. He tried his utmost to corrupt the pure principles my grandmother had instilled. He peopled my young mind with unclean images, such as only a vile monster could think of. I turned from him with disgust and hatred. But he was my master. I was compelled to live under the same roof with him — where I saw a man forty years my senior daily violating the most sacred command-

ments of nature.   He told me I was his property;
that I must be subject to his will in all things.   My
soul revolted against the mean tyranny.   But where
could I turn for protection ?   No matter whether the
slave girl be as black as ebony or as fair as her mistress.   In either case, there is no shadow of law to
protect her from insult, from violence, or even from
death ; all these are inflicted by fiends who bear the
shape of men.   The mistress, who ought to protect
the helpless victim, has no other feelings towards her
but those of jealousy and rage.   The degradation, the
wrongs, the vices, that grow out of slavery, are more
than I can describe.   They are greater than you would
willingly believe.   Surely, if you credited one half the
truths that are told you concerning the helpless millions suffering in this cruel bondage, you at the north
would not help to tighten the yoke.   You surely would
refuse to do for the master, on your own soil, the mean
and cruel work which trained bloodhounds and the
lowest class of whites do for him at the south.

Every where the years bring to all enough of sin
and sorrow ; but in slavery the very dawn of life is
darkened by these shadows.   Even the little child,
who is accustomed to wait on her mistress and her
children, will learn, before she is twelve years old,
why it is that her mistress hates such and such a one
among the slaves.   Perhaps the child's own mother
is among those hated ones.   She listens to violent
outbreaks of jealous passion, and cannot help understanding what is the cause.   She will become prematurely knowing in evil things.   Soon she will learn to
tremble when she hears her master's footfall.   She

will be compelled to realize that she is no longer a
child. If God has bestowed beauty upon her, it will
prove her greatest curse. That which commands ad-
miration in the white woman only hastens the degradation of the female slave. I know that some are too
much brutalized by slavery to feel the humiliation of
their position; but many slaves feel it most acutely,
and shrink from the memory of it. I cannot tell how
much I suffered in the presence of these wrongs, nor
how I am still pained by the retrospect. My master
met me at every turn, reminding me that I belonged
to him, and swearing by heaven and earth that he
would compel me to submit to him. If I went out for
a breath of fresh air, after a day of unwearied toil, his
footsteps dogged me. If I knelt by my mother's grave,
his dark shadow fell on me even there. The light
heart which nature had given me became heavy with
sad forebodings. The other slaves in my master's
house noticed the change. Many of them pitied me;
but none dared to ask the cause. They had no need
to inquire. They knew too well the guilty practices
under that roof; and they were aware that to speak
of them was an offence that never went unpunished.

I longed for some one to confide in. I would have
given the world to have laid my head on my grandmother's faithful bosom, and told her all my troubles.
But Dr. Flint swore he would kill me, if I was not as
silent as the grave. Then, although my grandmother
was all in all to me, I feared her as well as loved her.
I had been accustomed to look up to her with a respect bordering upon awe. I was very young, and
felt shamefaced about telling her such impure things,

especially as I knew her to be very strict on such subjects. Moreover, she was a woman of a high spirit. She was usually very quiet in her demeanor; but if her indignation was once roused, it was not very easily quelled. I had been told that she once chased a white gentleman with a loaded pistol, because he insulted one of her daughters. I dreaded the consequences of a violent outbreak; and both pride and fear kept me silent. But though I did not confide in my grandmother, and even evaded her vigilant watchfulness and inquiry, her presence in the neighborhood was some protection to me. Though she had been a slave, Dr. Flint was afraid of her. He dreaded her scorching rebukes. Moreover, she was known and patronized by many people; and he did not wish to have his villany made public. It was lucky for me that I did not live on a distant plantation, but in a town not so large that the inhabitants were ignorant of each other's affairs. Bad as are the laws and customs in a slaveholding community, the doctor, as a professional man, deemed it prudent to keep up some outward show of decency.

O, what days and nights of fear and sorrow that man caused me! Reader, it is not to awaken sympathy for myself that I am telling you truthfully what I suffered in slavery. I do it to kindle a flame of compassion in your hearts for my sisters who are still in bondage, suffering as I once suffered.

I once saw two beautiful children playing together. One was a fair white child; the other was her slave, and also her sister. When I saw them embracing each other, and heard their joyous laughter, I turned sadly away from the lovely sight. I foresaw the inevitable blight that would fall on the little slave's heart. I knew how soon her laughter would be changed to sighs. The fair child grew up to be a still fairer woman. From childhood to womanhood her pathway was blooming with flowers, and overarched by a sunny sky. Scarcely one day of her life had been clouded when the sun rose on her happy bridal morning.

How had those years dealt with her slave sister, the little playmate of her childhood? She, also, was very beautiful; but the flowers and sunshine of love were not for her. She drank the cup of sin, and shame, and misery, whereof her persecuted race are compelled to drink.

In view of these things, why are ye silent, ye free men and women of the north? Why do your tongues falter in maintenance of the right? Would that I had more ability! But my heart is so full, and my pen is so weak! There are noble men and women who plead for us, striving to help those who cannot help themselves. God bless them! God give them strength and courage to go on! God bless those, every where, who are laboring to advance the cause of humanity!

the conclusion that such an accomplishment might help to advance his favorite scheme. Before long, notes were often slipped into my hand. I would return them, saying, " I can't read them, sir." " Can't you ? " he replied ; " then I must read them to you." He always finished the reading by asking, " Do you understand ? " Sometimes he would complain of the heat of the tea room, and order his supper to be placed on a small table in the piazza. He would seat himself there with a well-satisfied smile, and tell me to stand by and brush away the flies. He would eat very slowly, pausing between the mouthfuls. These intervals were employed in describing the happiness I was so foolishly throwing away, and in threatening me with the penalty that finally awaited my stubborn disobedience. He boasted much of the forbearance he had exercised towards me, and reminded me that there was a limit to his patience. When I succeeded in avoiding opportunities for him to talk to me at home, I was ordered to come to his office, to do some errand. When there, I was obliged to stand and listen to such language as he saw fit to address to me. Sometimes I so openly expressed my contempt for him that he would become violently enraged, and I wondered why he did not strike me. Circumstanced as he was, he probably thought it was better policy to be forbearing. But the state of things grew worse and worse daily. In desperation I told him that I must and would apply to my grandmother for protection. He threatened me with death, and worse than death, if I made any complaint to her. Strange to say, I did not despair. I was naturally of a buoyant disposition, and always I had a hope of somehow getting out of his clutches. Like many a poor, simple slave before me, I trusted that some threads of joy would yet be woven into my dark destiny.

I had entered my sixteenth year, and every day it became more apparent that my presence was intolerable to Mrs. Flint. Angry words frequently passed between her and her husband. He had never punished me himself, and he would not allow any body else to punish me. In that respect, she was never satisfied; but, in her angry moods, no terms were too vile for her to bestow upon me. Yet I, whom she detested so bitterly, had far more pity for her than he had, whose duty it was to make her life happy. I never wronged her, or wished to wrong her; and one word of kindness from her would have brought me to her feet.

After repeated quarrels between the doctor and his wife, he announced his intention to take his youngest daughter, then four years old, to sleep in his apartment. It was necessary that a servant should sleep in the same room, to be on hand if the child stirred. I was selected for that office, and informed for what purpose that arrangement had been made. By managing to keep within sight of people, as much as possible, during the day time, I had hitherto succeeded in eluding my master, though a razor was often held to my throat to force me to change this line of policy. At night I slept by the side of my great aunt, where I felt safe. He was too prudent to come into her room. She was an old woman, and had been in the family many years. Moreover, as a married man, and a professional man, he deemed it necessary to save appearances in some degree. But he resolved to remove the obstacle in the way of his scheme ; and he thought he had planned it so that he should evade suspicion. He was well aware how much I prized my refuge by the side of my old aunt, and he determined to dispossess me of it. The first night the doctor had the little child in his room alone. The next morning, I was ordered to take my station as nurse the following night. A kind Providence interposed in my favor. During the day Mrs. Flint heard of this new arrangement, and a storm followed. I rejoiced to hear it rage.

After a while my mistress sent for me to come to her room. Her first question was, " Did you know you were to sleep in the doctor's room ? "

" Yes, ma'am."

" Who told you ? "

" My master."

" Will you answer truly all the questions I ask ? "

" Yes, ma'am."

" Tell me, then, as you hope to be forgiven, are you innocent of what I have accused you ? "

" I am."

She handed me a Bible, and said, " Lay your hand on your heart, kiss this holy book, and swear before God that you tell me the truth."

I took the oath she required, and I did it with a clear conscience.

" You have taken God's holy word to testify your innocence," said she. " If you have deceived me, beware ! Now take this stool, sit down, look me directly in the face, and tell me all that has passed between your master and you."

I did as she ordered. As I went on with my account her color changed frequently, she wept, and
sometimes groaned. She spoke in tones so sad, that I
was touched by her grief. The tears came to my
eyes; but I was soon convinced that her emotions
arose from anger and wounded pride. She felt that
her marriage vows were desecrated, her dignity insulted; but she had no compassion for the poor victim of her husband's perfidy. She pitied herself as
a martyr; but she was incapable of feeling for the
condition of shame and misery in which her unfortunate, helpless slave was placed.

Yet perhaps she had some touch of feeling for me;
for when the conference was ended, she spoke kindly,
and promised to protect me. I should have been
much comforted by this assurance if I could have had
confidence in it; but my experiences in slavery had
filled me with distrust. She was not a very refined
woman, and had not much control over her passions.
I was an object of her jealousy, and, consequently, of
her hatred; and I knew I could not expect kindness
or confidence from her under the circumstances in
which I was placed. I could not blame her. Slaveholders' wives feel as other women would under similar circumstances. The fire of her temper kindled
from small sparks, and now the flame became so intense that the doctor was obliged to give up his
intended arrangement.

I knew I had ignited the torch, and I expected to
suffer for it afterwards; but I felt too thankful to my
mistress for the timely aid she rendered me to care
much about that. She now took me to sleep in a

room adjoining her own. There I was an object of
her especial care, though not of her especial comfort,
for she spent many a sleepless night to watch over
me. Sometimes I woke up, and found her bending
over me. At other times she whispered in my ear, as
though it was her husband who was speaking to me,
and listened to hear what I would answer. If she
startled me, on such occasions, she would glide stealth-
ily away; and the next morning she would tell me I
had been talking in my sleep, and ask who I was talking to. At last, I began to be fearful for my life. It
had been often threatened; and you can imagine, better than I can describe, what an unpleasant sensation
it must produce to wake up in the dead of night and
find a jealous woman bending over you. Terrible as
this experience was, I had fears that it would give
place to one more terrible.

My mistress grew weary of her vigils; they did not
prove satisfactory. She changed her tactics. She
now tried the trick of accusing my master of crime,
in my presence, and gave my name as the author of
the accusation. To my utter astonishment, he replied,
"I don't believe it; but if she did acknowledge it, you
tortured her into exposing me." Tortured into exposing him! Truly, Satan had no difficulty in distin-
guishing the color of his soul! I understood his
object in making this false representation. It was to
show me that I gained nothing by seeking the protection of my mistress; that the power was still all in his
own hands. I pitied Mrs. Flint. She was a second
wife, many years the junior of her husband; and the
hoary-headed miscreant was enough to try the patience

of a wiser and better woman. She was completely
foiled, and knew not how to proceed. She would
gladly have had me flogged for my supposed false
oath ; but, as I have already stated, the doctor never
allowed any one to whip me. The old sinner was
politic. The application of the lash might have led to
remarks that would have exposed him in the eyes of
his children and grandchildren. How often did I rejoice that I lived in a town where all the inhabitants
knew each other! If I had been on a remote plantation, or lost among the multitude of a crowded city, I
should not be a living woman at this day.

The secrets of slavery are concealed like those of
the Inquisition. My master was, to my knowledge,
the father of eleven slaves But did the mothers dare
to tell who was the father of their children ? Did the
other slaves dare to allude to it, except in whispers
among themselves ? No, indeed ! They knew too
well the terrible consequences.

My grandmother could not avoid seeing things
which excited her suspicions. She was uneasy about
me, and tried various ways to buy me ; but the never-
changing answer was always repeated : " Linda does
not belong to *me*. She is my daughter's property, and
I have no legal right to sell her." The conscientious
man ! He was too scrupulous to *sell* me ; but he had
no scruples whatever about committing a much greater
wrong against the helpless young girl placed under his
guardianship, as his daughter's property. Sometimes
my persecutor would ask me whether I would like to
be sold. I told him I would rather be sold to any
body than to lead such a life as I did. On such occa-

sions he would assume the air of a very injured individual, and reproach me for my ingratitude. "Did I not take you into the house, and make you the companion of my own children?" he would say. "Have I ever treated you like a negro? I have never allowed you to be punished, not even to please your mistress. And this is the recompense I get, you ungrateful girl!" I answered that he had reasons of his own for screening me from punishment, and that the course he pursued made my mistress hate me and persecute me. If I wept, he would say, "Poor child! Don't cry! don't cry! I will make peace for you with your mistress. Only let me arrange matters in my own way. Poor, foolish girl! you don't know what is for your own good. I would cherish you. I would make a lady of you. Now go, and think of all I have promised you."

I did think of it.

Reader, I draw no imaginary pictures of southern homes. I am telling you the plain truth. Yet when victims make their escape from this wild beast of Slavery, northerners consent to act the part of bloodhounds, and hunt the poor fugitive back into his den, "full of dead men's bones, and all uncleanness." Nay, more, they are not only willing, but proud, to give their daughters in marriage to slaveholders. The poor girls have romantic notions of a sunny clime, and of the flowering vines that all the year round shade a happy home. To what disappointments are they destined! The young wife soon learns that the husband in whose hands she has placed her happiness pays no regard to his marriage vows. Children of every shade

of complexion play with her own fair babies, and too
well she knows that they are born unto him of his own
household. Jealousy and hatred enter the flowery
home, and it is ravaged of its loveliness.

Southern women often marry a man knowing that
he is the father of many little slaves. They do not
trouble themselves about it. They regard such children as property, as marketable as the pigs on the
plantation; and it is seldom that they do not make
them aware of this by passing them into the slave-
trader's hands as soon as possible, and thus getting
them out of their sight. I am glad to say there are
some honorable exceptions.

I have myself known two southern wives who exhorted their husbands to free those slaves towards
whom they stood in a " parental relation; " and their
request was granted. These husbands blushed before
the superior nobleness of their wives' natures. Though
they had only counselled them to do that which it was
their duty to do, it commanded their respect, and rendered their conduct more exemplary. Concealment
was at an end, and confidence took the place of distrust.

Though this bad institution deadens the moral sense,
even in white women, to a fearful extent, it is not altogether extinct. I have heard southern ladies say of
Mr. Such a one, " He not only thinks it no disgrace
to be the father of those little niggers, but he is not
ashamed to call himself their master. I declare, such
things ought not to be tolerated in any decent society ! "

VII.

THE LOVER.

WHY does the slave ever love? Why allow the tendrils of the heart to twine around objects which may at any moment be wrenched away by the hand of violence? When separations come by the hand of death, the pious soul can bow in resignation, and say, "Not my will, but thine be done, O Lord!" But when the ruthless hand of man strikes the blow, regardless of the misery he causes, it is hard to be submissive. I did not reason thus when I was a young girl. Youth will be youth. I loved, and I indulged the hope that the dark clouds around me would turn out a bright lining. I forgot that in the land of my birth the shadows are too dense for light to penetrate. A land

> "Where laughter is not mirth; nor thought the mind;
> Nor words a language; nor e'en men mankind.
> Where cries reply to curses, shrieks to blows,
> And each is tortured in his separate hell."

There was in the neighborhood a young colored carpenter; a free born man. We had been well acquainted in childhood, and frequently met together afterwards. We became mutually attached, and he proposed to marry me. I loved him with all the ardor of a young girl's first love. But when I reflected that I was a slave, and that the laws gave no sanction to the marriage of such, my heart sank within me. My lover wanted to buy me; but I knew that Dr. Flint was too wilful and arbitrary a man to consent to that arrangement. From him, I was sure of experiencing all sorts of opposition, and I had nothing to hope from my mistress. She would have been delighted to have got rid of me, but not in that way. It would have relieved her mind of a burden if she could have seen me sold to some distant state, but if I was married near home I should be just as much in her husband's power as I had previously been, — for the husband of a slave has no power to protect her. Moreover, my mistress, like many others, seemed to think that slaves had no right to any family ties of their own; that they were created merely to wait upon the family of the mistress. I once heard her abuse a young slave girl, who told her that a colored man wanted to make her his wife. "I will have you peeled and pickled, my lady," said she, "if I ever hear you mention that subject again. Do you suppose that I will have you tending *my* children with the children of that nigger?" The girl to whom she said this had a mulatto child, of course not acknowledged by its father. The poor black man who loved her would have been proud to acknowledge his helpless offspring.

Many and anxious were the thoughts I revolved in my mind. I was at a loss what to do. Above all things, I was desirous to spare my lover the insults that had cut so deeply into my own soul. I talked with my grandmother about it, and partly told her my fears. I did not dare to tell her the worst. She had long suspected all was not right, and if I confirmed her suspicions I knew a storm would rise that would prove the overthrow of all my hopes.

This love-dream had been my support through many trials; and I could not bear to run the risk of having it suddenly dissipated. There was a lady in the neighborhood, a particular friend of Dr. Flint's, who often visited the house. I had a great respect for her, and she had always manifested a friendly interest in me. Grandmother thought she would have great influence with the doctor. I went to this lady, and told her my story. I told her I was aware that my lover's being a free-born man would prove a great objection; but he wanted to buy me; and if Dr. Flint would consent to that arrangement, I felt sure he would be willing to pay any reasonable price. She knew that Mrs. Flint disliked me; therefore, I ventured to suggest that perhaps my mistress would approve of my being sold, as that would rid her of me. The lady listened with kindly sympathy, and promised to do her utmost to promote my wishes. She had an interview with the doctor, and I believe she pleaded my cause earnestly; but it was all to no purpose.

How I dreaded my master now! Every minute I expected to be summoned to his presence; but the day passed, and I heard nothing from him. The next morning, a message was brought to me: "Master wants you in his study." I found the door ajar, and I stood a moment gazing at the hateful man who claimed a right to rule me, body and soul. I entered, and tried to appear calm. I did not want him to know how my heart was bleeding. He looked fixedly at me, with an expression which seemed to say, "I have half a mind to kill you on the spot." At last he broke the silence, and that was a relief to both of us.

"So you want to be married, do you?" said he, "and to a free nigger."

"Yes, sir."

"Well, I'll soon convince you whether I am your master, or the nigger fellow you honor so highly. If you *must* have a husband, you may take up with one of my slaves."

What a situation I should be in, as the wife of one of *his* slaves, even if my heart had been interested!

I replied, "Don't you suppose, sir, that a slave can have some preference about marrying? Do you suppose that all men are alike to her?"

"Do you love this nigger?" said he, abruptly.

"Yes, sir."

"How dare you tell me so!" he exclaimed, in great wrath. After a slight pause, he added, "I supposed you thought more of yourself; that you felt above the insults of such puppies."

"I replied, "If he is a puppy I am a puppy, for we are both of the negro race. It is right and honorable for us to love each other. The man you call a puppy never insulted me, sir; and he would not love me if he did not believe me to be a virtuous woman."

He sprang upon me like a tiger, and gave me a stunning blow. It was the first time he had ever struck me; and fear did not enable me to control my anger. When I had recovered a little from the effects, I exclaimed, "You have struck me for answering you honestly. How I despise you!"

There was silence for some minutes. Perhaps he was deciding what should be my punishment; or, perhaps, he wanted to give me time to reflect on what I had said, and to whom I had said it. Finally, he asked, " Do you know what you have said ? "

" Yes, sir ; but your treatment drove me to it."

" Do you know that I have a right to do as I like with you, — that I can kill you, if I please ? "

" You have tried to kill me, and I wish you had ; but you have no right to do as you like with me."

" Silence ! " he exclaimed, in a thundering voice. " By heavens, girl, you forget yourself too far ! Are you mad ? If you are, I will soon bring you to your senses. Do you think any other master would bear what I have borne from you this morning ? Many masters would have killed you on the spot. How would you like to be sent to jail for your insolence ? "

" I know I have been disrespectful, sir," I replied ; " but you drove me to it ; I couldn't help it. As for the jail, there would be more peace for me there than there is here."

" You deserve to go there," said he, " and to be under such treatment, that you would forget the meaning of the word *peace*. It would do you good. It would take some of your high notions out of you. But I am not ready to send you there yet, notwithstanding your ingratitude for all my kindness and forbearance. You have been the plague of my life. I have wanted to make you happy, and I have been repaid with the basest ingratitude ; but though you have proved yourself incapable of appreciating my kindness, I will be lenient towards you, Linda. I will give you one more chance to redeem your character. If you behave yourself and do as I require, I will forgive you and treat you as I always have done ; but if you disobey me, I will punish you as I would the meanest slave on my plantation. Never let me hear that fellow's name mentioned again. If I ever know of your speaking to him, I will cowhide you both; and if I catch him lurking about my premises, I will shoot him as soon as I would a dog. Do you hear what I say? I'll teach you a lesson about marriage and free niggers! Now go, and let this be the last time I have occasion to speak to you on this subject."

Reader, did you ever hate? I hope not. I never did but once; and I trust I never shall again. Somebody has called it "the atmosphere of hell;" and I believe it is so.

For a fortnight the doctor did not speak to me. He thought to mortify me; to make me feel that I had disgraced myself by receiving the honorable addresses of a respectable colored man, in preference to the base proposals of a white man. But though his lips disdained to address me, his eyes were very loquacious. No animal ever watched its prey more narrowly than he watched me. He knew that I could write, though he had failed to make me read his letters; and he was now troubled lest I should exchange letters with another man. After a while he became weary of silence; and I was sorry for it. One morning, as he passed through the hall, to leave the house, he contrived to thrust a note into my hand. I thought I had better read it, and spare myself the vexation of having him read it to me. It expressed regret for the blow he had given me, and reminded me that I myself was wholly to blame for it. He hoped I had become convinced of the injury I was doing myself by incurring his displeasure. He wrote that he had made up his mind to go to Louisiana; that he should take several slaves with him, and intended I should be one of the number. My mistress would remain where she was; therefore I should have nothing to fear from that quarter. If I merited kindness from him, he assured me that it would be lavishly bestowed. He begged me to think over the matter, and answer the following day.

The next morning I was called to carry a pair of scissors to his room. I laid them on the table, with the letter beside them. He thought it was my answer, and did not call me back. I went as usual to attend my young mistress to and from school. He met me in the street, and ordered me to stop at his office on my way back. When I entered, he showed me his letter, and asked me why I had not answered it. I replied, " I am your daughter's property, and it is in your power to send me, or take me, wherever you please." He said he was very glad to find me so willing to go, and that we should start early in the autumn. He had a large practice in the town, and I rather thought he had made up the story merely to frighten me. However that might be, I was determined that I would never go to Louisiana with him.

Summer passed away, and early in the autumn Dr. Flint's eldest son was sent to Louisiana to examine the country, with a view to emigrating. That news did not disturb me. I knew very well that I should not be sent with *him*. That I had not been taken to the plantation before this time, was owing to the fact that his son was there. He was jealous of his son; and jealousy of the overseer had kept him from punishing me by sending me into the fields to work. Is it strange that I was not proud of these protectors? As for the overseer, he was a man for whom I had less respect than I had for a bloodhound.

Young Mr. Flint did not bring back a favorable report of Louisiana, and I heard no more of that scheme. Soon after this, my lover met me at the corner of the street, and I stopped to speak to him. Looking up, I saw my master watching us from his window. I hurried home, trembling with fear. I was sent for, immediately, to go to his room. He met me with a blow. "When is mistress to be married?" said he, in a sneering tone. A shower of oaths and imprecations followed. How thankful I was that my lover was a free man! that my tyrant had no power to flog him for speaking to me in the street!

Again and again I revolved in my mind how all this would end. There was no hope that the doctor would consent to sell me on any terms. He had an iron will, and was determined to keep me, and to conquer me. My lover was an intelligent and religious man. Even if he could have obtained permission to marry me while I was a slave, the marriage would give him no power to protect me from my master. It would have made him miserable to witness the insults I should have been subjected to. And then, if we had children, I knew they must "follow the condition of the mother." What a terrible blight that would be on the heart of a free, intelligent father! For *his* sake, I felt that I ought not to link his fate with my own unhappy destiny. He was going to Savannah to see about a little property left him by an uncle; and hard as it was to bring my feelings to it, I earnestly entreated him not to come back. I advised him to go to the Free States, where his tongue would not be tied, and where his intelligence would be of more avail to him. He left me, still hoping the day would come when I could be bought. With me the lamp of hope had gone out. The dream of my girlhood was over. I felt lonely and desolate.

Still I was not stripped of all. I still had my good grandmother, and my affectionate brother. When he put his arms round my neck, and looked into my eyes, as if to read there the troubles I dared not tell, I felt that I still had something to love. But even that pleasant emotion was chilled by the reflection that he might be torn from me at any moment, by some sudden freak of my master. If he had known how we loved each other, I think he would have exulted in separating us. We often planned together how we could get to the north. But, as William remarked, such things are easier said than done. My movements were very closely watched, and we had no means of getting any money to defray our expenses. As for grandmother, she was strongly opposed to her children's undertaking any such project. She had not forgotten poor Benjamin's sufferings, and she was afraid that if another child tried to escape, he would have a similar or a worse fate. To me, nothing seemed more dreadful than my present life. I said to myself, "William *must* be free. He shall go to the north, and I will follow him." Many a slave sister has formed the same plans.

VIII.

WHAT SLAVES ARE TAUGHT TO THINK OF THE NORTH.

SLAVEHOLDERS pride themselves upon being honorable men ; but if you were to hear the enormous lies they tell their slaves, you would have small respect for their veracity.   I have spoken plain English.   Pardon me.   I cannot use a milder term.   When they visit the north, and return home, they tell their slaves of the runaways they have seen, and describe them to be in the most deplorable condition.   A slaveholder once told me that he had seen a runaway friend of mine in New York, and that she besought him to take her back to her master, for she was literally dying of starvation ; that many days she had only one cold potato to eat, and at other times could get nothing at all.   He said he refused to take her, because he knew her master would not thank him for bringing such a miserable wretch to his house.   He ended by saying to me, " This is the punishment she brought on herself for running away from a kind master."

This whole story was false.   I afterwards staid with that friend in New York, and found her in comfortable circumstances.   She had never thought of such a thing as wishing to go back to slavery.   Many of the slaves believe such stories, and think it is not worth while to exchange slavery for such a hard kind of freedom.   It is difficult to persuade such that freedom could make them useful men, and enable them to protect their wives and children.   If those heathen in our Christian land had as much teaching as some Hindoos, they would think otherwise.   They would know that liberty is more valuable than life.   They would begin to understand their own capabilities, and exert themselves to become men and women.

But while the Free States sustain a law which hurls fugitives back into slavery, how can the slaves resolve to become men?   There are some who strive to protect wives and daughters from the insults of their masters; but those who have such sentiments have had advantages above the general mass of slaves.   They have been partially civilized and Christianized by favorable circumstances.   Some are bold enough to *utter* such sentiments to their masters.   O, that there were more of them!

Some poor creatures have been so brutalized by the lash that they will sneak out of the way to give their masters free access to their wives and daughters.   Do you think this proves the black man to belong to an inferior order of beings?   What would *you* be, if you had been born and brought up a slave, with generations of slaves for ancestors?   I admit that the black man *is* inferior.   But what is it that makes him so?   It is the ignorance in which white men compel him to live; it is the torturing whip that lashes manhood out of him; it is the fierce bloodhounds of the South, and the scarcely less cruel human bloodhounds of the north, who enforce the Fugitive Slave Law.   *They* do the work.

Southern gentlemen indulge in the most contempt-

uous expressions about the Yankees, while they, on
their part, consent to do the vilest work for them, such
as the ferocious bloodhounds and the despised negro-
hunters are employed to do at home. When southerners go to the north, they are proud to do them
honor; but the northern man is not welcome south of
Mason and Dixon's line, unless he suppresses every
thought and feeling at variance with their "peculiar
institution." Nor is it enough to be silent. The masters are not pleased, unless they obtain a greater degree of subservience than that; and they are generally accomodated. Do they respect the northerner
for this? I trow not. Even the slaves despise " a
northern man with southern principles;" and that is
the class they generally see. When northerners go to
the south to reside, they prove very apt scholars.
They soon imbibe the sentiments and disposition of
their neighbors, and generally go beyond their teachers.
Of the two, they are proverbially the hardest masters.

They seem to satisfy their consciences with the doctrine that God created the Africans to be sláves. What
a libel upon the heavenly Father, who " made of one
blood all nations of men!" And then who *are* Africans? Who can measure the amount of Anglo-Saxon
blood coursing in the veins of American slaves?

I have spoken of the pains slaveholders take to give
their slaves a bad opinion of the north; but, notwithstanding this, intelligent slaves are aware that they
have many friends in the Free States. Even the most
ignorant have some confused notions about it. They
knew that I could read; and I was often asked if I
had seen any thing in the newspapers about white folks

IX.

SKETCHES OF NEIGHBORING SLAVEHOLDERS.

THERE was a planter in the country, not far from us, whom I will call Mr. Litch. He was an ill-bred, un-educated man, but very wealthy. He had six hundred slaves, many of whom he did not know by sight. His extensive plantation was managed by well-paid overseers. There was a jail and a whipping post on his grounds; and whatever cruelties were perpetrated there, they passed without comment. He was so effectually screened by his great wealth that he was called to no account for his crimes, not even for murder.

Various were the punishments resorted to. A favorite one was to tie a rope round a man's body, and suspend him from the ground. A fire was kindled over him, from which was suspended a piece of fat pork. As this cooked, the scalding drops of fat continually fell on the bare flesh. On his own plantation, he required very strict obedience to the eighth commandment. But depredations on the neighbors were allowable, provided the culprit managed to evade detection or suspicion. If a neighbor brought a charge of theft against any of his slaves, he was browbeaten by the master, who assured him that his slaves had enough of every thing at home, and had no inducement to steal. No sooner was the neighbor's back turned, than the accused was sought out, and whipped for his lack of discretion. If a slave stole from him even a pound of meat or a peck of corn, if detection followed, he was put in chains and imprisoned, and so kept till his form was attenuated by hunger and suffering.

A freshet once bore his wine cellar and meat house miles away from the plantation. Some slaves followed, and secured bits of meat and bottles of wine. Two were detected; a ham and some liquor being found in their huts. They were summoned by their master. No words were used, but a club felled them to the ground. A rough box was their coffin, and their interment was a dog's burial. Nothing was said.

Murder was so common on his plantation that he feared to be alone after nightfall. He might have believed in ghosts.

His brother, if not equal in wealth, was at least equal in cruelty. His bloodhounds were well trained. Their pen was spacious, and a terror to the slaves. They were let loose on a runaway, and, if they tracked him, they literally tore the flesh from his bones. When this slaveholder died, his shrieks and groans were so frightful that they appalled his own friends. His last words were, "I am going to hell; bury my money with me."

After death his eyes remained open. To press the lids down, silver dollars were laid on them. These were buried with him. From this circumstance, a rumor went abroad that his coffin was filled with money. Three times his grave was opened, and his coffin taken out. The last time, his body was found on the ground, and a flock of buzzards were pecking at it. He was again interred, and a sentinel set over his grave. The perpetrators were never discovered.

Cruelty is contagious in uncivilized communities. Mr. Conant, a neighbor of Mr. Litch, returned from town one evening in a partial state of intoxication. His body servant gave him some offence. He was divested of his clothes, except his shirt, whipped, and tied to a large tree in front of the house. It was a stormy night in winter. The wind blew bitterly cold, and the boughs of the old tree crackled under falling sleet. A member of the family, fearing he would freeze to death, begged that he might be taken down ; but the master would not relent. He remained there three hours ; and, when he was cut down, he was more dead than alive. Another slave, who stole a pig from this master, to appease his hunger, was terribly flogged. In desperation, he tried to run away. But at the end of two miles, he was so faint with loss of blood, he thought he was dying. He had a wife, and he longed to see her once more. Too sick to walk, he crept back that long distance on his hands and knees. When he reached his master's, it was night. He had not strength to rise and open the gate. He moaned, and tried to call for help. I had a friend living in the same family. At last his cry reached her. She went out and found the prostrate man at the gate. She ran back to the house for assistance, and two men returned with her. They carried him in, and laid him on the floor. The back of his shirt was one clot of blood. By means of lard, my friend loosened it from the raw flesh. She bandaged him, gave him cool drink, and left him to rest. The master said he deserved a hundred more lashes. When his own labor was stolen from him, he had stolen food to appease his hunger. This was his crime.

Another neighbor was a Mrs. Wade. At no hour of the day was there cessation of the lash on her premises. Her labors began with the dawn, and did not cease till long after nightfall. The barn was her particular place of torture. There she lashed the slaves with the might of a man. An old slave of hers once said to me, " It is hell in missis's house. 'Pears I can never get out. Day and night I prays to die."

The mistress died before the old woman, and, when dying, entreated her husband not to permit any one of her slaves to look on her after death. A slave who had nursed her children, and had still a child in her care, watched her chance, and stole with it in her arms to the room where lay her dead mistress. She gazed a while on her, then raised her hand and dealt two blows on her face, saying, as she did so, " The devil is got you *now !* " She forgot that the child was looking on. She had just begun to talk ; and she said to her father, " I did see ma, and mammy did strike ma, so," striking her own face with her little hand. The master was startled. He could not imagine how the nurse could obtain access to the room where the corpse lay ; for he kept the door locked. He questioned her. She confessed that what the child had said was true, and told how she had procured the key. She was sold to Georgia.

In my childhood I knew a valuable slave, named Charity, and loved her, as all children did. Her young mistress married, and took her to Louisiana. Her little boy, James, was sold to a good sort of master. He became involved in debt, and James was sold again to a wealthy slaveholder, noted for his cruelty. With this man he grew up to manhood, receiving the treatment of a dog. After a severe whipping, to save himself from further infliction of the lash, with which he was threatened, he took to the woods. He was in a most miserable condition — cut by the cowskin, half naked, half starved, and without the means of procuring a crust of bread.

Some weeks after his escape, he was captured, tied, and carried back to his master's plantation. This man considered punishment in his jail, on bread and water, after receiving hundreds of lashes, too mild for the poor slave's offence. Therefore he decided, after the overseer should have whipped him to his satisfaction, to have him placed between the screws of the cotton gin, to stay as long as he had been in the woods. This wretched creature was cut with the whip from his head to his feet, then washed with strong brine, to prevent the flesh from mortifying, and make it heal sooner than it otherwise would. He was then put into the cotton gin, which was screwed down, only allowing him room to turn on his side when he could not lie on his back. Every morning a slave was sent with a piece of bread and bowl of water, which were placed within reach of the poor fellow. The slave was charged, under penalty of severe punishment, not to speak to him.

Four days passed, and the slave continued to carry the bread and water. On the second morning, he found the bread gone, but the water untouched.

When he had been in the press four days and five nights, the slave informed his master that the water had not been used for four mornings, and that a horrible stench came from the gin house. The overseer was sent to examine into it. When the press was unscrewed, the dead body was found partly eaten by rats and vermin. Perhaps the rats that devoured his bread had gnawed him before life was extinct. Poor Charity ! Grandmother and I often asked each other how her affectionate heart would bear the news, if she should ever hear of the murder of her son. We had known her husband, and knew that James was like him in manliness and intelligence. These were the qualities that made it so hard for him to be a plantation slave. They put him into a rough box, and buried him with less feeling than would have been manifested for an old house dog. Nobody asked any questions. He was a slave ; and the feeling was that the master had a right to do what he pleased with his own property. And what did *he* care for the value of a slave ? He had hundreds of them. When they had finished their daily toil, they must hurry to eat their little morsels, and be ready to extinguish their pine knots before nine o'clock, when the overseer went his patrol rounds. He entered every cabin, to see that men and their wives had gone to bed together, lest the men, from over-fatigue, should fall asleep in the chimney corner, and remain there till the morning horn called them to their daily task. Women are considered of no value, unless they continually increase their owner's stock. They are put on a par with animals. This same master shot a woman through the head, who had run away and been brought back to him. No one called him to account for it. If a slave resisted being whipped, the bloodhounds were unpacked, and set upon him, to tear his flesh from his bones. The master who did these things was highly educated, and styled a perfect gentleman. He also boasted the name and standing of a Christian, though Satan never had a truer follower.

I could tell of more slaveholders as cruel as those I have described. They are not exceptions to the general rule. I do not say there are no humane slaveholders. Such characters do exist, notwithstanding the hardening influences around them. But they are " like angels' visits — few and far between."

I knew a young lady who was one of these rare specimens. She was an orphan, and inherited as slaves a woman and her six children. Their father was a free man. They had a comfortable home of their own, parents and children living together. The mother and eldest daughter served their mistress during the day, and at night returned to their dwelling, which was on the premises. The young lady was very pious, and there was some reality in her religion. She taught her slaves to lead pure lives, and wished them to enjoy the fruit of their own industry. *Her* religion was not a garb put on for Sunday, and laid aside till Sunday returned again. The eldest daughter of the slave mother was promised in marriage to a free man ; and the day before the wedding this good mistress emancipated her, in order that her marriage might have the sanction of *law*.

Report said that this young lady cherished an unrequited affection for a man who had resolved to marry for wealth. In the course of time a rich uncle of hers died. He left six thousand dollars to his two sons by a colored woman, and the remainder of his property to this orphan niece. The metal soon attracted the magnet. The lady and her weighty purse became his. She offered to manumit her slaves — telling them that her marriage might make unexpected changes in their destiny, and she wished to insure their happiness. They refused to take their freedom, saying that she had always been their best friend, and they could not be so happy any where as with her. I was not surprised. I had often seen them in their comfortable home, and thought that the whole town did not contain a happier family. They had never felt slavery; and, when it was too late, they were convinced of its reality.

When the new master claimed this family as his property, the father became furious, and went to his mistress for protection. "I can do nothing for you now, Harry," said she. "I no longer have the power I had a week ago. I have succeeded in obtaining the freedom of your wife; but I cannot obtain it for your children." The unhappy father swore that nobody should take his children from him. He concealed them in the woods for some days; but they were discovered and taken. The father was put in jail, and the two oldest boys sold to Georgia. One little girl, too young to be of service to her master, was left with the wretched mother. The other three were carried to their master's plantation. The eldest soon became a mother ; and, when the slaveholder's wife looked at the babe, she wept bitterly. She knew that her own husband had violated the purity she had so carefully inculcated. She had a second child by her master, and then he sold her and his offspring to his brother. She bore two children to the brother, and was sold again. The next sister went crazy. The life she was compelled to lead drove her mad. The third one became the mother of five daughters. Before the birth of the fourth the pious mistress died. To the last, she rendered every kindness to the slaves that her unfortunate circumstances permitted. She passed away peacefully, glad to close her eyes on a life which had been made so wretched by the man she loved.

This man squandered the fortune he had received, and sought to retrieve his affairs by a second marriage; but, having retired after a night of drunken debauch, he was found dead in the morning. He was called a good master ; for he fed and clothed his slaves better than most masters, and the lash was not heard on his plantation so frequently as on many others. Had it not been for slavery, he would have been a better man, and his wife a happier woman.

No pen can give an adequate description of the all-pervading corruption produced by slavery. The slave girl is reared in an atmosphere of licentiousness and fear. The lash and the foul talk of her master and his sons are her teachers. When she is fourteen or fifteen, her owner, or his sons, or the overseer, or perhaps all of them, begin to bribe her with presents. If these fail to accomplish their purpose, she is whipped or starved into submission to their will. She may have had religious principles inculcated by some pious

mother or grandmother, or some good mistress; she
may have a lover, whose good opinion and peace of
mind are dear to her heart; or the profligate men who
have power over her may be exceedingly odious to
her. But resistance is hopeless.

> " The poor worm
> Shall prove her contest vain. Life's little day
> Shall pass, and she is gone!"

The slaveholder's sons are, of course, vitiated, even
while boys, by the unclean influences every where
around them. Nor do the master's daughters always
escape. Severe retributions sometimes come upon him
for the wrongs he does to the daughters of the slaves.
The white daughters early hear their parents quarrelling about some female slave. Their curiosity is
excited, and they soon learn the cause. They are
attended by the young slave girls whom their father
has corrupted; and they hear such talk as should
never meet youthful ears, or any other ears. They
know that the women slaves are subject to their father's authority in all things; and in some cases they
exercise the same authority over the men slaves. I
have myself seen the master of such a household whose
head was bowed down in shame; for it was known in
the neighborhood that his daughter had selected one
of the meanest slaves on his plantation to be the father
of his first grandchild. She did not make her advances to her equals, nor even to her father's more
intelligent servants. She selected the most brutalized,
over whom her authority could be exercised with less
fear of exposure. Her father, half frantic with rage,
sought to revenge himself on the offending black man;

but his daughter, foreseeing the storm that would arise, had given him free papers, and sent him out of the state.

In such cases the infant is smothered, or sent where it is never seen by any who know its history. But if the white parent is the *father*, instead of the mother, the offspring are unblushingly reared for the market. If they are girls, I have indicated plainly enough what will be their inevitable destiny.

You may believe what I say; for I write only that whereof I know. I was twenty-one years in that cage of obscene birds. I can testify, from my own experience and observation, that slavery is a curse to the whites as well as to the blacks. It makes the white fathers cruel and sensual; the sons violent and licentious; it contaminates the daughters, and makes the wives wretched. And as for the colored race, it needs an abler pen than mine to describe the extremity of their sufferings, the depth of their degradation.

Yet few slaveholders seem to be aware of the widespread moral ruin occasioned by this wicked system. Their talk is of blighted cotton crops — not of the blight on their children's souls.

If you want to be fully convinced of the abominations of slavery, go on a southern plantation, and call yourself a negro trader. Then there will be no concealment; and you will see and hear things that will seem to you impossible among human beings with immortal souls.

X.

A PERILOUS PASSAGE IN THE SLAVE GIRL'S LIFE.

After my lover went away, Dr. Flint contrived a new plan. He seemed to have an idea that my fear of my mistress was his greatest obstacle. In the blandest tones, he told me that he was going to build a small house for me, in a secluded place, four miles away from the town. I shuddered; but I was constrained to listen, while he talked of his intention to give me a home of my own, and to make a lady of me. Hitherto, I had escaped my dreaded fate, by being in the midst of people. My grandmother had already had high words with my master about me. She had told him pretty plainly what she thought of his character, and there was considerable gossip in the neighborhood about our affairs, to which the open-mouthed jealousy of Mrs. Flint contributed not a little. When my master said he was going to build a house for me, and that he could do it with little trouble and expense, I was in hopes something would happen to frustrate his scheme; but I soon heard that the house was actually begun. I vowed before my Maker that I would never enter it. I had rather toil on the plantation from dawn till dark; I had rather live and die in jail, than drag on, from day to day, through such a living death. I was determined that the master, whom I so hated and loathed, who had blighted the prospects of my youth, and made

my life a desert, should not, after my long struggle
with him, succeed at last in trampling his victim under
his feet. I would do any thing, every thing, for the sake
of defeating him. What *could* I do? I thought and
thought, till I became desperate, and made a plunge
into the abyss.

And now, reader, I come to a period in my unhappy
life, which I would gladly forget if I could. The remembrance fills me with sorrow and shame. It pains
me to tell you of it; but I have promised to tell you
the truth, and I will do it honestly, let it cost me what
it may. I will not try to screen myself behind
the plea of compulsion from a master; for it was
not so. Neither can I plead ignorance or thought-
lessness. For years, my master had done his utmost
to pollute my mind with foul images, and to destroy
the pure principles inculcated by my grandmother,
and the good mistress of my childhood. The influences of slavery had had the same effect on me that
they had on other young girls; they had made me
prematurely knowing, concerning the evil ways of
the world. I knew what I did, and I did it with de-
liberate calculation.

But, O, ye happy women, whose purity has been
sheltered from childhood, who have been free to choose
the objects of your affection, whose homes are protected
by law, do not judge the poor desolate slave girl too
severely! If slavery had been abolished, I, also, could
have married the man of my choice; I could have had
a home shielded by the laws; and I should have been
spared the painful task of confessing what I am now
about to relate; but all my prospects had been blighted

by slavery. I wanted to keep myself pure; and, under the most adverse circumstances, I tried hard to preserve my self-respect; but I was struggling alone in the powerful grasp of the demon Slavery; and the monster proved too strong for me. I felt as if I was forsaken by God and man; as if all my efforts must be frustrated; and I became reckless in my despair.

I have told you that Dr. Flint's persecutions and his wife's jealousy had given rise to some gossip in the neighborhood. Among others, it chanced that a white unmarried gentleman had obtained some knowledge of the circumstances in which I was placed. He knew my grandmother, and often spoke to me in the street. He became interested for me, and asked questions about my master, which I answered in part. He expressed a great deal of sympathy, and a wish to aid me. He constantly sought opportunities to see me, and wrote to me frequently. I was a poor slave girl, only fifteen years old.

So much attention from a superior person was, of course, flattering; for human nature is the same in all. I also felt grateful for his sympathy, and encouraged by his kind words. It seemed to me a great thing to have such a friend. By degrees, a more tender feeling crept into my heart. He was an educated and eloquent gentleman; too eloquent, alas, for the poor slave girl who trusted in him. Of course I saw whither all this was tending. I knew the impassable gulf between us; but to be an object of interest to a man who is not married, and who is not her master, is agreeable to the pride and feelings of a slave, if her miserable situation has left her any pride or sentiment. It seems less degrading to give one's self, than to submit to compulsion. There is something akin to freedom in having a lover who has no control over you, except that which he gains by kindness and attachment. A master may treat you as rudely as he pleases, and you dare not speak; moreover, the wrong does not seem so great with an unmarried man, as with one who has a wife to be made unhappy. There may be sophistry in all this; but the condition of a slave confuses all principles of morality, and, in fact, renders the practice of them impossible.

When I found that my master had actually begun to build the lonely cottage, other feelings mixed with those I have described. Revenge, and calculations of interest, were added to flattered vanity and sincere gratitude for kindness. I knew nothing would enrage Dr. Flint so much as to know that I favored another; and it was something to triumph over my tyrant even in that small way. I thought he would revenge himself by selling me, and I was sure my friend, Mr. Sands, would buy me. He was a man of more generosity and feeling than my master, and I thought my freedom could be easily obtained from him. The crisis of my fate now came so near that I was desperate. I shuddered to think of being the mother of children that should be owned by my old tyrant. I knew that as soon as a new fancy took him, his victims were sold far off to get rid of them; especially if they had children. I had seen several women sold, with his babies at the breast. He never allowed his offspring by slaves to remain long in sight of himself and his wife. Of a man who was not my master I could ask to have my children well supported; and in this case, I felt confident I should obtain the boon. I also felt quite sure that they would be made free. With all these thoughts revolving in my mind, and seeing no other way of escaping the doom I so much dreaded, I made a headlong plunge. Pity me, and pardon me, O virtuous reader! You never knew what it is to be a slave; to be entirely unprotected by law or custom; to have the laws reduce you to the condition of a chattel, entirely subject to the will of another. You never exhausted your ingenuity in avoiding the snares, and eluding the power of a hated tyrant; you never shuddered at the sound of his footsteps, and trembled within hearing of his voice. I know I did wrong. No one can feel it more sensibly than I do. The painful and humiliating memory will haunt me to my dying day. Still, in looking back, calmly, on the events of my life, I feel that the slave woman ought not to be judged by the same standard as others.

The months passed on. I had many unhappy hours. I secretly mourned over the sorrow I was bringing on my grandmother, who had so tried to shield me from harm. I knew that I was the greatest comfort of her old age, and that it was a source of pride to her that I had not degraded myself, like most of the slaves. I wanted to confess to her that I was no longer worthy of her love; but I could not utter the dreaded words.

As for Dr. Flint, I had a feeling of satisfaction and triumph in the thought of telling *him*. From time to time he told me of his intended arrangements, and I was silent. At last, he came and told me the cottage was completed, and ordered me to go to it. I told him I would never enter it. He said, " I have heard

enough of such talk as that. You shall go, if you are
carried by force; and you shall remain there."

I replied, " I will never go there. In a few months
I shall be a mother."

He stood and looked at me in dumb amazement, and
left the house without a word. I thought I should be
happy in my triumph over him. But now that the
truth was out, and my relatives would hear of it, I felt
wretched. Humble as were their circumstances, they
had pride in my good character. Now, how could I
look them in the face ? My self-respect was gone ! I
had resolved that I would be virtuous, though I was a
slave. I had said, " Let the storm beat ! I will brave
it till I die." And now, how humiliated I felt !

I went to my grandmother. My lips moved to make
confession, but the words stuck in my throat. I sat
down in the shade of a tree at her door and began to
sew. I think she saw something unusual was the
matter with me. The mother of slaves is very watchful. She knows there is no security for her children.
After they have entered their teens she lives in daily
expectation of trouble. This leads to many questions.
If the girl is of a sensitive nature, timidity keeps her
from answering truthfully, and this well-meant course
has a tendency to drive her from maternal counsels.
Presently, in came my mistress, like a mad woman,
and accused me concerning her husband. My grandmother, whose suspicions had been previously awakened, believed what she said. She exclaimed, " O
Linda ! has it come to this ? I had rather see you
dead than to see you as you now are. You are a disgrace to your dead mother." She tore from my fin-

gers my mother's wedding ring and her silver thimble.
" Go away ! " she exclaimed, " and never come to my
house, again." Her reproaches fell so hot and heavy,
that they left me no chance to answer. Bitter tears,
such as the eyes never shed but once, were my only
answer. I rose from my seat, but fell back again, sobbing. She did not speak to me; but the tears were
running down her furrowed cheeks, and they scorched
me like fire. She had always been so kind to me! *So*
kind ! How I longed to throw myself at her feet, and
tell her all the truth ! But she had ordered me to go,
and never to come there again. After a few minutes,
I mustered strength, and started to obey her. With
what feelings did I now close that little gate, which I
used to open with such an eager hand in my childhood ! It closed upon me with a sound I never
heard before.

Where could I go ? I was afraid to return to my master's. I walked on recklessly, not caring where I went,
or what would become of me. When I had gone four
or five miles, fatigue compelled me to stop. I sat
down on the stump of an old tree. The stars were
shining through the boughs above me. How they
mocked me, with their bright, calm light ! The hours
passed by, and as I sat there alone a chilliness and
deadly sickness came over me. I sank on the ground.
My mind was full of horrid thoughts. I prayed to die ;
but the prayer was not answered. At last, with great effort I roused myself, and walked some distance further,
to the house of a woman who had been a friend of my
mother. When I told her why I was there, she spoke
soothingly to me ; but I could not be comforted. I

thought I could bear my shame if I could only be re-
conciled to my grandmother. I longed to open my
heart to her. I thought if she could know the real
state of the case, and all I had been bearing for years,
she would perhaps judge me less harshly. My friend
advised me to send for her. I did so; but days of
agonizing suspense passed before she came. Had she
utterly forsaken me? No. She came at last. I knelt
before her, and told her the things that had poisoned
my life; how long I had been persecuted; that I saw
no way of escape; and in an hour of extremity I had
become desperate. She listened in silence. I told her
I would bear any thing and do any thing, if in time
I had hopes of obtaining her forgiveness. I begged
of her to pity me, for my dead mother's sake. And
she did pity me. She did not say, "I forgive you;"
but she looked at me lovingly, with her eyes full of
tears. She laid her old hand gently on my head, and
murmured, "Poor child! Poor child!"

8 *

XI.

THE NEW TIE TO LIFE.

I RETURNED to my good grandmother's house. She had an interview with Mr. Sands. When she asked him why he could not have left her one ewe lamb, — whether there were not plenty of slaves who did not care about character, — he made no answer ; but he spoke kind and encouraging words. He promised to care for my child, and to buy me, be the conditions what they might.

I had not seen Dr. Flint for five days. I had never seen him since I made the avowal to him. He talked of the disgrace I had brought on myself; how I had sinned against my master, and mortified my old grandmother. He intimated that if I had accepted his proposals, he, as a physician, could have saved me from exposure. He even condescended to pity me. Could he have offered wormwood more bitter ? He, whose persecutions had been the cause of my sin !

"Linda," said he, "though you have been criminal towards me, I feel for you, and I can pardon you if you obey my wishes. Tell me whether the fellow you wanted to marry is the father of your child. If you deceive me, you shall feel the fires of hell."

I did not feel as proud as I had done. My strongest weapon with him was gone. I was lowered in my own estimation, and had resolved to bear his abuse in silence. But when he spoke contemptuously of the lover who had always treated me honorably; when I remembered that but for *him* I might have been a virtuous, free, and happy wife, I lost my patience. "I have sinned against God and myself," I replied; "but not against you."

He clinched his teeth, and muttered, "Curse you!" He came towards me, with ill-suppressed rage, and exclaimed, "You obstinate girl! I could grind your bones to powder! You have thrown yourself away on some worthless rascal. You are weak-minded, and have been easily persuaded by those who don't care a straw for you. The future will settle accounts between us. You are blinded now; but hereafter you will be convinced that your master was your best friend. My lenity towards you is a proof of it. I might have punished you in many ways. I might have had you whipped till you fell dead under the lash. But I wanted you to live; I would have bettered your condition. Others cannot do it. You are my slave. Your mistress, disgusted by your conduct, forbids you to return to the house; therefore I leave you here for the present; but I shall see you often. I will call to-morrow."

He came with frowning brows, that showed a dissatisfied state of mind. After asking about my health, he inquired whether my board was paid, and who visited me. He then went on to say that he had neglected his duty; that as a physician there were certain things that he ought to have explained to me. Then followed talk such as would have made the most shameless blush. He ordered me to stand up before him. I obeyed. "I command you," said he, "to tell

me whether the father of your child is white or black."
I hesitated. "Answer me this instant!" he exclaimed.
I did answer. He sprang upon me like a wolf, and
grabbed my arm as if he would have broken it. "Do
you love him?" said he, in a hissing tone.

"I am thankful that I do not despise him," I replied.

He raised his hand to strike me; but it fell again.
I don't know what arrested the blow. He sat down,
with lips tightly compressed. At last he spoke. "I
came here," said he, "to make you a friendly proposition; but your ingratitude chafes me beyond endurance. You turn aside all my good intentions towards
you. I don't know what it is that keeps me from killing you." Again he rose, as if he had a mind to
strike me.

But he resumed. "On one condition I will forgive
your insolence and crime. You must henceforth
have no communication of any kind with the father
of your child. You must not ask any thing from him,
or receive any thing from him. I will take care of
you and your child. You had better promise this at
once, and not wait till you are deserted by him. This
is the last act of mercy I shall show towards you."

I said something about being unwilling to have my
child supported by a man who had cursed it and me
also. He rejoined, that a woman who had sunk to my
level had no right to expect any thing else. He asked,
for the last time, would I accept his kindness? I answered that I would not.

"Very well," said he; "then take the consequences
of your wayward course. Never look to me for help.

You are my slave, and shall always be my slave. I will never sell you, that you may depend upon."

Hope died away in my heart as he closed the door after him. I had calculated that in his rage he would sell me to a slave-trader ; and I knew the father of my child was on the watch to buy me.

About this time my uncle Phillip was expected to return from a voyage. The day before his departure I had officiated as bridesmaid to a young friend. My heart was then ill at ease, but my smiling countenance did not betray it. Only a year had passed ; but what fearful changes it had wrought ! My heart had grown gray in misery. Lives that flash in sunshine, and lives that are born in tears, receive their hue from circumstances. None of us know what a year may bring forth.

I felt no joy when they told me my uncle had come. He wanted to see me, though he knew what had happened. I shrank from him at first; but at last consented that he should come to my room. He received me as he always had done. O, how my heart smote me when I felt his tears on my burning cheeks ! The words of my grandmother came to my mind, — " Perhaps your mother and father are taken from the evil days to come." My disappointed heart could now praise God that it was so. But why, thought I, did my relatives ever cherish hopes for me ? What was there to save me from the usual fate of slave girls ? Many more beautiful and more intelligent than I had experienced a similar fate, or a far worse one. How could they hope that I should escape ?

My uncle's stay was short, and I was not sorry for

it. I was too ill in mind and body to enjoy my friends
as I had done. For some weeks I was unable to leave
my bed. I could not have any doctor but my master,
and I would not have him sent for. At last, alarmed
by my increasing illness, they sent for him. I was very
weak and nervous; and as soon as he entered the
room, I began to scream. They told him my state
was very critical. He had no wish to hasten me out
of the world, and he withdrew.

When my babe was born, they said it was premature.
It weighed only four pounds; but God let it live. I
heard the doctor say I could not survive till morning.
I had often prayed for death; but now I did not want
to die, unless my child could die too. Many weeks
passed before I was able to leave my bed. I was a
mere wreck of my former self. For a year there was
scarcely a day when I was free from chills and fever.
My babe also was sickly. His little limbs were often
racked with pain. Dr. Flint continued his visits, to
look after my health; and he did not fail to remind me
that my child was an addition to his stock of slaves.

I felt too feeble to dispute with him, and listened to
his remarks in silence. His visits were less frequent;
but his busy spirit could not remain quiet. He employed my brother in his office, and he was made the
medium of frequent notes and messages to me. William was a bright lad, and of much use to the doctor.
He had learned to put up medicines, to leech, cup, and
bleed. He had taught himself to read and spell. I
was proud of my brother; and the old doctor suspected as much. One day, when I had not seen him
for several weeks, I heard his steps approaching the

door. I dreaded the encounter, and hid myself. He inquired for me, of course; but I was nowhere to be found. He went to his office, and despatched William with a note. The color mounted to my brother's face when he gave it to me; and he said, "Don't you hate me, Linda, for bringing you these things?" I told him I could not blame him; he was a slave, and obliged to obey his master's will. The note ordered me to come to his office. I went. He demanded to know where I was when he called. I told him I was at home. He flew into a passion, and said he knew better. Then he launched out upon his usual themes, — my crimes against him, and my ingratitude for his forbearance. The laws were laid down to me anew, and I was dismissed. I felt humiliated that my brother should stand by, and listen to such language as would be addressed only to a slave. Poor boy! He was powerless to defend me; but I saw the tears, which he vainly strove to keep back. This manifestation of feeling irritated the doctor. William could do nothing to please him. One morning he did not arrive at the office so early as usual; and that circumstance afforded his master an opportunity to vent his spleen. He was put in jail. The next day my brother sent a trader to the doctor, with a request to be sold. His master was greatly incensed at what he called his insolence. He said he had put him there to reflect upon his bad conduct, and he certainly was not giving any evidence of repentance. For two days he harassed himself to find somebody to do his office work; but every thing went wrong without William. He was released, and ordered to take his old stand, with many threats, if he was not careful about his future behavior.

As the months passed on, my boy improved in health. When he was a year old, they called him beautiful. The little vine was taking deep root in my existence, though its clinging fondness excited a mixture of love and pain. When I was most sorely oppressed I found a solace in his smiles. I loved to watch his infant slumbers; but always there was a dark cloud over my enjoyment. I could never forget that he was a slave. Sometimes I wished that he might die in infancy. God tried me. My darling became very ill. The bright eyes grew dull, and the little feet and hands were so icy cold that I thought death had already touched them. I had prayed for his death, but never so earnestly as I now prayed for his life; and my prayer was heard. Alas, what mockery it is for a slave mother to try to pray back her dying child to life! Death is better than slavery. It was a sad thought that I had no name to give my child. His father caressed him and treated him kindly, whenever he had a chance to see him. He was not unwilling that he should bear his name; but he had no legal claim to it; and if I had bestowed it upon him, my master would have regarded it as a new crime, a new piece of insolence, and would, perhaps, revenge it on the boy. O, the serpent of Slavery has many and poisonous fangs!

XII.

FEAR OF INSURRECTION.

Not far from this time Nat Turner's insurrection broke out; and the news threw our town into great commotion. Strange that they should be alarmed, when their slaves were so " contented and happy " ! But so it was.

It was always the custom to have a muster every year. On that occasion every white man shouldered his musket. The citizens and the so-called country gentlemen wore military uniforms. The poor whites took their places in the ranks in every-day dress, some without shoes, some without hats. This grand occasion had already passed; and when the slaves were told there was to be another muster, they were surprised and rejoiced. Poor creatures ! They thought it was going to be a holiday. I was informed of the true state of affairs, and imparted it to the few I could trust. Most gladly would I have proclaimed it to every slave ; but I dared not. All could not be relied on. Mighty is the power of the torturing lash.

By sunrise, people were pouring in from every quarter within twenty miles of the town. I knew the houses were to be searched ; and I expected it would be done by country bullies and the poor whites. I knew nothing annoyed them so much as to see colored people living in comfort and respectability ; so I made arrangements for them with especial care. I arranged

9

every thing in my grandmother's house as neatly as possible. I put white quilts on the beds, and decorated some of the rooms with flowers. When all was arranged, I sat down at the window to watch. Far as my eye could reach, it rested on a motley crowd of soldiers. Drums and fifes were discoursing martial music. The men were divided into companies of sixteen, each headed by a captain. Orders were given, and the wild scouts rushed in every direction, wherever a colored face was to be found.

It was a grand opportunity for the low whites, who had no negroes of their own to scourge. They exulted in such a chance to exercise a little brief authority, and show their subserviency to the slaveholders; not reflecting that the power which trampled on the colored people also kept themselves in poverty, ignorance, and moral degradation. Those who never witnessed such scenes can hardly believe what I know was inflicted at this time on innocent men, women, and children, against whom there was not the slightest ground for suspicion. Colored people and slaves who lived in remote parts of the town suffered in an especial manner. In some cases the searchers scattered powder and shot among their clothes, and then sent other parties to find them, and bring them forward as proof that they were plotting insurrection. Every where men, women, and children were whipped till the blood stood in puddles at their feet. Some received five hundred lashes; others were tied hands and feet, and tortured with a bucking paddle, which blisters the skin terribly. The dwellings of the colored people, unless they happened to be protected by some influential white person, who was nigh at hand, were robbed of clothing and every thing else the marauders thought worth carrying away. All day long these unfeeling wretches went round, like a troop of demons, terrifying and tormenting the helpless. At night, they formed themselves into patrol bands, and went wherever they chose among the colored people, acting out their brutal will. Many women hid themselves in woods and swamps, to keep out of their way. If any of the husbands or fathers told of these outrages, they were tied up to the public whipping post, and cruelly scourged for telling lies about white men. The consternation was universal. No two people that had the slightest tinge of color in their faces dared to be seen talking together.

I entertained no positive fears about our household, because we were in the midst of white families who would protect us. We were ready to receive the soldiers whenever they came. It was not long before we heard the tramp of feet and the sound of voices. The door was rudely pushed open; and in they tumbled, like a pack of hungry wolves. They snatched at every thing within their reach. Every box, trunk, closet, and corner underwent a thorough examination. A box in one of the drawers containing some silver change was eagerly pounced upon. When I stepped forward to take it from them, one of the soldiers turned and said angrily, " What d'ye foller us fur? D'ye s'pose white folks is come to steal?"

I replied, " You have come to search; but you have searched that box, and I will take it, if you please."

At that moment I saw a white gentleman who was friendly to us; and I called to him, and asked him to have the goodness to come in and stay till the search was over. He readily complied. His entrance into the house brought in the captain of the company, whose business it was to guard the outside of the house, and see that none of the inmates left it. This officer was Mr. Litch, the wealthy slaveholder whom I mentioned, in the account of neighboring planters, as being notorious for his cruelty. He felt above soiling his hands with the search. He merely gave orders; and, if a bit of writing was discovered, it was carried to him by his ignorant followers, who were unable to read.

My grandmother had a large trunk of bedding and table cloths. When that was opened, there was a great shout of surprise; and one exclaimed, "Where'd the damned niggers git all dis sheet an' table clarf?"

My grandmother, emboldened by the presence of our white protector, said, "You may be sure we didn't pilfer 'em from *your* houses."

"Look here, mammy," said a grim-looking fellow without any coat, "you seem to feel mighty gran' 'cause you got all them 'ere fixens. White folks oughter have 'em all."

His remarks were interrupted by a chorus of voices shouting, "We's got 'em! We's got 'em! Dis 'ere yaller gal's got letters!"

There was a general rush for the supposed letter, which, upon examination, proved to be some verses written to me by a friend. In packing away my things, I had overlooked them. When their captain informed them of their contents, they seemed much disappointed. He inquired of me who wrote them.

I told him it was one of my friends. "Can you read them?" he asked. When I told him I could, he swore, and raved, and tore the paper into bits. "Bring me all your letters!" said he, in a commanding tone. I told him I had none. "Don't be afraid," he continued, in an insinuating way. "Bring them all to me. Nobody shall do you any harm." Seeing I did not move to obey him, his pleasant tone changed to oaths and threats. "Who writes to you? half free niggers?" inquired he. I replied, "O, no; most of my letters are from white people. Some request me to burn them after they are read, and some I destroy without reading."

An exclamation of surprise from some of the company put a stop to our conversation. Some silver spoons which ornamented an old-fashioned buffet had just been discovered. My grandmother was in the habit of preserving fruit for many ladies in the town, and of preparing suppers for parties; consequently she had many jars of preserves. The closet that contained these was next invaded, and the contents tasted. One of them, who was helping himself freely, tapped his neighbor on the shoulder, and said, "Wal done! Don't wonder de niggers want to kill all de white folks, when dey live on 'sarves" [meaning preserves]. I stretched out my hand to take the jar, saying, "You were not sent here to search for sweetmeats."

"And what *were* we sent for?" said the captain, bristling up to me. I evaded the question.

The search of the house was completed, and nothing found to condemn us. They next proceeded to the garden, and knocked about every bush and vine, with no better success. The captain called his men together, and, after a short consultation, the order to march was given. As they passed out of the gate, the captain turned back, and pronounced a malediction on the house. He said it ought to be burned to the ground, and each of its inmates receive thirty-nine lashes. We came out of this affair very fortunately; not losing any thing except some wearing apparel.

Towards evening the turbulence increased. The soldiers, stimulated by drink, committed still greater cruelties. Shrieks and shouts continually rent the air. Not daring to go to the door, I peeped under the window curtain. I saw a mob dragging along a number of colored people, each white man, with his musket upraised, threatening instant death if they did not stop their shrieks. Among the prisoners was a respectable old colored minister. They had found a few parcels of shot in his house, which his wife had for years used to balance her scales. For this they were going to shoot him on Court House Green. What a spectacle was that for a civilized country! A rabble, staggering under intoxication, assuming to be the administrators of justice!

The better class of the community exerted their influence to save the innocent, persecuted people; and in several instances they succeeded, by keeping them shut up in jail till the excitement abated. At last the white citizens found that their own property was not safe from the lawless rabble they had summoned to protect them. They rallied the drunken swarm, drove them back into the country, and set a guard over the town.

The next day, the town patrols were commissioned
to search colored people that lived out of the city;
and the most shocking outrages were committed with
perfect impunity. Every day for a fortnight, if I
looked out, I saw horsemen with some poor panting
negro tied to their saddles, and compelled by the lash
to keep up with their speed, till they arrived at the
jail yard. Those who had been whipped too unmer-
cifully to walk were washed with brine, tossed into a
cart, and carried to jail. One black man, who had
not fortitude to endure scourging, promised to give
information about the conspiracy. But it turned out
that he knew nothing at all. He had not even heard
the name of Nat Turner. The poor fellow had, however, made up a story, which augmented his own
sufferings and those of the colored people.

The day patrol continued for some weeks, and at
sundown a night guard was substituted. Nothing at
all was proved against the colored people, bond or free.
The wrath of the slaveholders was somewhat appeased
by the capture of Nat Turner. The imprisoned were
released. The slaves were sent to their masters, and
the free were permitted to return to their ravaged
homes. Visiting was strictly forbidden on the plantations. The slaves begged the privilege of again meeting at their little church in the woods, with their
burying ground around it. It was built by the colored
people, and they had no higher happiness than to meet
there and sing hymns together, and pour out their
hearts in spontaneous prayer. Their request was
denied, and the church was demolished. They were
permitted to attend the white churches, a certain por-

tion of the galleries being appropriated to their use. There, when every body else had partaken of the communion, and the benediction had been pronounced, the minister said, " Come down, now, my colored friends." They obeyed the summons, and partook of the bread and wine, in commemoration of the meek and lowly Jesus, who said, " God is your Father, and all ye are brethren."

XIII.

THE CHURCH AND SLAVERY.

AFTER the alarm caused by Nat Turner's insurrection had subsided, the slaveholders came to the conclusion that it would be well to give the slaves enough of religious instruction to keep them from murdering their masters. The Episcopal clergyman offered to hold a separate service on Sundays for their benefit. His colored members were very few, and also very respectable — a fact which I presume had some weight with him. The difficulty was to decide on a suitable place for them to worship. The Methodist and Baptist churches admitted them in the afternoon; but their carpets and cushions were not so costly as those at the Episcopal church. It was at last decided that they should meet at the house of a free colored man, who was a member.

I was invited to attend, because I could read. Sunday evening came, and, trusting to the cover of night, I ventured out. I rarely ventured out by daylight, for I always went with fear, expecting at every turn to encounter Dr. Flint, who was sure to turn me back, or order me to his office to inquire where I got my bonnet, or some other article of dress. When the Rev. Mr. Pike came, there were some twenty persons present. The reverend gentleman knelt in prayer, then seated himself, and requested all present, who could read, to open their books, while he gave out the portions he wished them to repeat or respond to.

His text was, " Servants, be obedient to them that
are your masters according to the flesh, with fear
and trembling, in singleness of your heart, as unto
Christ."

Pious Mr. Pike brushed up his hair till it stood upright, and, in deep, solemn tones, began : " Hearken,
ye servants !   Give strict heed unto my words.   You
are rebellious sinners.   Your hearts are filled with all
manner of evil.   'Tis the devil who tempts you.   God
is angry with you, and will surely punish you, if you
don't forsake your wicked ways.   You that live in
town are eye-servants behind your master's back.
Instead of serving your masters faithfully, which is
pleasing in the sight of your heavenly Master, you are
idle, and shirk your work.   God sees you.   You tell
lies.   God hears you.   Instead of being engaged in
worshipping him, you are hidden away somewhere,
feasting on your master's substance ; tossing coffee-
grounds with some wicked fortuneteller, or cutting
cards with another old hag.   Your masters may not
find you out, but God sees you, and will punish you.
O, the depravity of your hearts !   When your master's
work is done, are you quietly together, thinking of the
goodness of God to such sinful creatures ?   No ; you
are quarrelling, and tying up little bags of roots to
bury under the door-steps to poison each other with.
God sees you.   You men steal away to every grog
shop to sell your master's corn, that you may buy
rum to drink.   God sees you.   You sneak into the
back streets, or among the bushes, to pitch coppers.
Although your masters may not find you out, God
sees you ; and he will punish you.   You must forsake

your sinful ways, and be faithful servants. Obey your old master and your young master — your old mistress and your young mistress. If you disobey your earthly master, you offend your heavenly Master. You must obey God's commandments. When you go from here, don't stop at the corners of the streets to talk, but go directly home, and let your master and mistress see that you have come."

The benediction was pronounced. We went home, highly amused at brother Pike's gospel teaching, and we determined to hear him again. I went the next Sabbath evening, and heard pretty much a repetition of the last discourse. At the close of the meeting, Mr. Pike informed us that he found it very inconvenient to meet at the friend's house, and he should be glad to see us, every Sunday evening, at his own kitchen.

I went home with the feeling that I had heard the Reverend Mr. Pike for the last time. Some of his members repaired to his house, and found that the kitchen sported two tallow candles; the first time, I am sure, since its present occupant owned it, for the servants never had any thing but pine knots. It was so long before the reverend gentleman descended from his comfortable parlor that the slaves left, and went to enjoy a Methodist shout. They never seem so happy as when shouting and singing at religious meetings. Many of them are sincere, and nearer to the gate of heaven than sanctimonious Mr. Pike, and other long-faced Christians, who see wounded Samaritans, and pass by on the other side.

The slaves generally compose their own songs and

hymns; and they do not trouble their heads much about
the measure.   They often sing the following verses:

> " Old Satan is one busy ole man;
>   He rolls dem blocks all in my way;
> But Jesus is my bosom friend;
>   He rolls dem blocks away.

> "If I had died when I was young,
>   Den how my stam'ring tongue would have sung;
> But I am ole, and now I stand
>   A narrow chance for to tread dat heavenly land."

I well remember one occasion when I attended a
Methodist class meeting.   I went with a burdened
spirit, and happened to sit next a poor, bereaved
mother, whose heart was still heavier than mine.
The class leader was the town constable — a man who
bought and sold slaves, who whipped his brethren and
sisters of the church at the public whipping post, in
jail or out of jail.   He was ready to perform that
Christian office any where for fifty cents.   This white-
faced, black-hearted brother came near us, and said to
the stricken woman, " Sister, can't you tell us how the
Lord deals with your soul?   Do you love him as you
did formerly ? "

She rose to her feet, and said, in piteous tones,
" My Lord and Master, help me!   My load is more
than I can bear.   God has hid himself from me, and
I am left in darkness and misery."   Then, striking
her breast, she continued, " I can't tell you what is in
here!   They've got all my children.   Last week they
took the last one.   God only knows where they've
sold her.   They let me have her sixteen years, and
then——   O! O!   Pray for her brothers and sisters!

very different clergyman took his place. The change was very agreeable to the colored people, who said, " God has sent us a good man this time." They loved him, and their children followed him for a smile or a kind word. Even the slaveholders felt his influence. He brought to the rectory five slaves. His wife taught them to read and write, and to be useful to her and themselves. As soon as he was settled, he turned his attention to the needy slaves around him. He urged upon his parishioners the duty of having a meeting expressly for them every Sunday, with a sermon adapted to their comprehension. After much argument and importunity, it was finally agreed that they might occupy the gallery of the church on Sunday evenings. Many colored people, hitherto unaccustomed to attend church, now gladly went to hear the gospel preached. The sermons were simple, and they understood them. Moreover, it was the first time they had ever been addressed as human beings. It was not long before his white parishioners began to be dissatisfied. He was accused of preaching better sermons to the negroes than he did to them. He honestly confessed that he bestowed more pains upon those sermons than upon any others ; for the slaves were reared in such ignorance that it was a difficult task to adapt himself to their comprehension. Dissensions arose in the parish. Some wanted he should preach to them in the evening, and to the slaves in the afternoon. In the midst of these disputings his wife died, after a very short illness. Her slaves gathered round her dying bed in great sorrow. She said, " I have tried to do you good and promote your happiness ; and if I have failed, it has not been for want of interest in your welfare. Do not weep for me; but prepare for the new duties that lie before you. I leave you all free. May we meet in a better world." Her liberated slaves were sent away, with funds to establish them comfortably. The colored people will long bless the memory of that truly Christian woman. Soon after her death her husband preached his farewell sermon, and many tears were shed at his departure.

Several years after, he passed through our town and preached to his former congregation. In his afternoon sermon he addressed the colored people. "My friends," said he, "it affords me great happiness to have an opportunity of speaking to you again. For two years I have been striving to do something for the colored people of my own parish; but nothing is yet accomplished. I have not even preached a sermon to them. Try to live according to the word of God, my friends. Your skin is darker than mine; but God judges men by their hearts, not by the color of their skins." This was strange doctrine from a southern pulpit. It was very offensive to slaveholders. They said he and his wife had made fools of their slaves, and that he preached like a fool to the negroes.

I knew an old black man, whose piety and child-like trust in God were beautiful to witness. At fifty-three years old he joined the Baptist church. He had a most earnest desire to learn to read. He thought he should know how to serve God better if he could only read the Bible. He came to me, and begged me to teach him. He said he could not pay me, for he had no money ; but he would bring me nice fruit when the season for it came. I asked him if he didn't know it was contrary to law; and that slaves were whipped and imprisoned for teaching each other to read. This brought the tears into his eyes. " Don't be troubled, uncle Fred," said I. " I have no thoughts of refusing to teach you. I only told you of the law, that you might know the danger, and be on your guard." He thought he could plan to come three times a week without its being suspected. I selected a quiet nook, where no intruder was likely to penetrate, and there I taught him his A, B, C. Considering his age, his progress was astonishing. As soon as he could spell in two syllables he wanted to spell out words in the Bible. The happy smile that illuminated his face put joy into my heart. After spelling out a few words, he paused, and said, " Honey, it 'pears when I can read dis good book I shall be nearer to God. White man is got all de sense. He can larn easy. It ain't easy for ole black man like me. I only wants to read dis book, dat I may know how to live ; den I hab no fear 'bout dying."

I tried to encourage him by speaking of the rapid progress he had made. " Hab patience, child," he replied. " I larns slow."

I had no need of patience. His gratitude, and the happiness I imparted, were more than a recompense for all my trouble.

At the end of six months he had read through the New Testament, and could find any text in it. One day, when he had recited unusually well, I said,

"Uncle Fred, how do you manage to get your lessons so well?"

"Lord bress you, chile," he replied. "You nebber gibs me a lesson dat I don't pray to God to help me to understan' what I spells and what I reads. And he *does* help me, chile. Bress his holy name!"

There are thousands, who, like good uncle Fred, are thirsting for the water of life; but the law forbids it, and the churches withhold it. They send the Bible to heathen abroad, and neglect the heathen at home. I am glad that missionaries go out to the dark corners of the earth; but I ask them not to overlook the dark corners at home. Talk to American slaveholders as you talk to savages in Africa. Tell *them* it is wrong to traffic in men. Tell them it is sinful to sell their own children, and atrocious to violate their own daughters. Tell them that all men are brethren, and that man has no right to shut out the light of knowledge from his brother. Tell them they are answerable to God for sealing up the Fountain of Life from souls that are thirsting for it.

There are men who would gladly undertake such missionary work as this; but, alas! their number is small. They are hated by the south, and would be driven from its soil, or dragged to prison to die, as others have been before them. The field is ripe for the harvest, and awaits the reapers. Perhaps the great grandchildren of uncle Fred may have freely imparted to them the divine treasures, which he sought by stealth, at the risk of the prison and the scourge.

Are doctors of divinity blind, or are they hypocrites ? I suppose some are the one, and some the other; but I think if they felt the interest in the poor and the lowly, that they ought to feel, they would not be so *easily* blinded. A clergyman who goes to the south, for the first time, has usually some feeling, however vague, that slavery is wrong. The slave-holder suspects this, and plays his game accordingly. He makes himself as agreeable as possible; talks on theology, and other kindred topics. The reverend gentleman is asked to invoke a blessing on a table loaded with luxuries. After dinner he walks round the premises, and sees the beautiful groves and flowering vines, and the comfortable huts of favored household slaves. The southerner invites him to talk with these slaves. He asks them if they want to be free, and they say, " O, no, massa." This is sufficient to satisfy him. He comes home to publish a " South-Side View of Slavery," and to complain of the exaggerations of abolitionists. He assures people that he has been to the south, and seen slavery for himself; that it is a beautiful " patriarchal institution ; " that the slaves don't want their freedom ; that they have hallelujah meetings, and other religious privileges.

What does *he* know of the half-starved wretches toiling from dawn till dark on the plantations? of mothers shrieking for their children, torn from their arms by slave traders? of young girls dragged down into moral filth? of pools of blood around the whipping post? of hounds trained to tear human flesh? of men screwed into cotton gins to die? The slaveholder showed him none of these things, and the slaves dared not tell of them if he had asked them.

There is a great difference between Christianity and religion at the south. If a man goes to the communion table, and pays money into the treasury of the church, no matter if it be the price of blood, he is called religious. If a pastor has offspring by a woman not his wife, the church dismiss him, if she is a white woman; but if she is colored, it does not hinder his continuing to be their good shepherd.

When I was told that Dr. Flint had joined the Episcopal church, I was much surprised. I supposed that religion had a purifying effect on the character of men; but the worst persecutions I endured from him were after he was a communicant. The conversation of the doctor, the day after he had been confirmed, certainly gave *me* no indication that he had "renounced the devil and all his works." In answer to some of his usual talk, I reminded him that he had just joined the church. "Yes, Linda," said he. "It was proper for me to do so. I am getting in years, and my position in society requires it, and it puts an end to all the damned slang. You would do well to join the church, too, Linda."

"There are sinners enough in it already," rejoined I. "If I could be allowed to live like a Christian, I should be glad."

"You can do what I require; and if you are faithful to me, you will be as virtuous as my wife," he replied.

I answered that the Bible didn't say so.

His voice became hoarse with rage. "How dare you preach to me about your infernal Bible!" he exclaimed.   "What right have you, who are my negro, to talk to me about what you would like, and what you wouldn't like ?   I am your master, and you shall obey me."

No wonder the slaves sing, —

"Ole Satan's church is here below ;
Up to God's free church I hope to go."

XIV.

ANOTHER LINK TO LIFE.

I HAD not returned to my master's house since the birth of my child. The old man raved to have me thus, removed from his immediate power; but his wife vowed, by all that was good and great, she would kill me if I came back; and he did not doubt her word. Sometimes he would stay away for a season. Then he would come and renew the old threadbare discourse about his forbearance and my ingratitude. He labored, most unnecessarily, to convince me that I had lowered myself. The venomous old reprobate had no need of descanting on that theme. I felt humiliated enough. My unconscious babe was the ever-present witness of my shame. I listened with silent contempt when he talked about my having forfeited *his* good opinion; but I shed bitter tears that I was no longer worthy of being respected by the good and pure. Alas! slavery still held me in its poisonous grasp. There was no chance for me to be respectable. There was no prospect of being able to lead a better life.

Sometimes, when my master found that I still refused to accept what he called his kind offers, he would threaten to sell my child. "Perhaps that will humble you," said he.

Humble *me!* Was I not already in the dust? But his threat lacerated my heart. I knew the law gave him power to fulfil it; for slaveholders have been

cunning enough to enact that " the child shall follow
the condition of the *mother*," not of the *father*; thus
taking care that licentiousness shall not interfere with
avarice. This reflection made me clasp my innocent
babe all the more firmly to my heart. Horrid visions
passed through my mind when I thought of his lia-
bility to fall into the slave trader's hands. I wept
over him, and said, " O my child ! perhaps they will
leave you in some cold cabin to die, and then throw
you into a hole, as if you were a dog."

When Dr. Flint learned that I was again to be a
mother, he was exasperated beyond measure. He
rushed from the house, and returned with a pair of
shears. I had a fine head of hair; and he often
railed about my pride of arranging it nicely. He cut
every hair close to my head, storming and swearing
all the time. I replied to some of his abuse, and he
struck me. Some months before, he had pitched me
down stairs in a fit of passion ; and the injury I received was so serious that I was unable to turn myself
in bed for many days. He then said, " Linda, I swear
by God I will never raise my hand against you again;"
but I knew that he would forget his promise.

After he discovered my situation, he was like a
restless spirit from the pit. He came every day; and
I was subjected to such insults as no pen can describe.
I would not describe them if I could ; they were too
low, too revolting. I tried to keep them from my
grandmother's knowledge as much as I could. I
knew she had enough to sadden her life, without
having my troubles to bear. When she saw the
doctor treat me with violence, and heard him utter

oaths terrible enough to palsy a man's tongue, she could not always hold her peace. It was natural and motherlike that she should try to defend me ; but it only made matters worse.

When they told me my new-born babe was a girl, my heart was heavier than it had ever been before. Slavery is terrible for men ; but it is far more terrible for women. Superadded to the burden common to all, *they* have wrongs, and sufferings, and mortifications peculiarly their own.

Dr. Flint had sworn that he would make me suffer, to my last day, for this new crime against *him*, as he called it ; and as long as he had me in his power he kept his word. On the fourth day after the birth of my babe, he entered my room suddenly, and commanded me to rise and bring my baby to him. The nurse who took care of me had gone out of the room to prepare some nourishment, and I was alone. There was no alternative. I rose, took up my babe, and crossed the room to where he sat. "Now stand there," said he, "till I tell you to go back ! " My child bore a strong resemblance to her father, and to the deceased Mrs. Sands, her grandmother. He noticed this ; and while I stood before him, trembling with weakness, he heaped upon me and my little one every vile epithet he could think of. Even the grandmother in her grave did not escape his curses. In the midst of his vituperations I fainted at his feet. This recalled him to his senses. He took the baby from my arms, laid it on the bed, dashed cold water in my face, took me up, and shook me violently, to restore my consciousness before any one entered the room. Just then my grandmother

came in, and he hurried out of the house. I suffered
in consequence of this treatment; but I begged my
friends to let me die, rather than send for the doctor.
There was nothing I dreaded so much as his presence.
My life was spared; and I was glad for the sake of my
little ones. Had it not been for these ties to life, I
should have been glad to be released by death, though
I had lived only nineteen years.

Always it gave me a pang that my children had no
lawful claim to a name. Their father offered his; but,
if I had wished to accept the offer, I dared not while
my master lived. Moreover, I knew it would not be
accepted at their baptism. A Christian name they
were at least entitled to; and we resolved to call my
boy for our dear good Benjamin, who had gone far
away from us.

My grandmother belonged to the church; and she
was very desirous of having the children christened.
I knew Dr. Flint would forbid it, and I did not
venture to attempt it. But chance favored me. He
was called to visit a patient out of town, and was
obliged to be absent during Sunday. "Now is the
time," said my grandmother; "we will take the children to church, and have them christened."

When I entered the church, recollections of my
mother came over me, and I felt subdued in spirit.
There she had presented me for baptism, without any
reason to feel ashamed. She had been married, and
had such legal rights as slavery allows to a slave.
The vows had at least been sacred to *her*, and she had
never violated them. I was glad she was not alive, to
know under what different circumstances her grand-

children were presented for baptism. Why had my lot been so different from my mother's? *Her* master had died when she was a child; and she remained with her mistress till she married. She was never in the power of any master; and thus she escaped one class of the evils that generally fall upon slaves.

When my baby was about to be christened, the former mistress of my father stepped up to me, and proposed to give it her Christian name. To this I added the surname of my father, who had himself no legal right to it; for my grandfather on the paternal side was a white gentleman. What tangled skeins are the genealogies of slavery! I loved my father; but it mortified me to be obliged to bestow his name on my children.

When we left the church, my father's old mistress invited me to go home with her. She clasped a gold chain round my baby's neck. I thanked her for this kindness; but I did not like the emblem. I wanted no chain to be fastened on my daughter, not even if its links were of gold. How earnestly I prayed that she might never feel the weight of slavery's chain, whose iron entereth into the soul!

11

XV.

CONTINUED PERSECUTIONS.

My children grew finely; and Dr. Flint would often say to me, with an exulting smile, "These brats will bring me a handsome sum of money one of these days."

I thought to myself that, God being my helper, they should never pass into his hands. It seemed to me I would rather see them killed than have them given up to his power. The money for the freedom of myself and my children could be obtained; but I derived no advantage from that circumstance. Dr. Flint loved money, but he loved power more. After much discussion, my friends resolved on making another trial. There was a slaveholder about to leave for Texas, and he was commissioned to buy me. He was to begin with nine hundred dollars, and go up to twelve. My master refused his offers. " Sir," said he, " she don't belong to me. She is my daughter's property, and I have no right to sell her. I mistrust that you come from her paramour. If so, you may tell him that he cannot buy her for any money; neither can he buy her children."

The doctor came to see me the next day, and my heart beat quicker as he entered. I never had seen the old man tread with so majestic a step. He seated himself and looked at me with withering scorn. My children had learned to be afraid of him. The little one would shut her eyes and hide her face on my shoulder whenever she saw him; and Benny, who was now nearly five years old, often inquired, " What makes that bad man come here so many times ? Does he want to hurt us ? " I would clasp the dear boy in my arms, trusting that he would be free before he was old enough to solve the problem. And now, as the doctor sat there so grim and silent, the child left his play and came and nestled up by me. At last my tormentor spoke. " So you are left in disgust, are you ? " said he. " It is no more than I expected. You remember I told you years ago that you would be treated so. So he is tired of you ? Ha! ha! ha! The virtuous madam don't like to hear about it, does she ? Ha! ha! ha! " There was a sting in his calling me virtuous madam. I no longer had the power of answering him as I had formerly done. He continued : " So it seems you are trying to get up another intrigue. Your new paramour came to me, and offered to buy you ; but you may be assured you will not succeed. You are mine ; and you shall be mine for life. There lives no human being that can take you out of slavery. I would have done it ; but you rejected my kind offer."

I told him I did not wish to get up any intrigue ; that I had never seen the man who offered to buy me.

" Do you tell me I lie ? " exclaimed he, dragging me from my chair. " Will you say again that you never saw that man ? "

I answered, " I do say so."

He clinched my arm with a volley of oaths. Ben began to scream, and I told him to go to his grand-mother.

"Don't you stir a step, you little wretch!" said he. The child drew nearer to me, and put his arms round me, as if he wanted to protect me. This was too much for my enraged master. He caught him up and hurled him across the room. I thought he was dead, and rushed towards him to take him up.

"Not yet!" exclaimed the doctor. "Let him lie there till he comes to."

"Let me go! Let me go!" I screamed, "or I will raise the whole house." I struggled and got away; but he clinched me again. Somebody opened the door, and he released me. I picked up my insensible child, and when I turned my tormentor was gone. Anxiously I bent over the little form, so pale and still; and when the brown eyes at last opened, I don't know whether I was very happy.

All the doctor's former persecutions were renewed. He came morning, noon, and night. No jealous lover ever watched a rival more closely than he watched me and the unknown slaveholder, with whom he accused me of wishing to get up an intrigue. When my grandmother was out of the way he searched every room to find him.

In one of his visits, he happened to find a young girl, whom he had sold to a trader a few days previous. His statement was, that he sold her because she had been too familiar with the overseer. She had had a bitter life with him, and was glad to be sold. She had no mother, and no near ties. She had been torn from all her family years before. A few friends had entered into bonds for her safety, if the trader would allow her to spend with them the time that intervened between her sale and the gathering up of his human stock. Such a favor was rarely granted. It saved the trader the expense of board and jail fees, and though the amount was small, it was a weighty consideration in a slave-trader's mind.

Dr. Flint always had an aversion to meeting slaves after he had sold them. He ordered Rose out of the house; but he was no longer her master, and she took no notice of him. For once the crushed Rose was the conqueror. His gray eyes flashed angrily upon her; but that was the extent of his power. " How came this girl here ? " he exclaimed. " What right had you to allow it, when you knew I had sold her ? "

I answered " This is my grandmother's house, and Rose came to see her. I have no right to turn any body out of doors, that comes here for honest purposes."

He gave me the blow that would have fallen upon Rose if she had still been his slave. My grandmother's attention had been attracted by loud voices, and she entered in time to see a second blow dealt. She was not a woman to let such an outrage, in her own house, go unrebuked. The doctor undertook to explain that I had been insolent. Her indignant feelings rose higher and higher, and finally boiled over in words. " Get out of my house ! " she exclaimed. " Go home, and take care of your wife and children, and you will have enough to do, without watching my family."

He threw the birth of my children in her face, and accused her of sanctioning the life I was leading. She told him I was living with her by compulsion of his wife; that he needn't accuse her, for he was the one to blame; he was the one who had caused all the trouble. She grew more and more excited as she went on. " I tell you what, Dr. Flint," said she, " you ain't got many more years to live, and you'd better be saying your prayers. It will take 'em all, and more too, to wash the dirt off your soul."

" Do you know whom you are talking to ? " he exclaimed.

She replied, " Yes, I know very well who I am talking to."

He left the house in a great rage. I looked at my grandmother. Our eyes met. Their angry expression had passed away, but she looked sorrowful and weary — weary of incessant strife. I wondered that it did not lessen her love for me ; but if it did she never showed it. She was always kind, always ready to sympathize with my troubles. There might have been peace and contentment in that humble home if it had not been for the demon Slavery.

The winter passed undisturbed by the doctor. The beautiful spring came ; and when Nature resumes her loveliness, the human soul is apt to revive also. My drooping hopes came to life again with the flowers. I was dreaming of freedom again; more for my children's sake than my own. I planned and I planned. Obstacles hit against plans. There seemed no way of overcoming them ; and yet I hoped.

Back came the wily doctor. I was not at home when he called. A friend had invited me to a small party, and to gratify her I went. To my great consternation, a messenger came in haste to say that Dr. Flint was at my grandmother's, and insisted on seeing me. They did not tell him where I was, or he would have come

and raised a disturbance in my friend's house. They
sent me a dark wrapper; I threw it on and hurried
home. My speed did not save me; the doctor had gone
away in anger. I dreaded the morning, but I could
not delay it; it came, warm and bright. At an early
hour the doctor came and asked me where I had been
last night. I told him. He did not believe me, and
sent to my friend's house to ascertain the facts. He
came in the afternoon to assure me he was satisfied
that I had spoken the truth. He seemed to be in a
facetious mood, and I expected some jeers were coming.
"I suppose you need some recreation," said he, "but
I am surprised at your being there, among those negroes.
It was not the place for *you*. Are you *allowed* to visit
such people?"

I understood this covert fling at the white gentleman
who was my friend; but I merely replied, "I went to
visit my friends, and any company they keep is good
enough for me."

He went on to say, "I have seen very little of you
of late, but my interest in you is unchanged. When
I said I would have no more mercy on you I was rash.
I recall my words. Linda, you desire freedom for yourself and your children, and you can obtain it only
through me. If you agree to what I am about to pro-
pose, you and they shall be free. There must be no
communication of any kind between you and their
father. I will procure a cottage, where you and the
children can live together. Your labor shall be light,
such as sewing for my family. Think what is offered
you, Linda — a home and freedom! Let the past be
forgotten. If I have been harsh with you at times,

your wilfulness drove me to it. You know I exact obedience from my own children, and I consider you as yet a child."

He paused for an answer, but I remained silent.

" Why don't you speak ? " said he. . " What more do you wait for ? "

" Nothing, sir."

" Then you accept my offer ? "

" No, sir."

His anger was ready to break loose ; but he succeeded in curbing it, and replied, " You have answered without thought. But I must let you know there are two sides to my proposition ; if you reject the bright side, you will be obliged to take the dark one. You must either accept my offer, or you and your children shall be sent to your young master's plantation, there to remain till your young mistress is married ; and your children shall fare like the rest of the negro children. I give you a week to consider of it."

He was shrewd ; but I knew he was not to be trusted. I told him I was ready to give my answer now.

" I will not receive it now," he replied. " You act too much from impulse. Remember that you and your children can be free a week from to-day if you choose."

On what a monstrous chance hung the destiny of my children ! I knew that my master's offer was a snare, and that if I entered it escape would be impossible. As for his promise, I knew him so well that I was sure if he gave me free papers, they would be so managed as to have no legal value. The alternative was inevitable. I resolved to go to the plantation. But then I thought how completely I should be in his power, and the prospect was apalling. Even if I should kneel before him, and implore him to spare me, for the sake of my children, I knew he would spurn me with his foot, and my weakness would be his triumph.

Before the week expired, I heard that young Mr. Flint was about to be married to a lady of his own stamp. I foresaw the position I should occupy in his establishment. I had once been sent to the plantation for punishment, and fear of the son had induced the father to recall me very soon. My mind was made up ; I was resolved that I would foil my master and save my children, or I would perish in the attempt. I kept my plans to myself ; I knew that friends would try to dissuade me from them, and I would not wound their feelings by rejecting their advice.

On the decisive day the doctor came, and said he hoped I had made a wise choice.

" I am ready to go to the plantation, sir," I replied.

" Have you thought how important your decision is to your children ? " said he.

I told him I had.

" Very well. Go to the plantation, and my curse go with you," he replied. " Your boy shall be put to work, and he shall soon be sold ; and your girl shall be raised for the purpose of selling well. Go your own ways ! " He left the room with curses, not to be repeated.

As I stood rooted to the spot, my grandmother came and said, " Linda, child, what did you tell him ? "

I answered that I was going to the plantation.

" *Must* you go ? " said she. " Can't something be done to stop it ? "

I told her it was useless to try ; but she begged me not to give up. She said she would go to the doctor, and remind him how long and how faithfully she had served in the family, and how she had taken her own baby from her breast to nourish his wife. She would tell him I had been out of the family so long they would not miss me; that she would pay them for my time, and the money would procure a woman who had more strength for the situation than I had. I begged her not to go ; but she persisted in saying, " He will listen to *me*, Linda." She went, and was treated as I expected. He coolly listened to what he said, but denied her request. He told her that what he did was for my good, that my feelings were entirely above my situation, and that on the plantation I would receive treatment that was suitable to my behavior.

My grandmother was much cast down. I had my secret hopes ; but I must fight my battle alone. I had a woman's pride, and a mother's love for my children ; and I resolved that out of the darkness of this hour a brighter dawn should rise for them. My master had power and law on his side ; I had a determined will. There is might in each.

XVI.

SCENES AT THE PLANTATION.

EARLY the next morning I left my grandmother's with my youngest child. My boy was ill, and I left him behind. I had many sad thoughts as the old wagon jolted on. Hitherto, I had suffered alone; now, my little one was to be treated as a slave. As we drew near the great house, I thought of the time when I was formerly sent there out of revenge. I wondered for what purpose I was now sent. I could not tell. I resolved to obey orders so far as duty required; but within myself, I determined to make my stay as short as possible. Mr. Flint was waiting to receive us, and told me to follow him up stairs to receive orders for the day. My little Ellen was left below in the kitchen. It was a change for her, who had always been so carefully tended. My young master said she might amuse herself in the yard. This was kind of him, since the child was hateful to his sight. My task was to fit up the house for the reception of the bride. In the midst of sheets, tablecloths, towels, drapery, and carpeting, my head was as busy planning, as were my fingers with the needle. At noon I was allowed to go to Ellen. She had sobbed herself to sleep. I heard Mr. Flint say to a neighbor, "I've got her down here, and I'll soon take the town notions out of her head. My father is partly to blame for her nonsense. He ought to have broke her in long ago." The remark was made within my hearing, and it would have been quite as manly to have made it to my face. He *had* said things to my face which might, or might not, have surprised his neighbor if he had known of them. He was " a chip of the old block."

I resolved to give him no cause to accuse me of being too much of a lady, so far as work was concerned. I worked day and night, with wretchedness before me. When I lay down beside my child, I felt how much easier it would be to see her die than to see her master beat her about, as I daily saw him beat other little ones. The spirit of the mothers was so crushed by the lash, that they stood by, without courage to remonstrate. How much more must I suffer, before I should be " broke in" to that degree ?

I wished to appear as contented as possible. Sometimes I had an opportunity to send a few lines home ; and this brought up recollections that made it difficult, for a time, to seem calm and indifferent to my lot. Notwithstanding my efforts, I saw that Mr. Flint regarded me with a suspicious eye. Ellen broke down under the trials of her new life. Separated from me, with no one to look after her, she wandered about, and in a few days cried herself sick. One day, she sat under the window where I was at work, crying that weary cry which makes a mother's heart bleed. I was obliged to steel myself to bear it. After a while it ceased. I looked out, and she was gone. As it was near noon, I ventured to go down in search of her. The great house was raised two feet above the ground. I looked under it, and saw her about midway, fast asleep. I crept under and drew her out. As I held her in my arms, I thought how well it would be for her if she never waked up; and I uttered my thought aloud. I was startled to hear some one say, "Did you speak to me?" I looked up, and saw Mr. Flint standing beside me. He said nothing further, but turned, frowning, away. That night he sent Ellen a biscuit and a cup of sweetened milk. This generosity surprised me. I learned afterwards, that in the afternoon he had killed a large snake, which crept from under the house; and I supposed that incident had prompted his unusual kindness.

The next morning the old cart was loaded with shingles for town. I put Ellen into it, and sent her to her grandmother. Mr. Flint said I ought to have asked his permission. I told him the child was sick, and required attention which I had no time to give. He let it pass; for he was aware that I had accomplished much work in a little time.

I had been three weeks on the plantation, when I planned a visit home. It must be at night, after every body was in bed. I was six miles from town, and the road was very dreary. I was to go with a young man, who, I knew, often stole to town to see his mother. One night, when all was quiet, we started. Fear gave speed to our steps, and we were not long in performing the journey. I arrived at my grandmother's. Her bed room was on the first floor, and the window was open, the weather being warm. I spoke to her and she awoke. She let me in and closed the window, lest some late passer-by should see me. A light was brought, and the whole household gathered round me, some smiling

12

and some crying. I went to look at my children, and thanked God for their happy sleep. The tears fell as I leaned over them. As I moved to leave, Benny stirred. I turned back, and whispered, "Mother is here." After digging at his eyes with his little fist, they opened, and he sat up in bed, looking at me curiously. Having satisfied himself that it was I, he exclaimed, "O mother! you ain't dead, are you? They didn't cut off your head at the plantation, did they?"

My time was up too soon, and my guide was waiting for me. I laid Benny back in his bed, and dried his tears by a promise to come again soon. Rapidly we retraced our steps back to the plantation. About half way we were met by a company of four patrols. Luckily we heard their horse's hoofs before they came in sight, and we had time to hide behind a large tree. They passed, hallooing and shouting in a manner that indicated a recent carousal. How thankful we were that they had not their dogs with them! We hastened our footsteps, and when we arrived on the plantation we heard the sound of the hand-mill. The slaves were grinding their corn. We were safely in the house before the horn summoned them to their labor. I divided my little parcel of food with my guide, knowing that he had lost the chance of grinding his corn, and must toil all day in the field.

Mr. Flint often took an inspection of the house, to see that no one was idle. The entire management of the work was trusted to me, because he knew nothing about it; and rather than hire a superintendent he contented himself with my arrangements. He had often urged upon his father the necessity of having me at the plantation to take charge of his affairs, and make clothes for the slaves; but the old man knew him too well to consent to that arrangement.

When I had been working a month at the plantation, the great aunt of Mr. Flint came to make him a visit. This was the good old lady who paid fifty dollars for my grandmother, for the purpose of making her free, when she stood on the auction block. My grandmother loved this old lady, whom we all called Miss Fanny. She often came to take tea with us. On such occasions the table was spread with a snow-white cloth, and the china cups and silver spoons were taken from the old-fashioned buffet. There were hot muffins, tea rusks, and delicious sweetmeats. My grandmother kept two cows, and the fresh cream was Miss Fanny's delight. She invariably declared that it was the best in town. The old ladies had cosey times together. They would work and chat, and sometimes, while talking over old times, their spectacles would get dim with tears, and would have to be taken off and wiped. When Miss Fanny bade us good by, her bag was filled with grandmother's best cakes, and she was urged to come again soon.

There had been a time when Dr. Flint's wife came to take tea with us, and when her children were also sent to have a feast of "Aunt Marthy's" nice cooking. But after I became an object of her jealousy and spite, she was angry with grandmother for giving a shelter to me and my children. She would not even speak to her in the street. This wounded my grandmother's feelings, for she could not retain ill will against the woman whom she had nourished with her milk when a babe. The doctor's wife would gladly have prevented our intercourse with Miss Fanny if she could have done it, but fortunately she was not dependent on the bounty of the Flints. She had enough to be independent; and that is more than can ever be gained from charity, however lavish it may be.

Miss Fanny was endeared to me by many recollections, and I was rejoiced to see her at the plantation. The warmth of her large, loyal heart made the house seem pleasanter while she was in it. She staid a week, and I had many talks with her. She said her principal object in coming was to see how I was treated, and whether any thing could be done for me. She inquired whether she could help me in any way. I told her I believed not. She condoled with me in her own peculiar way; saying she wished that I and all my grandmother's family were at rest in our graves, for not until then should she feel any peace about us. The good old soul did not dream that I was planning to bestow peace upon her, with regard to myself and my children; not by death, but by securing our freedom.

Again and again I had traversed those dreary twelve miles, to and from the town; and all the way, I was meditating upon some means of escape for myself and my children. My friends had made every effort that ingenuity could devise to effect our purchase, but all their plans had proved abortive. Dr. Flint was suspicious, and determined not to loosen his grasp upon us. I could have made my escape alone; but it was more for my helpless children than for myself that I longed for freedom. Though the boon would have been precious to me, above all price, I would not have taken it at the expense of leaving them in slavery. Every trial I endured, every sacrifice I made for their sakes, drew them closer to my heart, and gave me fresh courage to beat back the dark waves that rolled and rolled over me in a seemingly endless night of storms.

The six weeks were nearly completed, when Mr. Flint's bride was expected to take possession of her new home. The arrangements were all completed, and Mr. Flint said I had done well. He expected to leave home on Saturday, and return with his bride the following Wednesday. After receiving various orders from him, I ventured to ask permission to spend Sunday in town. It was granted; for which favor I was thankful. It was the first I had ever asked of him, and I intended it should be the last. It needed more than one night to accomplish the project I had in view; but the whole of Sunday would give me an opportunity. I spent the Sabbath with my grandmother. A calmer, more beautiful day never came down out of heaven. To me it was a day of conflicting emotions. Perhaps it was the last day I should ever spend under that dear, old sheltering roof! Perhaps these were the last talks I should ever have with the faithful old friend of my whole life! Perhaps it was the last time I and my children should be together! Well, better so, I thought, than that they should be slaves. I knew the doom that awaited my fair baby in slavery, and I determined to save her from it, or perish in the attempt. I went to make this vow at the graves of my poor

12*

parents, in the burying-ground of the slaves. "There the wicked cease from troubling, and there the weary be at rest. There the prisoners rest together; they hear not the voice of the oppressor; the servant is free from his master." I knelt by the graves of my parents, and thanked God, as I had often done before, that they had not lived to witness my trials, or to mourn over my sins. I had received my mother's blessing when she died; and in many an hour of tribulation I had seemed to hear her voice, sometimes chiding me, sometimes whispering loving words into my wounded heart. I have shed many and bitter tears, to think that when I am gone from my children they cannot remember me with such entire satisfaction as I remembered my mother.

The graveyard was in the woods, and twilight was coming on. Nothing broke the death-like stillness except the occasional twitter of a bird. My spirit was overawed by the solemnity of the scene. For more than ten years I had frequented this spot, but never had it seemed to me so sacred as now. A black stump, at the head of my mother's grave, was all that remained of a tree my father had planted. His grave was marked by a small wooden board, bearing his name, the letters of which were nearly obliterated. I knelt down and kissed them, and poured forth a prayer to God for guidance and support in the perilous step I was about to take. As I passed the wreck of the old meeting house, where, before Nat Turner's time, the slaves had been allowed to meet for worship, I seemed to hear my father's voice come from it, bidding me not to tarry till I reached freedom or the grave. I rushed on with renovated hopes. My trust in God had been strengthened by that prayer among the graves.

My plan was to conceal myself at the house of a friend, and remain there a few weeks till the search was over. My hope was that the doctor would get discouraged, and, for fear of losing my value, and also of subsequently finding my children among the missing, he would consent to sell us; and I knew somebody would buy us. I had done all in my power to make my children comfortable during the time I expected to be separated from them. I was packing my things, when grandmother came into the room, and asked what I was doing. "I am putting my things in order," I replied. I tried to look and speak cheerfully; but her watchful eye detected something beneath the surface. She drew me towards her, and asked me to sit down. She looked earnestly at me, and said, "Linda, do you want to kill your old grandmother? Do you mean to leave your little, helpless children? I am old now, and cannot do for your babies as I once did for you."

I replied, that if I went away, perhaps their father would be able to secure their freedom.

"Ah, my child," said she, "don't trust too much to him. Stand by your own children, and suffer with them till death. Nobody respects a mother who forsakes her children; and if you leave them, you will never have a happy moment. If you go, you will make me miserable the short time I have to live. You would be taken and brought back, and your sufferings would be dreadful. Remember poor Benjamin. Do give it up, Linda. Try to bear a little longer. Things may turn out better than we expect."

My courage failed me, in view of the sorrow I should bring on that faithful, loving old heart. I promised that I would try longer, and that I would take nothing out of her house without her knowledge.

Whenever the children climbed on my knee, or laid their heads on my lap, she would say, "Poor little souls! what would you do without a mother? She don't love you as I do." And she would hug them to her own bosom, as if to reproach me for my want of affection ; but she knew all the while that I loved them better than my life. I slept with her that night, and it was the last time. The memory of it haunted me for many a year.

On Monday I returned to the plantation, and busied myself with preparations for the important day. Wednesday came. It was a beautiful day, and the faces of the slaves were as bright as the sunshine. The poor creatures were merry. They were expecting little presents from the bride, and hoping for better times under her administration. I had no such hopes for them. I knew that the young wives of slaveholders often thought their authority and importance would be best established and maintained by cruelty ; and what I had heard of young Mrs. Flint gave me no reason to expect that her rule over them would be less severe than that of the master and overseer. Truly, the colored race are the most cheerful and forgiving people on the face of the earth. That their masters sleep in safety is owing to their superabundance of heart ; and yet they look upon their sufferings with less

pity than they would bestow on those of a horse or
a dog.

I stood at the door with others to receive the bride-
groom and bride. She was a handsome, delicate-look-
ing girl, and her face flushed with emotion at sight of
her new home. I thought it likely that visions of a
happy future were rising before her. It made me sad ;
for I knew how soon clouds would come over her sunshine. She examined every part of the house, and
told me she was delighted with the arrangements I
had made. I was afraid old Mrs. Flint had tried to
prejudice her against me, and I did my best to please
her.

All passed off smoothly for me until dinner time
arrived. I did not mind the embarrassment of waiting on a dinner party, for the first time in my life,
half so much as I did the meeting with Dr. Flint and
his wife, who would be among the guests. It was a
mystery to me why Mrs. Flint had not made her appearance at the plantation during all the time I was
putting the house in order. I had not met her, face to
face, for five years, and I had no wish to see her now.
She was a praying woman, and, doubtless, considered
my present position a special answer to her prayers.
Nothing could please her better than to see me hum-
bled and trampled upon. I was just where she would
have me — in the power of a hard, unprincipled master. She did not speak to me when she took her seat
at table ; but her satisfied, triumphant smile, when I
handed her plate, was more eloquent than words.
The old doctor was not so quiet in his demonstrations.
He ordered me here and there, and spoke with pecu-

liar emphasis when he said " your *mistress.*" I was
drilled like a disgraced soldier. When all was over,
and the last key turned, I sought my pillow, thankful that God had appointed a season of rest for the
weary.

The next day my new mistress began her housekeep-
ing. I was not exactly appointed maid of all work;
but I was to do whatever I was told. Monday evening
came. It was always a busy time. On that night the
slaves received their weekly allowance of food. Three
pounds of meat, a peck of corn, and perhaps a dozen
herring were allowed to each man. Women received
a pound and a half of meat, a peck of corn, and the
same number of herring. Children over twelve years
old had half the allowance of the women. The meat
was cut and weighed by the foreman of the field hands,
and piled on planks before the meat house. Then the
second foreman went behind the building, and when
the first foreman called out, " Who takes this piece of
meat ? " he answered by calling somebody's name.
This method was resorted to as a means of preventing
partiality in distributing the meat. The young mistress came out to see how things were done on her
plantation, and she soon gave a specimen of her character. Among those in waiting for their allowance
was a very old slave, who had faithfully served the
Flint family through three generations. When he
hobbled up to get his bit of meat, the mistress said he
was too old to have any allowance ; that when niggers
were too old to work, they ought to be fed on grass.
Poor old man ! He suffered much before he found
rest in the grave.

My mistress and I got along very well together. At the end of a week, old Mrs. Flint made us another visit, and was closeted a long time with her daughter-in-law. I had my suspicions what was the subject of the conference. The old doctor's wife had been informed that I could leave the plantation on one condition, and she was very desirous to keep me there. If she had trusted me, as I deserved to be trusted by her, she would have had no fears of my accepting that condition. When she entered her carriage to return home, she said to young Mrs. Flint, " Don't neglect to send for them as quick as possible." My heart was on the watch all the time, and I at once concluded that she spoke of my children. The doctor came the next day, and as I entered the room to spread the tea table, I heard him say, " Don't wait any longer. Send for them to-morrow." I saw through the plan. They thought my children's being there would fetter me to the spot, and that it was a good place to break us all in to abject submission to our lot as slaves. After the doctor left, a gentleman called, who had always manifested friendly feelings towards my grandmother and her family. Mr. Flint carried him over the plantation to show him the results of labor performed by men and women who were unpaid, miserably clothed, and half famished. The cotton crop was all they thought of. It was duly admired, and the gentleman returned with specimens to show his friends. I was ordered to carry water to wash his hands. As I did so, he said, " Linda, how do you like your new home ? " I told him I liked it as well as I expected. He replied, " They don't think you are contented, and to-morrow they are going

to bring your children to be with you.   I am sorry for
you, Linda.   I hope they will treat you kindly."   I
hurried from the room, unable to thank him.   My
suspicions were correct.   My children were to be
brought to the plantation to be " broke in."

To this day I feel grateful to the gentleman who
gave me this timely information.   It nerved me to
immediate action.

XVII.

THE FLIGHT.

Mr. Flint was hard pushed for house servants, and rather than lose me he had restrained his malice. I did my work faithfully, though not, of course, with a willing mind. They were evidently afraid I should leave them. Mr. Flint wished that I should sleep in the great house instead of the servants' quarters. His wife agreed to the proposition, but said I mustn't bring my bed into the house, because it would scatter feathers on her carpet. I knew when I went there that they would never think of such a thing as furnishing a bed of any kind for me and my little one. I therefore carried my own bed, and now I was forbidden to use it. I did as I was ordered. But now that I was certain my children were to be put in their power, in order to give them a stronger hold on me, I resolved to leave them that night. I remembered the grief this step would bring upon my dear old grandmother; and nothing less than the freedom of my children would have induced me to disregard her advice. I went about my evening work with trembling steps. Mr. Flint twice called from his chamber door to inquire why the house was not locked up. I replied that I had not done my work. "You have had time enough to do it," said he. "Take care how you answer me!"

I shut all the windows, locked all the doors, and went up to the third story, to wait till midnight. How

long those hours seemed, and how fervently I prayed
that God would not forsake me in this hour of utmost
need! I was about to risk every thing on the throw
of a die; and if I failed, O what would become of me
and my poor children? They would be made to suffer
for my fault.

At half past twelve I stole softly down stairs. I
stopped on the second floor, thinking I heard a noise.
I felt my way down into the parlor, and looked out of
the window. The night was so intensely dark that I
could see nothing. I raised the window very softly
and jumped out. Large drops of rain were falling,
and the darkness bewildered me. I dropped on my
knees, and breathed a short prayer to God for guidance
and protection. I groped my way to the road, and
rushed towards the town with almost lightning speed.
I arrived at my grandmother's house, but dared not
see her. She would say, "Linda, you are killing me;"
and I knew that would unnerve me. I tapped softly
at the window of a room, occupied by a woman, who
had lived in the house several years. I knew she was
a faithful friend, and could be trusted with my secret.
I tapped several times before she heard me. At last
she raised the window, and I whispered, "Sally, I have
run away. Let me in, quick." She opened the door
softly, and said in low tones, "For God's sake, don't.
Your grandmother is trying to buy you and de chillern.
Mr. Sands was here last week. He tole her he was
going away on business, but he wanted her to go ahead
about buying you and de chillern, and he would help
her all he could. Don't run away, Linda. Your
grandmother is all bowed down wid trouble now."

I replied, " Sally, they are going to carry my children to the plantation to-morrow ; and they will never sell them to any body so long as they have me in their power. Now, would you advise me to go back ? "

" No, chile, no," answered she. " When dey finds you is gone, dey won't want de plague ob de chillern ; but where is you going to hide ? Dey knows ebery inch ob dis house."

I told her I had a hiding-place, and that was all it was best for her to know. I asked her to go into my room as soon as it was light, and take all my clothes out of my trunk, and pack them in hers ; for I knew Mr. Flint and the constable would be there early to search my room. I feared the sight of my children would be too much for my full heart ; but I could not go out into the uncertain future without one last look. I bent over the bed where lay my little Benny and baby Ellen. Poor little ones ! fatherless and motherless ! Memories of their father came over me. He wanted to be kind to them ; but they were not all to him, as they were to my womanly heart. I knelt and prayed for the innocent little sleepers. I kissed them lightly, and turned away.

As I was about to open the street door, Sally laid her hand on my shoulder, and said, " Linda, is you gwine all alone ? Let me call your uncle."

" No, Sally," I replied, " I want no one to be brought into trouble on my account."

I went forth into the darkness and rain. I ran on till I came to the house of the friend who was to conceal me.

Early the next morning Mr. Flint was at my grandmother's inquiring for me. She told him she had not seen me, and supposed I was at the plantation. He watched her face narrowly, and said, " Don't you know any thing about her running off?" She assured him that she did not. He went on to say, " Last night she ran off without the least provocation. We had treated her very kindly. My wife liked her. She will soon be found and brought back. Are her children with you?" When told that they were, he said, " I am very glad to hear that. If they are here, she cannot be far off. If I find out that any of my niggers have had any thing to do with this damned business, I'll give 'em five hundred lashes." As he started to go to his father's, he turned round and added, persuasively, " Let her be brought back, and she shall have her children to live with her."

The tidings made the old doctor rave and storm at a furious rate. It was a busy day for them. My grandmother's house was searched from top to bottom. As my trunk was empty, they concluded I had taken my clothes with me. Before ten o'clock every vessel northward bound was thoroughly examined, and the law against harboring fugitives was read to all on board. At night a watch was set over the town. Knowing how distressed my grandmother would be, I wanted to send her a message; but it could not be done. Every one who went in or out of her house was closely watched. The doctor said he would take my children, unless she became responsible for them; which of course she willingly did. The next day was spent in searching. Before night, the following advertisement was posted at every corner, and in every public place for miles round : —

"$300 Reward! Ran away from the subscriber, an intelligent, bright, mulatto girl, named Linda, 21 years of age. Five feet four inches high. Dark eyes, and black hair inclined to curl; but it can be made straight. Has a decayed spot on a front tooth. She can read and write, and in all probability will try to get to the Free States. All persons are forbidden, under penalty of the law, to harbor or employ said slave. $150 will be given to whoever takes her in the state, and $300 if taken out of the state and delivered to me, or lodged in jail.

Dr. Flint."

13 *

XVIII.

MONTHS OF PERIL.

THE search for me was kept up with more perse-verence than I had anticipated. I began to think that escape was impossible. I was in great anxiety lest I should implicate the friend who harbored me. I knew the consequences would be frightful ; and much as I dreaded being caught, even that seemed better than causing an innocent person to suffer for kindness to me. A week had passed in terrible suspense, when my pursuers came into such close vicinity that I concluded they had tracked me to my hiding-place. I flew out of the house, and concealed myself in a thicket of bushes. There I remained in an agony of fear for two hours. Suddenly, a reptile of some kind seized my leg. In my fright, I struck a blow which loosened its hold, but I could not tell whether I had killed it ; it was so dark, I could not see what it was ; I only knew it was something cold and slimy. The pain I felt soon indicated that the bite was poisonous. I was compelled to leave my place of concealment, and I groped my way back into the house. The pain had become intense, and my friend was startled by my look of anguish. I asked her to prepare a poultice of warm ashes and vinegar, and I applied it to my leg, which was already much swollen. The application gave me some relief, but the swelling did not abate. The dread of being disabled was greater than the physical pain I endured.

My friend asked an old woman, who doctored among the slaves, what was good for the bite of a snake or a lizard. She told her to steep a dozen coppers in vinegar, over night, and apply the cankered vinegar to the inflamed part.*

I had succeeded in cautiously conveying some messages to my relatives. They were harshly threatened, and despairing of my having a chance to escape, they advised me to return to my master, ask his forgiveness, and let him make an example of me. But such counsel had no influence with me. When I started upon this hazardous undertaking, I had resolved that, come what would, there should be no turning back. "Give me liberty, or give me death," was my motto. When my friend contrived to make known to my relatives the painful situation I had been in for twenty-four hours, they said no more about my going back to my master. Something must be done, and that speedily ; but where to turn for help, they knew not. God in his mercy raised up "a friend in need."

Among the ladies who were acquainted with my grandmother, was one who had known her from childhood, and always been very friendly to her. She had also known my mother and her children, and felt interested for them. At this crisis of affairs she called to see my grandmother, as she not unfrequently did. She observed the sad and troubled expression of her face, and asked if she knew where Linda was, and whether

* The poison of a snake is a powerful acid, and is counteracted by powerful alkalies, such as potash, ammonia, &c. The Indians are accustomed to apply wet ashes, or plunge the limb into strong lie. White men, employed to lay out railroads in snaky places, often carry ammonia with them as an antidote. — EDITOR.

she was safe. My grandmother shook her head, without answering. " Come, Aunt Martha," said the kind lady, " tell me all about it. Perhaps I can do something to help you." The husband of this lady held many slaves, and bought and sold slaves. She also held a number in her own name ; but she treated them kindly, and would never allow any of them to be sold. She was unlike the majority of slaveholders' wives. My grandmother looked earnestly at her. Something in the expression of her face said " Trust me ! " and she did trust her. She listened attentively to the details of my story, and sat thinking for a while. At last she said, " Aunt Martha, I pity you both. If you think there is any chance of Linda's getting to the Free States, I will conceal her for a time. But first you must solemnly promise that my name shall never be mentioned. If such a thing should become known, it would ruin me and my family. No one in my house must know of it, except the cook. She is so faithful that I would trust my own life with her ; and I know she likes Linda. It is a great risk ; but I trust no harm will come of it. Get word to Linda to be ready as soon as it is dark, before the patrols are out. I will send the housemaids on errands, and Betty shall go to meet Linda." The place where we were to meet was designated and agreed upon. My grandmother was unable to thank the lady for this noble deed ; overcome by her emotions, she sank on her knees and sobbed like a child.

I received a message to leave my friend's house at such an hour, and go to a certain place where a friend would be waiting for me. As a matter of prudence no names were mentioned. I had no means of conjectur-

ing who I was to meet, or where I was going. I did
not like to move thus blindfolded, but I had no choice.
It would not do for me to remain where I was. I disguised myself, summoned up courage to meet the worst,
and went to the appointed place. My friend Betty was
there; she was the last person I expected to see. We
hurried along in silence. The pain in my leg was so
intense that it seemed as if I should drop; but fear
gave me strength. We reached the house and entered
unobserved. Her first words were : " Honey, now you
is safe. Dem devils ain't coming to search *dis* house.
When I get you into missis' safe place, I will bring
some nice hot supper. I specs you need it after all dis
skeering." Betty's vocation led her to think eating
the most important thing in life. She did not realize
that my heart was too full for me to care much about
supper.

The mistress came to meet us, and led me up stairs
to a small room over her own sleeping apartment.
" You will be safe here, Linda," said she; "I keep this
room to store away things that are out of use. The
girls are not accustomed to be sent to it, and they will
not suspect any thing unless they hear some noise. I
always keep it locked, and Betty shall take care of the
key. But you must be very careful, for my sake as
well as your own ; and you must never tell my secret;
for it would ruin me and my family. I will keep the
girls busy in the morning, that Betty may have a chance
to bring your breakfast ; but it will not do for her to
come to you again till night. I will come to see you
sometimes. Keep up your courage. I hope this state
of things will not last long." Betty came with the

"nice hot supper," and the mistress hastened down stairs to keep things straight till she returned. How my heart overflowed with gratitude! Words choked in my throat; but I could have kissed the feet of my benefactress. For that deed of Christian womanhood, may God forever bless her!

I went to sleep that night with the feeling that I was for the present the most fortunate slave in town. Morning came and filled my little cell with light. I thanked the heavenly Father for this safe retreat. Opposite my window was a pile of feather beds. On the top of these I could lie perfectly concealed, and command a view of the street through which Dr. Flint passed to his office. Anxious as I was, I felt a gleam of satisfaction when I saw him. Thus far I had outwitted him, and I triumphed over it. Who can blame slaves for being cunning? They are constantly compelled to resort to it. It is the only weapon of the weak and oppressed against the strength of their tyrants.

I was daily hoping to hear that my master had sold my children; for I knew who was on the watch to buy them. But Dr. Flint cared even more for revenge than he did for money. My brother William, and the good aunt who had served in his family twenty years, and my little Benny, and Ellen, who was a little over two years old, were thrust into jail, as a means of compelling my relatives to give some information about me. He swore my grandmother should never see one of them again till I was brought back. They kept these facts from me for several days. When I heard that my little ones were in a loathsome jail, my first impulse was to go to them. I was encountering dangers for the sake of freeing them, and must I be the cause of their death? The thought was agonizing. My benefactress tried to soothe me by telling me that my aunt would take good care of the children while they remained in jail. But it added to my pain to think that the good old aunt, who had always been so kind to her sister's orphan children, should be shut up in prison for no other crime than loving them. I suppose my friends feared a reckless movement on my part, knowing, as they did, that my life was bound up in my children. I received a note from my brother William. It was scarcely legible, and ran thus: "Wherever you are, dear sister, I beg of you not to come here. We are all much better off than you are. If you come, you will ruin us all. They would force you to tell where you had been, or they would kill you. Take the advice of your friends; if not for the sake of me and your children, at least for the sake of those you would ruin."

Poor William! He also must suffer for being my brother. I took his advice and kept quiet. My aunt was taken out of jail at the end of a month, because Mrs. Flint could not spare her any longer. She was tired of being her own housekeeper. It was quite too fatiguing to order her dinner and eat it too. My children remained in jail, where brother William did all he could for their comfort. Betty went to see them sometimes, and brought me tidings. She was not permitted to enter the jail; but William would hold them up to the grated window while she chatted with them. When she repeated their prattle, and told me how they

wanted to see their ma, my tears would flow.   Old
Betty would exclaim, " Lors, chile ! what's you crying
'bout ?   Dem young uns vil kill you dead.   Don't be
so chick'n hearted ! If you does, you vil nebber git
thro' dis world."

Good old soul ! She had gone through the world
childless. She had never had little ones to clasp their
arms round her neck ; she had never seen their soft
eyes looking into hers ; no sweet little voices had called
her mother ; she had never pressed her own infants to
her heart, with the feeling that even in fetters there
was something to live for.   How could she realize my
feelings ?   Betty's husband loved children dearly, and
wondered why God had denied them to him.   He expressed great sorrow when he came to Betty with the
tidings that Ellen had been taken out of jail and
carried to Dr. Flint's. She had the measles a short
time before they carried her to jail, and the disease
had left her eyes affected. The doctor had taken her
home to attend to them.   My children had always been
afraid of the doctor and his wife. They had never
been inside of their house. Poor little Ellen cried all
day to be carried back to prison. The instincts of
childhood are true. She knew she was loved in the
jail.   Her screams and sobs annoyed Mrs. Flint. Before night she called one of the slaves, and said, " Here,
Bill, carry this brat back to the jail. I can't stand
her noise. If she would be quiet I should like to
keep the little minx. She would make a handy waiting-maid for my daughter by and by. But if she
staid here, with her white face, I suppose I should
either kill her or spoil her. I hope the doctor will

sell them as far as wind and water can carry them. As for their mother, her ladyship will find out yet what she gets by running away. She hasn't so much feeling for her children as a cow has for its calf. If she had, she would have come back long ago, to get them out of jail, and save all this expense and trouble. The good-for-nothing hussy! When she is caught, she shall stay in jail, in irons, for one six months, and then be sold to a sugar plantation. I shall see her broke in yet. What do you stand there for, Bill? Why don't you go off with the brat? Mind, now, that you don't let any of the niggers speak to her in the street!"

When these remarks were reported to me, I smiled at Mrs. Flint's saying that she should either kill my child or spoil her. I thought to myself there was very little danger of the latter. I have always considered it as one of God's special providences that Ellen screamed till she was carried back to jail.

That same night Dr. Flint was called to a patient, and did not return till near morning. Passing my grandmother's, he saw a light in the house, and thought to himself, "Perhaps this has something to do with Linda." He knocked, and the door was opened. "What calls you up so early?" said he. "I saw your light, and I thought I would just stop and tell you that I have found out where Linda is. I know where to put my hands on her, and I shall have her before twelve o'clock." When he had turned away, my grandmother and my uncle looked anxiously at each other. They did not know whether or not it was merely one of the doctor's tricks to frighten them. In their uncertainty, they thought it was best to have a

14

message conveyed to my friend Betty. Unwilling to
alarm her mistress, Betty resolved to dispose of me
herself. She came to me, and told me to rise and
dress quickly. We hurried down stairs, and across
the yard, into the kitchen. She locked the door, and
lifted up a plank in the floor. A buffalo skin and a
bit of carpet were spread for me to lie on, and a quilt
thrown over me. "Stay dar," said she, "till I sees if
dey know 'bout you. Dey say dey vil put thar hans
on you afore twelve o'clock. If dey *did* know whar
you are, dey won't know *now*. Dey'll be disapinted
dis time. Dat's all I got to say. If dey comes rum-
magin 'mong *my* tings, dey'll get one bressed sarssin
from dis 'ere nigger." In my shallow bed I had but
just room enough to bring my hands to my face to
keep the dust out of my eyes; for Betty walked over
me twenty times in an hour, passing from the dresser
to the fireplace. When she was alone, I could hear
her pronouncing anathemas over Dr. Flint and all his
tribe, every now and then saying, with a chuckling
laugh, "Dis nigger's too cute for 'em dis time."
When the housemaids were about, she had sly ways
of drawing them out, that I might hear what they
would say. She would repeat stories she had heard
about my being in this, or that, or the other place. To
which they would answer, that I was not fool enough
to be staying round there; that I was in Philadelphia
or New York before this time. When all were abed
and asleep, Betty raised the plank, and said, "Come
out, chile; come out. Dey don't know nottin 'bout
you. 'Twas only white folks' lies, to skeer de niggers."
Some days after this adventure I had a much worse

fright. As I sat very still in my retreat above stairs, cheerful visions floated through my mind. I thought Dr. Flint would soon get discouraged, and would be willing to sell my children, when he lost all hopes of making them the means of my discovery. I knew who was ready to buy them. Suddenly I heard a voice that chilled my blood. The sound was too familiar to me, it had been too dreadful, for me not to recognize at once my old master. He was in the house, and I at once concluded he had come to seize me. I looked round in terror. There was no way of escape. The voice receded. I supposed the constable was with him, and they were searching the house. In my alarm I did not forget the trouble I was bringing on my generous benefactress. It seemed as if I were born to bring sorrow on all who befriended me, and that was the bitterest drop in the bitter cup of my life. After a while I heard approaching footsteps; the key was turned in my door. I braced myself against the wall to keep from falling. I ventured to look up, and there stood my kind benefactress alone. I was too much overcome to speak, and sunk down upon the floor.

"I thought you would hear your master's voice," she said; "and knowing you would be terrified, I came to tell you there is nothing to fear. You may even indulge in a laugh at the old gentleman's expense. He is so sure you are in New York, that he came to borrow five hundred dollars to go in pursuit of you. My sister had some money to loan on interest. He has obtained it, and proposes to start for New York to-night. So, for the present, you see you are safe. The doctor will merely lighten his pocket hunting after the bird he has left behind."

XIX.

THE CHILDREN SOLD.

The doctor came back from New York, of course
without accomplishing his purpose. He had expended
considerable money, and was rather disheartened. My
brother and the children had now been in jail two
months, and that also was some expense. My friends
thought it was a favorable time to work on his discouraged feelings. Mr. Sands sent a speculator to
offer him nine hundred dollars for my brother William, and eight hundred for the two children. These
were high prices, as slaves were then selling; but the
offer was rejected. If it had been merely a question
of money, the doctor would have sold any boy of
Benny's age for two hundred dollars; but he could
not bear to give up the power of revenge. But he
was hard pressed for money, and he revolved the matter
in his mind. He knew that if he could keep Ellen till
she was fifteen, he could sell her for a high price; but
I presume he reflected that she might die, or might be
stolen away. At all events, he came to the conclusion
that he had better accept the slave-trader's offer.
Meeting him in the street, he inquired when he would
leave town. "To-day, at ten o'clock," he replied.
"Ah, do you go so soon?" said the doctor; "I have
been reflecting upon your proposition, and I have concluded to let you have the three negroes if you will
say nineteen hundred dollars." After some parley,

the trader agreed to his terms. He wanted the bill of sale drawn up and signed immediately, as he had a great deal to attend to during the short time he remained in town. The doctor went to the jail and told William he would take him back into his service if he would promise to behave himself; but he replied that he would rather be sold. "And you *shall* be sold, you ungrateful rascal!" exclaimed the doctor. In less than an hour the money was paid, the papers were signed, sealed, and delivered, and my brother and children were in the hands of the trader.

It was a hurried transaction; and after it was over, the doctor's characteristic caution returned. He went back to the speculator, and said, "Sir, I have come to lay you under obligations of a thousand dollars not to sell any of those negroes in this state." "You come too late," replied the trader; "our bargain is closed." He had, in fact, already sold them to Mr. Sands, but he did not mention it. The doctor required him to put irons on "that rascal, Bill," and to pass through the back streets when he took his gang out of town. The trader was privately instructed to concede to his wishes. My good old aunt went to the jail to bid the children good by, supposing them to be the speculator's property, and that she should never see them again. As she held Benny in her lap, he said, "Aunt Nancy, I want to show you something." He led her to the door and showed her a long row of marks, saying, "Uncle Will taught me to count. I have made a mark for every day I have been here, and it is sixty days. It is a long time; and the speculator is going to take me and Ellen away. He's a bad man. It's

14 *

wrong for him to take grandmother's children. I want
to go to my mother."

My grandmother was told that the children would
be restored to her, but she was requested to act as if
they were really to be sent away. Accordingly, she
made up a bundle of clothes and went to the jail.
When she arrived, she found William handcuffed
among the gang, and the children in the trader's cart.
The scene seemed too much like reality. She was
afraid there might have been some deception or mistake. She fainted, and was carried home.

When the wagon stopped at the hotel, several gentlemen came out and proposed to purchase William, but
the trader refused their offers, without stating that he
was already sold. And now came the trying hour for
that drove of human beings, driven away like cattle, to
be sold they knew not where. Husbands were torn from
wives, parents from children, never to look upon each
other again this side the grave. There was wringing
of hands and cries of despair.

Dr. Flint had the supreme satisfaction of seeing the
wagon leave town, and Mrs. Flint had the gratification
of supposing that my children were going " as far as
wind and water would carry them." According to
agreement, my uncle followed the wagon some miles,
until they came to an old 'farm house. There the
trader took the irons from William, and as he did so,
he said, " You are a damned clever fellow. I should
like to own you myself. Them gentlemen that wanted
to buy you said you was a bright, honest chap, and I
must git you a good home. I guess your old master
will swear to-morrow, and call himself an old fool for

selling the children. I reckon he'll never git their mammy back agin. I expect she's made tracks for the north. Good by, old boy. Remember, I have done you a good turn. You must thank me by coaxing all the pretty gals to go with me next fall. That's going to be my last trip. This trading in' niggers is a bad business for a fellow that's got any heart. Move on, you fellows!" And the gang went on, God alone knows where.

Much as I despise and detest the class of slave-traders, whom I regard as the vilest wretches on earth, I must do this man the justice to say that he seemed to have some feeling. He took a fancy to William in the jail, and wanted to buy him. When he heard the story of my children, he was willing to aid them in getting out of Dr. Flint's power, even without charging the customary fee.

My uncle procured a wagon and carried William and the children back to town. Great was the joy in my grandmother's house! The curtains were closed, and the candles lighted. The happy grandmother cuddled the little ones to her bosom. They hugged her, and kissed her, and clapped their hands, and shouted. She knelt down and poured forth one of her heartfelt prayers of thanksgiving to God. The father was present for a while; and though such a "parental relation" as existed between him and my children takes slight hold of the hearts or consciences of slaveholders, it must be that he experienced some moments of pure joy in witnessing the happiness he had imparted.

I had no share in the rejoicings of that evening.

The events of the day had not come to my knowledge. And now I will tell you something that happened to me; though you will, perhaps, think it illustrates the superstition of slaves. I sat in my usual place on the floor near the window, where I could hear much that was said in the street without being seen. The family had retired for the night, and all was still. I sat there thinking of my children, when I heard a low strain of music. A band of serenaders were under the window, playing "Home, sweet home." I listened till the sounds did not seem like music, but like the moaning of children. It seemed as if my heart would burst. I rose from my sitting posture, and knelt. A streak of moonlight was on the floor before me, and in the midst of it appeared the forms of my two children. They vanished; but I had seen them distinctly. Some will call it a dream, others a vision. I know not how to account for it, but it made a strong impression on my mind, and I felt certain something had happened to my little ones.

I had not seen Betty since morning. Now I heard her softly turning the key. As soon as she entered, I clung to her, and begged her to let me know whether my children were dead, or whether they were sold; for I had seen their spirits in my room, and I was sure something had happened to them. "Lor, chile," said she, putting her arms round me, "you's got de highsterics. I'll sleep wid you to-night, 'cause you'll make a noise, and ruin missis. Something has stirred you up mightily. When you is done cryin, I'll talk wid you. De chillern is well, and mighty happy. I seed 'em my-self. Does dat satisfy you? Dar, chile, be still! Somebody vill hear you." I tried to obey her. She lay down, and was soon sound asleep; but no sleep would come to my eyelids.

At dawn, Betty was up and off to the kitchen. The hours passed on, and the vision of the night kept constantly recurring to my thoughts. After a while I heard the voices of two women in the entry. In one of them I recognized the housemaid. The other said to her, "Did you know Linda Brent's children was sold to the speculator yesterday. They say ole massa Flint was mighty glad to see 'em drove out of town; but they say they've come back agin. I 'spect it's all their daddy's doings. They say he's bought William too. Lor! how it will take hold of ole massa Flint! I'm going roun' to aunt Marthy's to see 'bout it."

I bit my lips till the blood came to keep from crying out. Were my children with their grandmother, or had the speculator carried them off? The suspense was dreadful. Would Betty *never* come, and tell me the truth about it? At last she came, and I eagerly repeated what I had overheard. Her face was one broad, bright smile. "Lor, you foolish ting!" said she. "I'se gwine to tell you all 'bout it. De gals is eating thar breakfast, and missus tole me to let her tell you; but, poor creeter! t'aint right to keep you waitin', and I'se gwine to tell you. Brudder, chillern, all is bought by de daddy! I'se laugh more dan nuff, tinking 'bout ole massa Flint. Lor, how he *vill* swar! He's got ketched dis time, any how; but I must be getting out o' dis, or dem gals vill come and ketch *me*."

Betty went off laughing; and I said to myself, "Can it be true that my children are free? I have not suffered for them in vain. Thank God!"

Great surprise was expressed when it was known that my children had returned to their grandmother's. The news spread through the town, and many a kind word was bestowed on the little ones.

Dr. Flint went to my grandmother's to ascertain who was the owner of my children, and she informed him. " I expected as much," said he. " I am glad to hear it. I have had news from Linda lately, and I shall soon have her. You need never expect to see *her* free. She shall be my slave as long as I live, and when I am dead she shall be the slave of my children. If I ever find out that you or Phillip had any thing to do with her running off I'll kill him. And if I meet William in the street, and he presumes to look at me, I'll flog him within an inch of his life. Keep those brats out of my sight! "

As he turned to leave, my grandmother said something to remind him of his own doings. He looked back upon her, as if he would have been glad to strike her to the ground.

I had my season of joy and thanksgiving. It was the first time since my childhood that I had experienced any real happiness. I heard of the old doctor's threats, but they no longer had the same power to trouble me. The darkest cloud that hung over my life had rolled away. Whatever slavery might do to me, it could not shackle my children. If I fell a sacrifice, my little ones were saved. It was well for me that my simple heart believed all that had been promised for their welfare. It is always better to trust than to doubt.

XX.

NEW PERILS.

The doctor, more exasperated than ever, again tried to revenge himself on my relatives. He arrested uncle Phillip on the charge of having aided my flight. He was carried before a court, and swore truly that he knew nothing of my intention to escape, and that he had not seen me since I left my master's plantation. The doctor then demanded that he should give bail for five hundred dollars that he would have nothing to do with me. Several gentlemen offered to be security for him; but Mr. Sands told him he had better go back to jail, and he would see that he came out without giving bail.

The news of his arrest was carried to my grandmother, who conveyed it to Betty. In the kindness of her heart, she again stowed me away under the floor; and as she walked back and forth, in the performance of her culinary duties, she talked apparently to herself, but with the intention that I should hear what was going on. I hoped that my uncle's imprisonment would last but few days; still I was anxious. I thought it likely Dr. Flint would do his utmost to taunt and insult him, and I was afraid my uncle might lose control of himself, and retort in some way that would be construed into a punishable offence; and I was well aware that in court his word would not be taken against any white man's. The search for me was renewed. Something had excited suspicions that I was in the vicinity. They searched the house I was in. I heard their steps and their voices. At night, when all were asleep, Betty came to release me from my place of confinement. The fright I had undergone, the constrained posture, and the dampness of the ground, made me ill for several days. My uncle was soon after taken out of prison; but the movements of all my relatives, and of all our friends, were very closely watched.

We all saw that I could not remain where I was much longer. I had already staid longer than was intended, and I knew my presence must be a source of perpetual anxiety to my kind benefactress. During this time, my friends had laid many plans for my escape, but the extreme vigilance of my persecutors made it impossible to carry them into effect.

One morning I was much startled by hearing somebody trying to get into my room. Several keys were tried, but none fitted. I instantly conjectured it was one of the housemaids; and I concluded she must either have heard some noise in the room, or have noticed the entrance of Betty. When my friend came, at her usual time, I told her what had happened. " I knows who it was," said she. " 'Pend upon it, 'twas dat Jenny. Dat nigger allers got de debble in her." I suggested that she might have seen or heard something that excited her curiosity.

" Tut! tut! chile!" exclaimed Betty, " she ain't seen notin', nor hearn notin'. She only 'spects someting. Dat's all. She wants to fine out who hab cut and make my gownd. But she won't nebber know. Dat's sartin. I'll git missis to fix her."

I reflected a moment, and said, " Betty, I must leave here to-night."

" Do as you tink best, poor chile," she replied. " I'se mighty 'fraid dat 'ere nigger vill pop on you some time."

She reported the incident to her mistress, and received orders to keep Jenny busy in the kitchen till she could see my uncle Phillip. He told her he would send a friend for me that very evening. She told him she hoped I was going to the north, for it was very dangerous for me to remain any where in the vicinity. Alas, it was not an easy thing, for one in my situation, to go to the north. In order to leave the coast quite clear for me, she went into the country to spend the day with her brother, and took Jenny with her. She was afraid to come and bid me good by, but she left a kind message with Betty. I heard her carriage roll from the door, and I never again saw her who had so generously befriended the poor, trembling fugitive! Though she was a slaveholder, to this day my heart blesses her!

I had not the slightest idea where I was going. Betty brought me a suit of sailor's clothes, — jacket, trowsers, and tarpaulin hat. She gave me a small bundle, saying I might need it where I was going. In cheery tones, she exclaimed, " I'se *so* glad you is gwine to free parts! Don't forget ole Betty. P'raps I'll come 'long by and by."

I tried to tell her how grateful I felt for all her kindness, but she interrupted me. "I don't want no tanks, honey. I'se glad I could help you, and I hope de good Lord vill open de path for you. I'se gwine wid

you to de lower gate. Put your hands in your pock-
ets, and walk ricketty, like de sailors."

I performed to her satisfaction. At the gate I found
Peter, a young colored man, waiting for me. I had
known him for years. He had been an apprentice to
my father, and had always borne a good character. I
was not afraid to trust to him. Betty bade me a hurried good by, and we walked off. "Take courage,
Linda," said my friend Peter. "I've got a dagger,
and no man shall take you from me, unless he passes
over my dead body."

It was a long time since I had taken a walk out of
doors, and the fresh air revived me. It was also pleasant to hear a human voice speaking to me above a whisper. I passed several people whom I knew, but they
did not recognize me in my disguise. I prayed inter-
nally that, for Peter's sake, as well as my own, nothing
might occur to bring out his dagger. We walked on
till we came to the wharf. My aunt Nancy's husband
was a seafaring man, and it had been deemed necessary to let him into our secret. He took me into his
boat, rowed out to a vessel not far distant, and hoisted
me on board. We three were the only occupants of
the vessel. I now ventured to ask what they proposed
to do with me. They said I was to remain on board
till near dawn, and then they would hide me in Snaky
Swamp, till my uncle Phillip had prepared a place of
concealment for me. If the vessel had been bound
north, it would have been of no avail to me, for it
would certainly have been searched. About four
o'clock, we were again seated in the boat, and rowed
three miles to the swamp. My fear of snakes had been

increased by the venomous bite I had received, and I
dreaded to enter this hiding-place. But I was in no
situation to choose, and I gratefully accepted the best
that my poor, persecuted friends could do for me.

Peter landed first, and with a large knife cut a path
through bamboos and briers of all descriptions. He
came back, took me in his arms, and carried me to a
seat made among the bamboos. Before we reached it,
we were covered with hundreds of mosquitos. In an
hour's time they had so poisoned my flesh that I was
a pitiful sight to behold. As the light increased, I saw
snake after snake crawling round us. I had been
accustomed to the sight of snakes all my life, but these
were larger than any I had ever seen. To this day I
shudder when I remember that morning. As evening
approached, the number of snakes increased so much
that we were continually obliged to thrash them with
sticks to keep them from crawling over us. The bamboos were so high and so thick that it was impossible
to see beyond a very short distance. Just before it
became dark we procured a seat nearer to the entrance
of the swamp, being fearful of losing our way back to
the boat. It was not long before we heard the paddle
of oars, and the low whistle, which had been agreed
upon as a signal. We made haste to enter the boat,
and were rowed back to the vessel. I passed a wretched
night; for the heat of the swamp, the mosquitos, and
the constant terror of snakes, had brought on a burning fever. I had just dropped asleep, when they came
and told me it was time to go back to that horrid
swamp. I could scarcely summon courage to rise.
But even those large, venomous snakes were less dread-

ful to my imagination than the white men in that
community called civilized.   This time Peter took a
quantity of tobacco to burn, to keep off the mosquitos.   It produced the desired effect on them, but gave
me nausea and severe headache.   At dark we returned
to the vessel.   I had been so sick during the day, that
Peter declared I should go home that night, if the
devil himself was on patrol.   They told me a place of
concealment had been provided for me at my grandmother's.   I could not imagine how it was possible to
hide me in her house, every nook and corner of which
was known to the Flint family.   They told me to wait
and see.   We were rowed ashore, and went boldly
through the streets, to my grandmother's.   I wore my
sailor's clothes, and had blackened my face with charcoal.   I passed several people whom I knew.   The
father of my children came so near that I brushed
against his arm; but he had no idea who it was.

"You must make the most of this walk," said my
friend Peter, "for you may not have another very
soon."

I thought his voice sounded sad.   It was kind of
him to conceal from me what a dismal hole was to be
my home for a long, long time.

XXI.

THE LOOPHOLE OF RETREAT.

A SMALL shed had been added to my grandmother's house years ago. Some boards were laid across the joists at the top, and between these boards and the roof was a very small garret, never occupied by any thing but rats and mice. It was a pent roof, covered with nothing but shingles, according to the southern custom for such buildings. The garret was only nine feet long and seven wide. The highest part was three feet high, and sloped down abruptly to the loose board floor. There was no admission for either light or air. My uncle Philip, who was a carpenter, had very skilfully made a concealed trap-door, which communicated with the storeroom. He had been doing this while I was waiting in the swamp. The storeroom opened upon a piazza. To this hole I was conveyed as soon as I entered the house. The air was stifling; the darkness total. A bed had been spread on the floor. I could sleep quite comfortably on one side; but the slope was so sudden that I could not turn on the other without hitting the roof. The rats and mice ran over my bed; but I was weary, and I slept such sleep as the wretched may, when a tempest has passed over them. Morning came. I knew it only by the noises I heard; for in my small den day and night were all the same. I suffered for air even more than for light. But I was not comfortless. I heard the voices of my children.

15 *

There was joy and there was sadness in the sound. It
made my tears flow. How I longed to speak to them!
I was eager to look on their faces; but there was no
hole, no crack, through which I could peep. This continued darkness was oppressive. It seemed horrible to
sit or lie in a cramped position day after day, without one
gleam of light. Yet I would have chosen this, rather
than my lot as a slave, though white people considered
it an easy one; and it was so compared with the fate
of others. I was never cruelly over-worked; I was
never lacerated with the whip from head to foot; I was
never so beaten and bruised that I could not turn from
one side to the other; I never had my heel-strings cut
to prevent my running away; I was never chained to
a log and forced to drag it about, while I toiled in the
fields from morning till night; I was never branded
with hot iron, or torn by bloodhounds. On the contrary, I had always been kindly treated, and tenderly
cared for, until I came into the hands of Dr. Flint.
I had never wished for freedom till then. But though
my life in slavery was comparatively devoid of hardships, God pity the woman who is compelled to lead
such a life!

My food was passed up to me through the trap-door
my uncle had contrived; and my grandmother, my
uncle Phillip, and aunt Nancy would seize such opportunities as they could, to mount up there and chat with
me at the opening. But of course this was not safe in
the daytime. It must all be done in darkness. It was
impossible for me to move in an erect position, but I
crawled about my den for exercise. One day I hit my
head against something, and found it was a gimlet.

My uncle had left it sticking there when he made the trap-door. I was as rejoiced as Robinson Crusoe could have been at finding such a treasure. It put a lucky thought into my head. I said to myself, " Now I will have some light. Now I will see my children." I did not dare to begin my work during the daytime, for fear of attracting attention. But I groped round ; and having found the side next the street, where I could frequently see my children, I stuck the gimlet in and waited for evening. I bored three rows of holes, one above another ; then I bored out the interstices between. I thus succeeded in making one hole about an inch long and an inch broad. I sat by it till late into the night, to enjoy the little whiff of air that floated in. In the morning I watched for my children. The first person I saw in the street was Dr. Flint. I had a shuddering, superstitious feeling that it was a bad omen. Several familiar faces passed by. At last I heard the merry laugh of children, and presently two sweet little faces were looking up at me, as though they knew I was there, and were conscious of the joy they imparted. How I longed to *tell* them I was there !

My condition was now a little improved. But for weeks I was tormented by hundreds of little red insects, fine as a needle's point, that pierced through my skin, and produced an intolerable burning. The good grandmother gave me herb teas and cooling medicines, and finally I got rid of them. The heat of my den was intense, for nothing but thin shingles protected me from the scorching summer's sun. But I had my consolations. Through my peeping-hole I could watch the children, and when they were near enough, I could hear their talk.

Aunt Nancy brought me all the news she could hear at Dr. Flint's. From her I learned that the doctor had written to New York to a colored woman, who had been born and raised in our neighborhood, and had breathed his contaminating atmosphere. He offered her a reward if she could find out any thing about me. I know not what was the nature of her reply; but he soon after started for New York in haste, saying to his family that he had business of importance to transact. I peeped at him as he passed on his way to the steamboat. It was a satisfaction to have miles of land and water between us, even for a little while; and it was a still greater satisfaction to know that he believed me to be in the Free States. My little den seemed less dreary than it had done. He returned, as he did from his former journey to New York, without obtaining any satisfactory information. When he passed our house next morning, Benny was standing at the gate. He had heard them say that he had gone to find me, and he called out, "Dr. Flint, did you bring my mother home? I want to see her." The doctor stamped his foot at him in a rage, and exclaimed, "Get out of the way, you little damned rascal! If you don't, I'll cut off your head."

Benny ran terrified into the house, saying, "You can't put me in jail again. I don't belong to you now." It was well that the wind carried the words away from the doctor's ear. I told my grandmother of it, when we had our next conference at the trap-door; and begged of her not to allow the children to be impertinent to the irascible old man.

Autumn came, with a pleasant abatement of heat.

My eyes had become accustomed to the dim light, and
by holding my book or work in a certain position near
the aperture I contrived to read and sew.   That was a
great relief to the tedious monotony of my life.   But
when winter came, the cold penetrated through the thin
shingle roof, and I was dreadfully chilled.   The winters
there are not so long, or so severe, as in northern lati-
tudes ; but the houses are not built to shelter from cold,
and my little den was peculiarly comfortless.   The kind
grandmother brought me bed-clothes and warm drinks.
Often I was obliged to lie in bed all day to keep comfortable ; but with all my precautions, my shoulders
and feet were frostbitten.   O, those long, gloomy days,
with no object for my eye to rest upon, and no thoughts
to occupy my mind, except the dreary past and the uncertain future !   I was thankful when there came a day
sufficiently mild for me to wrap myself up and sit at
the loophole to watch the passers by.   Southerners
have the habit of stopping and talking in the streets,
and I heard many conversations not intended to meet
my ears.   I heard slave-hunters planning how to catch
some poor fugitive.   Several times I heard allusions to
Dr. Flint, myself, and the history of my children, who,
perhaps, were playing near the gate.   One would say,
" I wouldn't move my little finger to catch her, as old
Flint's property."   Another would say, "I'll catch *any*
nigger for the reward.   A man ought to have what
belongs to him, if he *is* a damned brute."   The opinion was often expressed that I was in the Free States.
Very rarely did any one suggest that I might be in the
vicinity.   Had the least suspicion rested on my grandmother's house, it would have been burned to the ground.

But it was the last place they thought of. Yet there was no place, where slavery existed, that could have afforded me so good a place of concealment.

Dr. Flint and his family repeatedly tried to coax and bribe my children to tell something they had heard said about me. One day the doctor took them into a shop, and offered them some bright little silver pieces and gay handkerchiefs if they would tell where their mother was. Ellen shrank away from him, and would not speak ; but Benny spoke up, and said, " Dr. Flint, I don't know where my mother is. I guess she's in New York ; and when you go there again, I wish you'd ask her to come home, for I want to see her ; but if you put her in jail, or tell her you'll cut her head off, I'll tell her to go right back."

XXII.

CHRISTMAS FESTIVITIES.

CHRISTMAS was approaching. Grandmother brought me materials, and I busied myself making some new garments and little playthings for my children. Were it not that hiring day is near at hand, and many families are fearfully looking forward to the probability of separation in a few days, Christmas might be a happy season for the poor slaves. Even slave mothers try to gladden the hearts of their little ones on that occasion. Benny and Ellen had their Christmas stockings filled. Their imprisoned mother could not have the privilege of witnessing their surprise and joy. But I had the pleasure of peeping at them as they went into the street with their new suits on. I heard Benny ask a little playmate whether Santa Claus brought him any thing. "Yes," replied the boy; "but Santa Claus ain't a real man. It's the children's mothers that put things into the stockings." "No, that can't be," replied Benny, "for Santa Claus brought Ellen and me these new clothes, and my mother has been gone this long time."

How I longed to tell him that his mother made those garments, and that many a tear fell on them while she worked!

Every child rises early on Christmas morning to see the Johnkannaus. Without them, Christmas would

be shorn of its greatest attraction. They consist of
companies of slaves from the plantations, generally of
the lower class. Two athletic men, in calico wrappers,
have a net thrown over them, covered with all manner of bright-colored stripes. Cows' tails are fastened
to their backs, and their heads are decorated with
horns. A box, covered with sheepskin, is called the
gumbo box. A dozen beat on this, while others strike
triangles and jawbones, to which bands of dancers
keep time. For a month previous they are composing
songs, which are sung on this occasion. These companies, of a hundred each, turn out early in the morning, and are allowed to go round till twelve o'clock,
begging for contributions. Not a door is left unvisited
where there is the least chance of obtaining a penny
or a glass of rum. They do not drink while they are
out, but carry the rum home in jugs, to have a carousal.
These Christmas donations frequently amount to twenty
or thirty dollars. It is seldom that any white man or
child refuses to give them a trifle. If he does, they
regale his ears with the following song: —

> " Poor massa, so dey say ;
>   Down in de heel, so dey say ;
>   Got no money, so dey say ;
>   Not one shillin, so dey say ;
>   God A'mighty bress you, so dey say."

Christmas is a day of feasting, both with white and
colored people. Slaves, who are lucky enough to have
a few shillings, are sure to spend them for good eating;
and many a turkey and pig is captured, without saying, " By your leave, sir." Those who cannot obtain

these, cook a 'possum, or a raccoon, from which savory dishes can be made. My grandmother raised poultry and pigs for sale; and it was her established custom to have both a turkey and a pig roasted for Christmas dinner.

On this occasion, I was warned to keep extremely quiet, because two guests had been invited. One was the town constable, and the other was a free colored man, who tried to pass himself off for white, and who was always ready to do any mean work for the sake of currying favor with white people. My grandmother had a motive for inviting them. She managed to take them all over the house. All the rooms on the lower floor were thrown open for them to pass in and out; and after dinner, they were invited up stairs to look at a fine mocking bird my uncle had just brought home. There, too, the rooms were all thrown open, that they might look in. When I heard them talking on the piazza, my heart almost stood still. I knew this colored man had spent many nights hunting for me. Every body knew he had the blood of a slave father in his veins; but for the sake of passing himself off for white, he was ready to kiss the slaveholders' feet. How I despised him! As for the constable, he wore no false colors. The duties of his office were despicable, but he was superior to his companion, inasmuch as he did not pretend to be what he was not. Any white man, who could raise money enough to buy a slave, would have considered himself degraded by being a constable; but the office enabled its possessor to exercise authority. If he found any slave out after nine o'clock, he could

16

whip him as much as he liked; and that was a privilege to be coveted. When the guests were ready to
depart, my grandmother gave each of them some of
her nice pudding, as a present for their wives. Through
my peep-hole I saw them go out of the gate, and I
was glad when it closed after them. So passed the
first Christmas in my den.

XXIII.

STILL IN PRISON.

WHEN spring returned, and I took in the little patch of green the aperture commanded, I asked myself how many more summers and winters I must be condemned to spend thus. I longed to draw in a plentiful draught of fresh air, to stretch my cramped limbs, to have room to stand erect, to feel the earth under my feet again. My relatives were constantly on the lookout for a chance of escape; but none offered that seemed practicable, and even tolerably safe. The hot summer came again, and made the turpentine drop from the thin roof over my head.

During the long nights I was restless for want of air, and I had no room to toss and turn. There was but one compensation; the atmosphere was so stifled that even mosquitos would not condescend to buzz in it. With all my detestation of Dr. Flint, I could hardly wish him a worse punishment, either in this world or that which is to come, than to suffer what I suffered in one single summer. Yet the laws allowed *him* to be out in the free air, while I, guiltless of crime, was pent up here, as the only means of avoiding the cruelties the laws allowed him to inflict upon me! I don't know what kept life within me. Again and again, I thought I should die before long; but I saw the leaves of another autumn whirl through the air, and felt the touch of another winter. In summer the most terrible thunder storms were acceptable, for the rain came through the roof, and I rolled up my bed that it might cool the hot boards under it. Later in the season, storms sometimes wet my clothes through and through, and that was not comfortable when the air grew chilly. Moderate storms I could keep out by filling the chinks with oakum.

But uncomfortable as my situation was, I had glimpses of things out of doors, which made me thankful for my wretched hiding-place. One day I saw a slave pass our gate, muttering, " It's his own, and he can kill it if he will." My grandmother told me that woman's history. Her mistress had that day seen her baby for the first time, and in the lineaments of its fair face she saw a likeness to her husband. She turned the bondwoman and her child out of doors, and forbade her ever to return. The slave went to her master, and told him what had happened. He promised to talk with her mistress, and make it all right. The next day she and her baby were sold to a Georgia trader.

Another time I saw a woman rush wildly by, pursued by two men. She was a slave, the wet nurse of her mistress's children. For some trifling offence her mistress ordered her to be stripped and whipped. To escape the degradation and the torture, she rushed to the river, jumped in, and ended her wrongs in death.

Senator Brown, of Mississippi, could not be ignorant of many such facts as these, for they are of frequent occurrence in every Southern State. Yet he stood up in the Congress of the United States, and declared that slavery was " a great moral, social, and political bless-

ing; a blessing to the master, and a blessing to the
slave!"

I suffered much more during the second winter than
I did during the first. My limbs were benumbed by
inaction, and the cold filled them with cramp. I had
a very painful sensation of coldness in my head; even
my face and tongue stiffened, and I lost the power of
speech. Of course it was impossible, under the circumstances, to summon any physician. My brother
William came and did all he could for me. Uncle
Phillip also watched tenderly over me; and poor grandmother crept up and down to inquire whether there
were any signs of returning life. I was restored to
consciousness by the dashing of cold water in my face,
and found myself leaning against my brother's arm,
while he bent over me with streaming eyes. He afterwards told me he thought I was dying, for I had been
in an unconscious state sixteen hours. I next became
delirious, and was in great danger of betraying myself
and my friends. To prevent this, they stupefied me
with drugs. I remained in bed six weeks, weary in
body and sick at heart. How to get medical advice
was the question. William finally went to a Thompso-
nian doctor, and described himself as having all my
pains and aches. He returned with herbs, roots, and
ointment. He was especially charged to rub on the
ointment by a fire; but how could a fire be made in my
little den? Charcoal in a furnace was tried, but there
was no outlet for the gas, and it nearly cost me my life.
Afterwards coals, already kindled, were brought up in
an iron pan, and placed on bricks. I was so weak, and
it was so long since I had enjoyed the warmth of a fire,

that those few coals actually made me weep. I think the medicines did me some good; but my recovery was very slow. Dark thoughts passed through my mind as I lay there day after day. I tried to be thankful for my little cell, dismal as it was, and even to love it, as part of the price I had paid for the redemption of my children. Sometimes I thought God was a compassionate Father, who would forgive my sins for the sake of my sufferings. At other times, it seemed to me there was no justice or mercy in the divine government. I asked why the curse of slavery was permitted to exist, and why I had been so persecuted and wronged from youth upward. These things took the shape of mystery, which is to this day not so clear to my soul as I trust it will be hereafter.

In the midst of my illness, grandmother broke down under the weight of anxiety and toil. The idea of losing her, who had always been my best friend and a mother to my children, was the sorest trial I had yet had. O, how earnestly I prayed that she might recover! How hard it seemed, that I could not tend upon her, who had so long and so tenderly watched over me!

One day the screams of a child nerved me with strength to crawl to my peeping-hole, and I saw my son covered with blood. A fierce dog, usually kept chained, had seized and bitten him. A doctor was sent for, and I heard the groans and screams of my child while the wounds were being sewed up. O, what torture to a mother's heart, to listen to this and be unable to go to him!

But childhood is like a day in spring, alternately

shower and sunshine. Before night Benny was bright
and lively, threatening the destruction of the dog ; and
great was his delight when the doctor told him the
next day that the dog had bitten another boy and been
shot. Benny recovered from his wounds ; but it was
long before he could walk.

When my grandmother's illness became known,
many ladies, who were her customers, called to bring
her some little comforts, and to inquire whether she
had every thing she wanted. Aunt Nancy one night
asked permission to watch with her sick mother, and
Mrs. Flint replied, "I don't see any need of your going. I can't spare you." But when she found other
ladies in the neighborhood were so attentive, not wishing to be outdone in Christian charity, she also sallied
forth, in magnificent condescension, and stood by the
bedside of her who had loved her in her infancy, and
who had been repaid by such grievous wrongs. She
seemed surprised to find her so ill, and scolded uncle
Phillip for not sending for Dr. Flint. She herself sent
for him immediately, and he came. Secure as I was in
my retreat, I should have been terrified if I had known
he was so near me. He pronounced my grandmother
in a very critical situation, and said if her attending
physician wished it, he would visit her. Nobody wished
to have him coming to the house at all hours, and we
were not disposed to give him a chance to make out a
long bill.

As Mrs. Flint went out, Sally told her the reason Benny was lame was, that a dog had bitten him. "I'm glad
of it," replied she. "I wish he had killed him. It would
be good news to send to his mother. *Her* day will come.

The dogs will grab *her* yet." With these Christian words she and her husband departed, and, to my great satisfaction, returned no more.

I heard from uncle Phillip, with feelings of unspeakable joy and gratitude, that the crisis was passed and grandmother would live. I could now say from my heart, " God is merciful. He has spared me the anguish of feeling that I caused her death."

The day before his departure for Washington I made arrangements, towards evening, to get from my hiding-place into the storeroom below. I found myself so stiff and clumsy that it was with great difficulty I could hitch from one resting place to another. When I reached the storeroom my ankles gave way under me, and I sank exhausted on the floor. It seemed as if I could never use my limbs again. But the purpose I had in view roused all the strength I had. I crawled on my hands and knees to the window, and, screened behind a barrel, I waited for his coming. The clock struck nine, and I knew the steamboat would leave between ten and eleven. My hopes were failing. But presently I heard his voice, saying to some one, " Wait for me a moment. I wish to see aunt Martha." When he came out, as he passed the window, I said, " Stop one moment, and let me speak for my children." He started, hesitated, and then passed on, and went out of the gate. I closed the shutter I had partially opened, and sank down behind the barrel. I had suffered much; but seldom had I experienced a keener pang than I then felt. Had my children, then, become of so little consequence to him? And had he so little feeling for their wretched mother that he would not listen a moment while she pleaded for them? Painful memories were so busy within me, that I forgot I had not hooked the shutter, till I heard some one opening it. I looked up. He had come back. " Who called me ? " said he, in a low tone. " I did," I replied. " Oh, Linda," said he, " I knew your voice ; but I was afraid to answer, lest my friend should hear me. Why do you come here ? Is it pos-

sible you risk yourself in this house? They are mad
to allow it. I shall expect to hear that you are all
ruined." I did not wish to implicate him, by letting
him know my place of concealment; so I merely said,
"I thought you would come to bid grandmother good
by, and so I came here to speak a few words to you
about emancipating my children. Many changes may
take place during the six months you are gone to
Washington, and it does not seem right for you to
expose them to the risk of such changes. I want nothing for myself; all I ask is, that you will free my
children, or authorize some friend to do it, before
you go."

He promised he would do it, and also expressed a
readiness to make any arrangements whereby I could
be purchased.

I heard footsteps approaching, and closed the shutter hastily. I wanted to crawl back to my den, without
letting the family know what I had done; for I knew
they would deem it very imprudent. But he stepped
back into the house, to tell my grandmother that he
had spoken with me at the storeroom window, and to
beg of her not to allow me to remain in the house over
night. He said it was the height of madness for me
to be there; that we should certainly all be ruined.
Luckily, he was in too much of a hurry to wait for a
reply, or the dear old woman would surely have told
him all.

I tried to go back to my den, but found it more
difficult to go up than I had to come down. Now that
my mission was fulfilled, the little strength that had
supported me through it was gone, and I sank help-

less on the floor.   My grandmother, alarmed at the
risk I had run, came into the storeroom in the dark,
and locked the door behind her.   "Linda," she whispered, " where are you ? "

"I am here by the window," I replied.   "I *couldn't*
have him go away without emancipating the children.
Who knows what may happen ? "

"Come, come, child," said she, "it won't do for
you to stay here another minute.   You've done wrong;
but I can't blame you, poor thing ! "

I told her I could not return without assistance, and
she must call my uncle.   Uncle Phillip came, and pity
prevented him from scolding me.   He carried me back
to my dungeon, laid me tenderly on the bed, gave me
some medicine, and asked me if there was any thing
more he could do.   Then he went away, and I was left
with my own thoughts — starless as the midnight darkness around me.

My friends feared I should become a cripple for life;
and I was so weary of my long imprisonment that,
had it not been for the hope of serving my children, I
should have been thankful to die; but, for their sakes,
I was willing to bear on.

XXV.

COMPETITION IN CUNNING.

Dr. Flint had not given me up. Every now and then he would say to my grandmother that I would yet come back, and voluntarily surrender myself; and that when I did, I could be purchased by my relatives, or any one who wished to buy me. I knew his cunning nature too well not to percieve that this was a trap laid for me; and so all my friends understood it. I resolved to match my cunning against his cunning. In order to make him believe that I was in New York, I resolved to write him a letter dated from that place. I sent for my friend Peter, and asked him if he knew any trustworthy seafaring person, who would carry such a letter to New York, and put it in the post office there. He said he knew one that he would trust with his own life to the ends of the world. I reminded him that it was a hazardous thing for him to undertake. He said he knew it, but he was willing to do any thing to help me. I expressed a wish for a New York paper, to ascertain the names of some of the streets. He run his hand into his pocket, and said, "Here is half a one, that was round a cap I bought of a pedler yesterday." I told him the letter would be ready the next evening. He bade me good by, adding, "Keep up your spirits, Linda; brighter days will come by and by."

My uncle Phillip kept watch over the gate until

our brief interview was over. Early the next morning, I seated myself near the little aperture to examine the newspaper. It was a piece of the New York Herald; and, for once, the paper that systematically abuses the colored people, was made to render them a service. Having obtained what information I wanted concerning streets and numbers, I wrote two letters, one to my grandmother, the other to Dr. Flint. I reminded him how he, a gray-headed man, had treated a helpless child, who had been placed in his power, and what years of misery he had brought upon her. To my grandmother, I expressed a wish to have my children sent to me at the north, where I could teach them to respect themselves, and set them a virtuous example; which a slave mother was not allowed to do at the south. I asked her to direct her answer to a certain street in Boston, as I did not live in New York, though I went there sometimes. I dated these letters ahead, to allow for the time it would take to carry them, and sent a memorandum of the date to the messenger. When my friend came for the letters, I said, " God bless and reward you, Peter, for this disinterested kindness. Pray be careful. If you are detected, both you and I will have to suffer dreadfully. I have not a relative who would dare to do it for me." He replied, "You may trust to me, Linda. I don't forget that your father was my best friend, and I will be a friend to his children so long as God lets me live."

It was necessary to tell my grandmother what I had done, in order that she might be ready for the letter, and prepared to hear what Dr. Flint might say about my being at the north. She was sadly troubled.

She felt sure mischief would come of it. I also told my plan to aunt Nancy, in order that she might report to us what was said at Dr. Flint's house. I whispered it to her through a crack, and she whispered back, "I hope it will succeed. I shan't mind being a slave all *my* life, if I can only see you and the children free."

I had directed that my letters should be put into the New York post office on the 20th of the month. On the evening of the 24th my aunt came to say that Dr. Flint and his wife had been talking in a low voice about a letter he had received, and that when he went to his office he promised to bring it when he came to tea. So I concluded I should hear my letter read the next morning. I told my grandmother Dr. Flint would be sure to come, and asked her to have him sit near a certain door, and leave it open, that I might hear what he said. The next morning I took my station within sound of that door, and remained motionless as a statue. It was not long before I heard the gate slam, and the well-known footsteps enter the house. He seated himself in the chair that was placed for him, and said, "Well, Martha, I've brought you a letter from Linda. She has sent me a letter, also. I know exactly where to find her; but I don't choose to go to Boston for her. I had rather she would come back of her own accord, in a respectable manner. Her uncle Phillip is the best person to go for her. With *him*, she would feel perfectly free to act. I am willing to pay his expenses going and returning. She shall be sold to her friends. Her children are free; at least I suppose they are; and when you obtain her freedom, you'll make a happy family. I suppose, Martha, you have no objection to my reading to you the letter Linda has written to you."

He broke the seal, and I heard him read it. The old villain! He had suppressed the letter I wrote to grandmother, and prepared a substitute of his own, the purport of which was as follows : —

"Dear Grandmother: I have long wanted to write to you ; but the disgraceful manner in which I left you and my children made me ashamed to do it. If you knew how much I have suffered since I ran away, you would pity and forgive me. I have purchased freedom at a dear rate. If any arrangement could be made for me to return to the south without being a slave, I would gladly come. If not, I beg of you to send my children to the north. I cannot live any longer without them. Let me know in time, and I will meet them in New York or Philadelphia, which-ever place best suits my uncle's convenience. Write as soon as possible to your unhappy daughter,

LINDA."

"It is very much as I expected it would be," said the old hypocrite, rising to go. "You see the foolish girl has repented of her rashness, and wants to re-turn. We must help her to do it, Martha. Talk with Phillip about it. If he will go for her, she will trust to him, and come back. I should like an answer to-morrow. Good morning, Martha."

As he stepped out on the piazza, he stumbled over

my little girl. "Ah, Ellen, is that you?" he said, in his most gracious manner. "I didn't see you. How do you do?"

"Pretty well, sir," she replied. "I heard you tell grandmother that my mother is coming home. I want to see her."

"Yes, Ellen, I am going to bring her home very soon," rejoined he; "and you shall see her as much as you like, you little curly-headed nigger."

This was as good as a comedy to me, who had heard it all; but grandmother was frightened and distressed, because the doctor wanted my uncle to go for me.

The next evening Dr. Flint called to talk the matter over. My uncle told him that from what he had heard of Massachusetts, he judged he should be mobbed if he went there after a runaway slave. "All stuff and nonsense, Phillip!" replied the doctor. "Do you suppose I want you to kick up a row in Boston? The business can all be done quietly. Linda writes that she wants to come back. You are her relative, and she would trust *you*. The case would be different if I went. She might object to coming with *me*; and the damned abolitionists, if they knew I was her master, would not believe me, if I told them she had begged to go back. They would get up a row; and I should not like to see Linda dragged through the streets like a common negro. She has been very ungrateful to me for all my kindness; but I forgive her, and want to act the part of a friend towards her. I have no wish to hold her as my slave. Her friends can buy her as soon as she arrives here."

Finding that his arguments failed to convince my
uncle, the doctor " let the cat out of the bag," by saying that he had written to the mayor of Boston, to ascertain whether there was a person of my description
at the street and number from which my letter was
dated. He had omitted this date in the letter he had
made up to read to my grandmother. If I had dated
from New York, the old man would probably have
made another journey to that city. But even in that
dark region, where knowledge is so carefully excluded
from the slave, I had heard enough about Massachusetts to come to the conclusion that slaveholders did
not consider it a comfortable place to go to in search
of a runaway. That was before the Fugitive Slave
Law was passed; before Massachusetts had consented
to become a " nigger hunter " for the south.

My grandmother, who had become skittish by seeing
her family always in danger, came to me with a very
distressed countenance, and said, " What will you do
if the mayor of Boston sends him word that you
haven't been there? Then he will suspect the letter
was a trick; and maybe he'll find out something about
it, and we shall all get into trouble. O Linda, I wish
you had never sent the letters."

" Don't worry yourself, grandmother," said I.
" The mayor of Boston won't trouble himself to hunt
niggers for Dr. Flint. The letters will do good in the
end. I shall get out of this dark hole some time or
other."

" I hope you will, child," replied the good, patient
old friend. · " You have been here a long time; almost
five years ; but whenever you do go, it will break your

old grandmother's heart. I should be expecting every day to hear that you were brought back in irons and put in jail God help you, poor child! Let us be thankful that some time or other we shall go " where the wicked cease from troubling, and the weary are at rest." My heart responded, Amen.

The fact that Dr. Flint had written to the mayor of Boston convinced me that he believed my letter to be genuine, and of course that he had no suspicion of my being any where in the vicinity. It was a great object to keep up this delusion, for it made me and my friends feel less anxious, and it would be very convenient whenever there was a chance to escape. I resolved, therefore, to continue to write letters from the north from time to time.

Two or three weeks passed, and as no news came from the mayor of Boston, grandmother began to listen to my entreaty to be allowed to leave my cell, sometimes, and exercise my limbs to prevent my becoming a cripple. I was allowed to slip down into the small storeroom, early in the morning, and remain there a little while. The room was all filled up with barrels, except a small open space under my trap-door. This faced the door, the upper part of which was of glass, and purposely left uncurtained, that the curious might look in. The air of this place was close; but it was so much better than the atmosphere of my cell, that I dreaded to return. I came down as soon as it was light, and remained till eight o'clock, when people began to be about, and there was danger that some one might come on the piazza. I had tried various applications to bring warmth and feeling into my limbs, but without avail. They were so numb and stiff that it was a painful effort to move; and had my enemies come upon me during the first mornings I tried to exercise them a little in the small unoccupied space of the storeroom, it would have been impossible for me to have escaped.

XXVI.

IMPORTANT ERA IN MY BROTHER'S LIFE.

I MISSED the company and kind attentions of my brother William, who had gone to Washington with his master, Mr. Sands. We received several letters from him, written without any allusion to me, but expressed in such a manner that I knew he did not forget me. I disguised my hand, and wrote to him in the same manner. It was a long session; and when it closed, William wrote to inform us that Mr. Sands was going to the north, to be gone some time, and that he was to accompany him. I knew that his master had promised to give him his freedom, but no time had been specified. Would William trust to a slave's chances ? I remembered how we used to talk together, in our young days, about obtaining our freedom, and I thought it very doubtful whether he would come back to us.

Grandmother received a letter from Mr. Sands, saying that William had proved a most faithful servant, and he would also say a valued friend ; that no mother had ever trained a better boy. He said he had travelled through the Northern States and Canada ; and though the abolitionists had tried to decoy him away, they had never succeeded. He ended by saying they should be at home shortly.

We expected letters from William, describing the novelties of his journey, but none came. In time, it was reported that Mr. Sands would return late in the autumn, accompanied by a bride. Still no letters from William. I felt almost sure I should never see him again on southern soil ; but had he no word of comfort to send to his friends at home ? to the poor captive in her dungeon ? My thoughts wandered through the dark past, and over the uncertain future. Alone in my cell, where no eye but God's could see me, I wept bitter tears. How earnestly I prayed to him to restore me to my children, and enable me to be a useful woman and a good mother !

At last the day arrived for the return of the travellers. Grandmother had made loving preparations to welcome her absent boy back to the old hearthstone. When the dinner table was laid, William's plate occupied its old place. The stage coach went by empty. My grandmother waited dinner. She thought perhaps he was necessarily detained by his master. In my prison I listened anxiously, expecting every moment to hear my dear brother's voice and step. In the course of the afternoon a lad was sent by Mr. Sands to tell grandmother that William did not return with him ; that the abolitionists had decoyed him away. But he begged her not to feel troubled about it, for he felt confident she would see William in a few days. As soon as he had time to reflect he would come back, for he could never expect to be so well off at the north as he had been with him.

If you had seen the tears, and heard the sobs, you would have thought the messenger had brought tidings of death instead of freedom. Poor old grandmother felt that she should never see her darling boy again. And I was selfish. I thought more of what I had lost, than of what my brother had gained. A new anxiety began to trouble me. Mr. Sands had expended a good deal of money, and would naturally feel irritated by the loss he had incurred. I greatly feared this might injure the prospects of my children, who were now becoming valuable property. I longed to have their emancipation made certain. The more so, because their master and father was now married. I was too familiar with slavery not to know that promises made to slaves, though with kind intentions, and sincere at the time, depend upon many contingencies for their fulfilment.

Much as I wished William to be free, the step he had taken made me sad and anxious. The following Sabbath was calm and clear; so beautiful that it seemed like a Sabbath in the eternal world. My grandmother brought the children out on the piazza, that I might hear their voices. She thought it would comfort me in my despondency; and it did. They chatted merrily, as only children can. Benny said, " Grandmother, do you think uncle Will has gone for good ? Won't he ever come back again ? May be he'll find mother. If he does, *won't* she be glad to see him ! Why don't you and uncle Phillip, and all of us, go and live where mother is ? I should like it; wouldn't you, Ellen ? "

" Yes, I should like it," replied Ellen ; " but how could we find her ? Do you know the place, grandmother ? I don't remember how mother looked — do you, Benny ? "

Benny was just beginning to describe me when they were interrupted by an old slave woman, a near neigh-

bor, named Aggie. This poor creature had witnessed
the sale of her children, and seen them carried off to
parts unknown, without any hopes of ever hearing from
them again. She saw that my grandmother had been
weeping, and she said, in a sympathizing tone, " What's
the matter, aunt Marthy ? "

" O Aggie," she replied, " it seems as if I shouldn't
have any of my children or grandchildren left to hand
me a drink when I'm dying, and lay my old body in
the ground. My boy didn't come back with Mr. Sands.
He staid at the north."

Poor old Aggie clapped her hands for joy. " Is *dat*
what you's crying fur ? " she exclaimed. " Git down
on your knees and bress de Lord ! I don't know whar
my poor chillern is, and I nebber . 'spect to know.
You don't know whar poor Linda's gone to ; but you *do*
know whar her brudder is. He's in free parts ; and
dat's de right place. Don't murmur at de Lord's doings, but git down on your knees and tank him for
his goodness."

My selfishness was rebuked by what poor Aggie said.
She rejoiced over the escape of one who was merely her
fellow-bondman, while his own sister was only thinking
what his good fortune might cost her children. I knelt
and prayed God to forgive me ; and I thanked him from
my heart, that one of my family was saved from the
grasp of slavery.

It was not long before we received a letter from William. He wrote that Mr. Sands had always treated
him kindly, and that he had tried to do his duty to
him faithfully. But ever since he was a boy, he had
longed to be free ; and he had already gone through

enough to convince him he had better not lose the chance that offered. He concluded by saying, " Don't worry about me, dear grandmother. I shall think of you always; and it will spur me on to work hard and try to do right. When I have earned money enough to give you a home, perhaps you will come to the north, and we can all live happy together."

Mr. Sands told my uncle Phillip the particulars about William's leaving him. He said, " I trusted him as if he were my own brother, and treated him as kindly. The abolitionists talked to him in several places ; but I had no idea they could tempt him. However, I don't blame William. He's young and inconsiderate, and those Northern rascals decoyed him. I must confess the scamp was very bold about it. I met him coming down the steps of the Astor House with his trunk on his shoulder, and I asked him where he was going. He said he was going to change his old trunk. I told him it was rather shabby, and asked if he didn't need some money. He said, No, thanked me, and went off. He did not return so soon as I expected ; but I waited patiently. At last I went to see if our trunks were packed, ready for our journey. I found them locked, and a sealed note on the table informed me where I could find the keys. The fellow even tried to be religious. He wrote that he hoped God would always bless me, and reward me for my kindness ; that he was not unwilling to serve me ; but he wanted to be a free man ; and that if I thought he did wrong, he hoped I would forgive him. I intended to give him his freedom in five years. He might have trusted me. He has shown himself ungrateful ; but I

18

shall not go for him, or send for him.   I feel confident
that he will soon return to me."

I afterwards heard an account of the affair from
William himself.   He had not been urged away by
abolitionists.   He needed no information they could
give him about slavery to stimulate his desire for
freedom.   He looked at his hands, and remembered
that they were once in irons.   What security had he
that they would not be so again ?   Mr. Sands was
kind to him; but he might indefinitely postpone the
promise he had made to give him his freedom.   He
might come under pecuniary embarrassments, and his
property be seized by creditors ; or he might die, without making any arrangements in his favor.   He had
too often known such accidents to happen to slaves
who had kind masters, and he wisely resolved to make
sure of the present opportunity to own himself.   He
was scrupulous about taking any money from his
master on false pretences ; so he sold his best clothes
to pay for his passage to Boston.   The slaveholders
pronounced him a base, ungrateful wretch, for thus
requiting his master's indulgence.   What would *they*
have done under similar circumstances ?

When Dr. Flint's family heard that William had
deserted Mr. Sands, they chuckled greatly over the
news.   Mrs. Flint made her usual manifestations of
Christian feeling, by saying, "I'm glad of it.   I hope
he'll never get him again.   I like to see people paid
back in their own coin.   I reckon Linda's children
will have to pay for it.   I should be glad to see them
in the speculator's hands again, for I'm tired of seeing
those little niggers march about the streets."

XXVII.

NEW DESTINATION FOR THE CHILDREN.

MRS. FLINT proclaimed her intention of informing Mrs. Sands who was the father of my children. She likewise proposed to tell her what an artful devil I was; that I had made a great deal of trouble in her family; that when Mr. Sands was at the north, she didn't doubt I had followed him in disguise, and persuaded William to run away. She had some reason to entertain such an idea; for I had written from the north, from time to time, and I dated my letters from various places. Many of them fell into Dr. Flint's hands, as I expected they would; and he must have come to the conclusion that I travelled about a good deal. He kept a close watch over my children, thinking they would eventually lead to my detection.

A new and unexpected trial was in store for me. One day, when Mr. Sands and his wife were walking in the street, they met Benny. The lady took a fancy to him, and exclaimed, " What a pretty little negro! Whom does he belong to ? "

Benny did not hear the answer; but he came home very indignant with the stranger lady, because she had called him a negro. A few days afterwards, Mr. Sands called on my grandmother, and told her he wanted her to take the children to his house. He said he had informed his wife of his relation to them, and told her they were motherless; and she wanted to see them.

When he had gone, my grandmother came and asked what I would do. The question seemed a mockery. What *could* I do ? They were Mr. Sands's slaves, and their mother was a slave, whom he had represented to be dead. Perhaps he thought I was. I was too much pained and puzzled to come to any decision ; and the children were carried without my knowledge.

Mrs. Sands had a sister from Illinois staying with her. This lady, who had no children of her own, was so much pleased with Ellen, that she offered to adopt her, and bring her up as she would a daughter. Mrs. Sands wanted to take Benjamin. When grandmother reported this to me, I was tried almost beyond endurance. Was this all I was to gain by what I had suffered for the sake of having my children free ? True, the prospect *seemed* fair ; but I knew too well how lightly slaveholders held such " parental relations." If pecuniary troubles should come, or if the new wife required more money than could conveniently be spared, my children might be thought of as a convenient means of raising funds. I had no trust in thee, O Slavery ! Never should I know peace till my children were emancipated with all due formalities of law.

I was too proud to ask Mr. Sands to do any thing for my own benefit; but I could bring myself to become a supplicant for my children. I resolved to remind him of the promise he had made me, and to throw myself upon his honor for the performance of it. I persuaded my grandmother to go to him, and tell him I was not dead, and that I earnestly entreated him to keep the promise he had made me ; that I had heard of the recent proposals concerning my children, and did not feel easy to accept them; that he had promised to emancipate them, and it was time for him to redeem his pledge. I knew there was some risk in thus betraying that I was in the vicinity; but what will not a mother do for her children? He received the message with surprise, and said, "The children are free. I have never intended to claim them as slaves. Linda may decide their fate. In my opinion, they had better be 'sent to the north. I don't think they are quite safe here. Dr. Flint boasts that they are still in his power. He says they were his daughter's property, and as she was not of age when they were sold, the contract is not legally binding."

So, then, after all I had endured for their sakes, my poor children were between two fires; between my old master and their new master! And I was powerless. There was no protecting arm of the law for me to invoke. Mr. Sands proposed that Ellen should go, for the present, to some of his relatives, who had removed to Brooklyn, Long Island. It was promised that she should be well taken care of, and sent to school. I consented to it, as the best arrangement I could make for her. My grandmother, of course, negotiated it all; and Mrs. Sands knew of no other person in the transaction. She proposed that they should take Ellen with them to Washington, and keep her till they had a good chance of sending her, with friends, to Brooklyn. She had an infant daughter. I had had a glimpse of it, as the nurse passed with it in her arms. It was not a pleasant thought to me, that the bondwoman's child should tend her free-born sister; but there was no al-

ternative.   Ellen was made ready for the journey.   O,
how it tried my heart to send her away, so young, alone,
among strangers!   Without a mother's love to shelter
her from the storms of life; almost without memory
of a mother!   I doubted whether she and Benny would
have for me the natural affection that children feel for
a parent.   I thought to myself that I might perhaps
never see my daughter again, and I had a great desire
that she should look upon me, before she went, that
she might take my image with her in her memory. ' It
seemed to me cruel to have her brought to my dungeon.   It was sorrow enough for her young heart to
know that her mother was a victim of slavery, without
seeing the wretched hiding-place to which it had driven
her.   I begged permission to pass the last night in one
of the open chambers, with my little girl.   They
thought I was crazy to think of trusting such a young
child with my perilous secret.   I told them I had
watched her character, and I felt sure she would not
betray me; that I was determined to have an interview, and if they would not facilitate it, I would take
my own way to obtain it.   They remonstrated against
the rashness of such a proceeding; but finding they
could not change my purpose, they yielded.   I slipped
through the trap-door into the storeroom, and my uncle
kept watch at the gate, while I passed into the piazza
and went up stairs, to the room I used to occupy.   It
was more than five years since I had seen it; and how
the memories crowded on me!   There I had taken
shelter when my mistress drove me from her house;
there came my old tyrant, to mock, insult, and curse
me; there my children were first laid in my arms;

there I had watched over them, each day with a deeper and sadder love; there I had knelt to God, in anguish of heart, to forgive the wrong I had done. How vividly it all came back! And after this long, gloomy interval, I stood there such a wreck!

In the midst of these meditations, I heard footsteps on the stairs. The door opened, and my uncle Phillip came in, leading Ellen by the hand. I put my arms round her, and said, "Ellen, my dear child, I am your mother." She drew back a little, and looked at me; then, with sweet confidence, she laid her cheek against mine, and I folded her to the heart that had been so long desolated. She was the first to speak. Raising her head, she said, inquiringly, "You really *are* my mother?" I told her I really was; that during all the long time she had not seen me, I had loved her most tenderly; and that now she was going away, I wanted to see her and talk with her, that she might remember me. With a sob in her voice, she said, "I'm glad you've come to see me; but why didn't you ever come before? Benny and I have wanted so much to see you! He remembers you, and sometimes he tells me about you. Why didn't you come home when Dr. Flint went to bring you?"

I answered, "I couldn't come before, dear. But now that I am with you, tell me whether you like to go away." "I don't know," said she, crying. "Grandmother says I ought not to cry; that I am going to a good place, where I can learn to read and write, and that by and by I can write her a letter. But I shan't have Benny, or grandmother, or uncle Phillip, or anybody to love me. Can't you go with me? O, *do* go, dear mother!"

I told her I couldn't go now; but sometime I would come to her, and then she and Benny and I would live together, and have happy times. She wanted to run and bring Benny to see me now. I told her he was going to the north, before long, with uncle Phillip, and then I would come to see him before he went away. I asked if she would like to have me stay all night and sleep with her. " O, yes," she replied. Then, turning to her uncle, she said, pleadingly, " *May* I stay ? Please, uncle ! She is my own mother." He laid his hand on her head, and said, solemnly, " Ellen, this is the secret you have promised grandmother never to tell. If you ever speak of it to any body, they will never let you see your grandmother again, and your mother can never come to Brooklyn." " Uncle," she replied, " I will never tell." He told her she might stay with me ; and when he had gone, I took her in my arms and told her I was a slave, and that was the reason she must never say she had seen me. I exhorted her to be a good child, to try to please the people where she was going, and that God would raise her up friends. I told her to say her prayers, and remember always to pray for her poor mother, and that God would permit us to meet again. She wept, and I did not check her tears. Perhaps she would never again have a chance to pour her tears into a mother's bosom. All night she nestled in my arms, and I had no inclination to slumber. The moments were too precious to lose any of them. Once, when I thought she was asleep, I kissed her forehead softly, and she said, " I am not asleep, dear mother."

Before dawn they came to take me back to my den.

I drew aside the window curtain, to take a last look of
my child. The moonlight shone on her face, and I
bent over her, as I had done years before, that wretched
night when I ran away. I hugged her close to my
throbbing heart; and tears, too sad for such young
eyes to shed, flowed down her cheeks, as she gave her
last kiss, and whispered in my ear, "Mother, I will
never tell." And she never did.

When I got back to my den, I threw myself on the
bed and wept there alone in the darkness. It seemed
as if my heart would burst. When the time for Ellen's departure drew nigh, I could hear neighbors and
friends saying to her, "Good by, Ellen. I hope your
poor mother will find you out. *Won't* you be glad to
see her!" She replied, "Yes, ma'am;" and they
little dreamed of the weighty secret that weighed down
her young heart. She was an affectionate child, but
naturally very reserved, except with those she loved,
and I felt secure that my secret would be safe with her.
I heard the gate close after her, with such feelings as
only a slave mother can experience. During the day
my meditations were very sad. Sometimes I feared I
had been very selfish not to give up all claim to her,
and let her go to Illinois, to be adopted by Mrs. Sands's
sister. It was my experience of slavery that decided
me against it. I feared that circumstances might arise
that would cause her to be sent back. I felt confident
that I should go to New York myself; and then I
should be able to watch over her, and in some degree
protect her.

Dr. Flint's family knew nothing of the proposed
arrangement till after Ellen was gone, and the news

displeased them greatly.   Mrs. Flint called on Mrs.
Sands's sister to inquire into the matter.   She expressed her opinion very freely as to the respect Mr.
Sands showed for his wife, and for his own character,
in acknowledging those "young niggers."   And as for
sending Ellen away, she pronounced it to be just as
much stealing as it would be for him to come and take
a piece of furniture out of her parlor.   She said her
daughter was not of age to sign the bill of sale, and
the children were her property ; and when she became
of age, or was married, she could take them, wherever
she could lay hands on them.

Miss Emily Flint, the little girl to whom I had been
bequeathed, was now in her sixteenth year.   Her
mother considered it all right and honorable for her,
or her future husband, to steal my children ; but she
did not understand how any body could hold up their
heads in respectable society, after they had purchased
their own children, as Mr. Sands had done.   Dr. Flint
said very little.   Perhaps he thought that Benny would
be less likely to be sent away if he kept quiet.   One
of my letters, that fell into his hands, was dated from
Canada ; and he seldom spoke of me now.   This state
of things enabled me to slip down into the storeroom
more frequently, where I could stand upright, and
move my limbs more freely.

Days, weeks, and months passed, and there came no
news of Ellen.   I sent a letter to Brooklyn, written in
my grandmother's name, to inquire whether she had
arrived there.   Answer was returned that she had not.
I wrote to her in Washington ; but no notice was taken
of it.   There was one person there, who ought to have

had some sympathy with the anxiety of the child's
friends at home ; but the links of such relations as he
had formed with me, are easily broken and cast away
as rubbish.   Yet how protectingly and persuasively
he once talked to the poor, helpless slave girl !   And
how entirely I trusted him !   But now suspicions darkened my mind.   Was my child dead, or had they deceived me, and sold her ?

If the secret memoirs of many members of Congress
should be published, curious details would be unfolded.
I once saw a letter from a member of Congress to a
slave, who was the mother of six of his children.   He
wrote to request that she would send her children away
from the great house before his return, as he expected
to be accompanied by friends.   The woman could not
read, and was obliged to employ another to read the
letter.   The existence of the colored children did not
trouble this gentleman, it was only the fear that
friends might recognize in their features a resemblance to him.

At the end of six months, a letter came to my grandmother, from Brooklyn.   It was written by a young
lady in the family, and announced that Ellen had just
arrived.   It contained the following message from her:
" I do try to do just as you told me to, and I pray for
you every night and morning."   I understood that
these words were meant for me ; and they were a
balsam to my heart.   The writer closed her letter by
saying, " Ellen is a nice little girl, and we shall like to
have her with us.   My cousin, Mr. Sands, has given
her to me, to be my little waiting maid.   I shall send
her to school, and I hope some day she will write to

you herself." This letter perplexed and troubled me. Had my child's father merely placed her there till she was old enough to support herself? Or had he given her to his cousin, as a piece of property? If the last idea was correct, his cousin might return to the south at any time, and hold Ellen as a slave. I tried to put away from me the painful thought that such a foul wrong could have been done to us. I said to myself, "Surely there must be *some* justice in man;" then I remembered, with a sigh, how slavery perverted all the natural feelings of the human heart. It gave me a pang to look on my light-hearted boy. He believed himself free; and to have him brought under the yoke of slavery, would be more than I could bear. How I longed to have him safely out of the reach of its power!

XXVIII.

AUNT NANCY.

I HAVE mentioned my great-aunt, who was a slave in Dr. Flint's family, and who had been my refuge during the shameful persecutions I suffered from him. This aunt had been married at twenty years of age ; that is, as far as slaves *can* marry. She had the consent of her master and mistress, and a clergyman performed the ceremony. But it was a mere form, without any legal value. Her master or mistress could annul it any day they pleased. She had always slept on the floor in the entry, near Mrs. Flint's chamber door, that she might be within call. When she was married, she was told she might have the use of a small room in an out-house. Her mother and her husband furnished it. He was a seafaring man, and was allowed to sleep there when he was at home. But on the wedding evening, the bride was ordered to her old post on the entry floor.

Mrs. Flint, at that time, had no children ; but she was expecting to be a mother, and if she should want a drink of water in the night, what could she do without her slave to bring it ? So my aunt was compelled to lie at her door, until one midnight she was forced to leave, to give premature birth to a child. In a fortnight she was required to resume her place on the entry floor, because Mrs. Flint's babe needed her attentions. She kept her station there through summer and winter, until she had given premature birth to six children ;

and all the while she was employed as night-nurse to Mrs. Flint's children. Finally, toiling all day, and being deprived of rest at night, completely broke down her constitution, and Dr. Flint declared it was impossible she could ever become the mother of a living child. The fear of losing so valuable a servant by death, now induced them to allow her to sleep in her little room in the out-house, except when there was sickness in the family. She afterwards had two feeble babes, one of whom died in a few days, and the other in four weeks. I well remember her patient sorrow as she held the last dead baby in her arms. " I wish it could have lived," she said; " it is not the will of God that any of my children should live. But I will try to be fit to meet their little spirits in heaven."

Aunt Nancy was housekeeper and waiting-maid in Dr. Flint's family. Indeed, she was the *factotum* of the household. Nothing went on well without her. She was my mother's twin sister, and, as far as was in her power, she supplied a mother's place to us orphans. I slept with her all the time I lived in my old master's house, and the bond between us was very strong. When my friends tried to discourage me from running away, she always encouraged me. When they thought I had better return and ask my master's pardon, because there was no possibility of escape, she sent me word never to yield. She said if I persevered I might, perhaps, gain the freedom of my children ; and even if I perished in doing it, that was better than to leave them to groan under the same persecutions that had blighted my own life. After I was shut up in my dark cell, she stole away, whenever she could, to bring me the news and say something cheering. Hcw often did I kneel down to listen to her words of consolation, whispered through a crack! " I am old, and have not long to live," she used to say; " and I could die happy if I could only see you and the children free. You must pray to God, Linda, as I do for you, that he will lead you out of this darkness." I would beg her not to worry herself on my account; that there was an end of all suffering sooner or later, and that whether I lived in chains or in freedom, I should always remember her as the good friend who had been the comfort of my life. A word from her always strengthened me; and not me only. The whole family relied upon her judgment, and were guided by her advice.

I had been in my cell six years when my grandmother was summoned to the bedside of this, her last remaining daughter. She was very ill, and they said she would die. Grandmother had not entered Dr. Flint's house for several years. They had treated her cruelly, but she thought nothing of that now. She was grateful for permission to watch by the death-bed of her child. They had always been devoted to each other; and now they sat looking into each other's eyes, longing to speak of the secret that had weighed so much on the hearts of both. My aunt had been stricken with paralysis. She lived but two days, and the last day she was speechless. Before she lost the power of utterance, she told her mother not to grieve if she could not speak to her; that she would try to hold up her hand, to let her know that all was well with her. Even the hard-hearted doctor was a little softened when he saw the dying woman try to smile on the aged

mother, who was kneeling by her side. His eyes
moistened for a moment, as he said she had always been
a faithful servant, and they should never be able to
supply her place. Mrs. Flint took to her bed, quite
overcome by the shock. While my grandmother sat
alone with the dead, the doctor came in, leading his
youngest son, who had always been a great pet with
aunt Nancy, and was much attached to her. "Martha," said he, "aunt Nancy loved this child, and when
he comes where you are, I hope you will be kind to
him, for her sake." She replied, "Your wife was my
foster-child, Dr. Flint, the foster-sister of my poor
Nancy, and you little know me if you think I can feel
any thing but good will for her children."

"I wish the past could be forgotten, and that we
might never think of it," said he; "and that Linda
would come to supply her aunt's place. She would be
worth more to us than all the money that could be paid
for her. I wish it for your sake also, Martha. Now
that Nancy is taken away from you, she would be a
great comfort to your old age."

He knew he was touching a tender chord. Almost
choking with grief, my grandmother replied, "It was
not I that drove Linda away. My grandchildren are
gone; and of my nine children only one is left. God
help me!"

To me, the death of this kind relative was an inex-
pressible sorrow. I knew that she had been slowly
murdered; and I felt that my troubles had helped to
finish the work. After I heard of her illness, I listened
constantly to hear what news was brought from the
great house; and the thought that I could not go to

her made me utterly miserable. At last, as uncle
Phillip came into the house, I heard some one inquire,
"How is she?" and he answered, "She is dead."
My little cell seemed whirling round, and I knew nothing more till I opened my eyes and found uncle Phillip
bending over me. I had no need to ask any questions.
He whispered, "Linda, she died happy." I could not
weep. My fixed gaze troubled him. "Don't look
so," he said. "Don't add to my poor mother's
trouble. Remember how much she has to bear, and
that we ought to do all we can to comfort her." Ah,
yes, that blessed old grandmother, who for seventy-
three years had borne the pelting storms of a slave-
mother's life. She did indeed need consolation!

Mrs. Flint had rendered her poor foster-sister childless, apparently without any compunction; and with
cruel selfishness had ruined her health by years of incessant, unrequited toil, and broken rest. But now she
became very sentimental. I suppose she thought it
would be a beautiful illustration of the attachment existing between slaveholder and slave, if the body of
her old worn-out servant was buried at her feet. She
sent for the clergyman and asked if he had any objection to burying aunt Nancy in the doctor's family
burial-place. No colored person had ever been allowed
interment in the white people's burying-ground, and
the minister knew that all the deceased of our family
reposed together in the old graveyard of the slaves.
He therefore replied, "I have no objection to comply-
ing with your wish; but perhaps aunt Nancy's *mother*
may have some choice as to where her remains shall be
deposited."

It had never occurred to Mrs. Flint that slaves could have any feelings. When my grandmother was consulted, she at once said she wanted Nancy to lie with all the rest of her family, and where her own old body would be buried. Mrs. Flint graciously complied with her wish, though she said it was painful to her to have Nancy buried away from *her*. She might have added with touching pathos, " I was so long *used* to sleep with her lying near me, on the entry floor."

My uncle Phillip asked permission to bury his sister at his own expense ; and slaveholders are always ready to grant *such* favors to slaves and their relatives. The arrangements were very plain, but perfectly respectable. She was buried on the Sabbath, and Mrs. Flint's minister read the funeral service. There was a large concourse of colored people, bond and free, and a few white persons who had always been friendly to our family. Dr. Flint's carriage was in the procession ; and when the body was deposited in its humble resting place, the mistress dropped a tear, and returned to her carriage, probably thinking she had performed her duty nobly.

It was talked of by the slaves as a mighty grand funeral. Northern travellers, passing through the place, might have described this tribute of respect to the humble dead as a beautiful feature in the " patriarchal institution ; " a touching proof of the attachment between slaveholders and their servants ; and tenderhearted Mrs. Flint would have confirmed this impression, with handkerchief at her eyes. *We* could have told them a different story. We could have given them a chapter of wrongs and sufferings, that would have touched their hearts, if they *had* any hearts to feel for the colored people. We could have told them how the poor old slave-mother had toiled, year after year, to earn eight hundred dollars to buy her son Phillip's right to his own earnings ; and how that same Phillip paid the expenses of the funeral, which they regarded as doing so much credit to the master. We could also have told them of a poor, blighted young creature, shut up in a living grave for years, to avoid the tortures that would be inflicted on her, if she ventured to come out and look on the face of her departed friend.

All this, and much more, I thought of, as I sat at my loophole, waiting for the family to return from the grave ; sometimes weeping, sometimes falling asleep, dreaming strange dreams of the dead and the living.

It was sad to witness the grief of my bereaved grandmother. She had always been strong to bear, and now, as ever, religious faith supported her. But her dark life had become still darker, and age and trouble were leaving deep traces on her withered face. She had four places to knock for me to come to the trap-door, and each place had a different meaning. She now came oftener than she had done, and talked to me of her dead daughter, while tears trickled slowly down her furrowed cheeks. I said all I could to comfort her ; but it was a sad reflection, that instead of being able to help her, I was a constant source of anxiety and trouble. The poor old back was fitted to its burden. It bent under it, but did not break.

XXIX.

PREPARATIONS FOR ESCAPE.

I HARDLY expect that the reader will credit me, when I affirm that I lived in that little dismal hole, almost deprived of light and air, and with no space to move my limbs, for nearly seven years. But it is a fact; and to me a sad one, even now; for my body still suffers from the effects of that long imprisonment, to say nothing of my soul. Members of my family, now living in New York and Boston, can testify to the truth of what I say.

Countless were the nights that I sat late at the little loophole scarcely large enough to give me a glimpse of one twinkling star. There, I heard the patrols and slave-hunters conferring together about the capture of runaways, well knowing how rejoiced they would be to catch me.

Season after season, year after year, I peeped at my children's faces, and heard their sweet voices, with a heart yearning all the while to say, "Your mother is here." Sometimes it appeared to me as if ages had rolled away since I entered upon that gloomy, monotonous existence. At times, I was stupefied and listless; at other times I became very impatient to know when these dark years would end, and I should again be allowed to feel the sunshine, and breathe the pure air.

After Ellen left us, this feeling increased. Mr. Sands had agreed that Benny might go to the north

whenever his uncle Phillip could go with him; and
I was anxious to be there also, to watch over my
children, and protect them so far as I was able. Moreover, I was likely to be drowned out of my den, if I
remained much longer; for the slight roof was getting
badly out of repair, and uncle Phillip was afraid to remove the shingles, lest some one should get a glimpse
of me. When storms occurred in the night, they
spread mats and bits of carpet, which in the morning
appeared to have been laid out to dry; but to cover
the roof in the daytime might have attracted attention. Consequently, my clothes and bedding were
often drenched; a process by which the pains and
aches in my cramped and stiffened limbs were greatly
increased. I revolved various plans of escape in my
mind, which I sometimes imparted to my grandmother,
when she came to whisper with me at the trap-door.
The kind-hearted old woman had an intense sympathy
for runaways. She had known too much of the
cruelties inflicted on those who were captured. Her
memory always flew back at once to the sufferings of her
bright and handsome son, Benjamin, the youngest and
dearest of her flock. So, whenever I alluded to the
subject, she would groan out, " O, don't think of it,
child. You'll break my heart." I had no good old
aunt Nancy now to encourage me; but my brother
William and my children were continually beckoning
me to the north.

And now I must go back a few months in my story.
I have stated that the first of January was the time
for selling slaves, or leasing them out to new masters.
If time were counted by heart-throbs, the poor slaves

might reckon years of suffering during that festival so joyous to the free.   On the New Year's day preceding my aunt's death, one of my friends, named Fanny, was to be sold at auction, to pay her master's debts.   My thoughts were with her during all the day, and at night I anxiously inquired what had been her fate.   I was told that she had been sold to one master, and her four little girls to another master, far distant; that she had escaped from her purchaser, and was not to be found.   Her mother was the old Aggie I have spoken of.   She lived in a small tenement belonging to my grandmother, and built on the same lot with her own house.   Her dwelling was searched and watched, and that brought the patrols so near me that I was obliged to keep very close in my den.   The hunters were somehow eluded; and not long afterwards Benny accidentally caught sight of Fanny in her mother's hut. He told his grandmother, who charged him never to speak of it, explaining to him the frightful consequences; and he never betrayed the trust.   Aggie little dreamed that my grandmother knew where her daughter was concealed, and that the stooping form of her old neighbor was bending under a similar burden of anxiety and fear; but these dangerous secrets deepened the sympathy between the two old persecuted mothers.

My friend Fanny and I remained many weeks hidden within call of each other; but she was unconscious of the fact.   I longed to have her share my den, which seemed a more secure retreat than her own; but I had brought so much trouble on my grandmother, that it seemed wrong to ask her to incur greater risks.   My

restlessness increased. I had lived too long in bodily
pain and anguish of spirit. Always I was in dread
that by some accident, or some contrivance, slavery
would succeed in snatching my children from me. This
thought drove me nearly frantic, and I determined to
steer for the North Star at all hazards. At this crisis,
Providence opened an unexpected way for me to escape. My friend Peter came one evening, and asked
to speak with me. "Your day has come, Linda," said
he. "I have found a chance for you to go to the Free
States. You have a fortnight to decide." The news
seemed too good to be true; but Peter explained his
arrangements, and told me all that was necessary was
for me to say I would go. I was going to answer him
with a joyful yes, when the thought of Benny came
to my mind. I told him the temptation was exceedingly strong, but I was terribly afraid of Dr. Flint's
alleged power over my child, and that I could not go
and leave him behind. Peter remonstrated earnestly.
He said such a good chance might never occur again;
that Benny was free, and could be sent to me; and
that for the sake of my children's welfare I ought not
to hesitate a moment. I told him I would consult with
uncle Phillip. My uncle rejoiced in the plan, and
bade me go by all means. He promised, if his life
was spared, that he would either bring or send my son
to me as soon as I reached a place of safety. I resolved to go, but thought nothing had better be said to
my grandmother till very near the time of departure.
But my uncle thought she would feel it more keenly
if I left her so suddenly. "I will reason with her,"
said he, "and convince her how necessary it is, not

only for your sake, but for hers also. You cannot be
blind to the fact that she is sinking under her burdens." I was not blind to it. I knew that my concealment was an ever-present source of anxiety, and
that the older she grew the more nervously fearful
she was of discovery. My uncle talked with her, and
finally succeeded in persuading her that it was abso-
lutely necessary for me to seize the chance so unexpectedly offered.

The anticipation of being a free woman proved almost too much for my weak frame. The excitement
stimulated me, and at the same time bewildered me.
I made busy preparations for my journey, and for my
son to follow me. I resolved to have an interview with
him before I went, that I might give him cautions and
advice, and tell him how anxiously I should be waiting
for him at the north. Grandmother stole up to me as
often as possible to whisper words of counsel. She
insisted upon my writing to Dr. Flint, as soon as I
arrived in the Free States, and asking him to sell me to
her. She said she would sacrifice her house, and all
she had in the world, for the sake of having me safe
with my children in any part of the world. If she
could only live to know *that* she could die in peace.
I promised the dear old faithful friend that I would
write to her as soon as I arrived, and put the letter in
a safe way to reach her; but in my own mind I resolved that not another cent of her hard earnings
should be spent to pay rapacious slaveholders for what
they called their property. And even if I had not
been unwilling to buy what I had already a right to
possess, common humanity would have prevented me

from accepting the generous offer, at the expense of turning my aged relative out of house and home, when she was trembling on the brink of the grave.

I was to escape in a vessel; but I forbear to mention any further paticulars. I was in readiness, but the vessel was unexpectedly detained several days. Meantime, news came to town of a most horrible murder committed on a fugitive slave, named James. Charity, the mother of this unfortunate young man, had been an old acquaintance of ours. I have told the shocking particulars of his death, in my description of some of the neighboring slaveholders. My grandmother, always nervously sensitive about runaways, was terribly frightened. She felt sure that a similar fate awaited me, if I did not desist from my enterprise. She sobbed, and groaned, and entreated me not to go. Her excessive fear was somewhat contagious, and my heart was not proof against her extreme agony. I was grievously disappointed, but I promised to relinquish my project.

When my friend Peter was apprised of this, he was both disappointed and vexed. He said, that judging from our past experience, it would be a long time before I had such another chance to throw away. I told him it need not be thrown away; that I had a friend concealed near by, who would be glad enough to take the place that had been provided for me. I told him about poor Fanny, and the kind-hearted, noble fellow, who never turned his back upon any body in distress, white or black, expressed his readiness to help her. Aggie was much surprised when she found that we knew her secret. She was rejoiced to hear of such a chance for Fanny,

and arrangements were made for her to go on board
the vessel the next night.   They both supposed that I
had long been at the north, therefore my name was not
mentioned in the transaction.   Fanny was carried on
board at the appointed time, and stowed away in
a very small cabin.   This accommodation had been
purchased at a price that would pay for a voyage to
England.   But when one proposes to go to fine old
England, they stop to calculate whether they can afford
the cost of the pleasure ; while in making a bargain to
escape from slavery, the trembling victim is ready to
say, " Take all I have, only don't betray me ! "

The next morning I peeped through my loophole,
and saw that it was dark and cloudy.   At night I received news that the wind was ahead, and the vessel
had not sailed.   I was exceedingly anxious about
Fanny, and Peter too, who was running a tremendous
risk at my instigation.   Next day the wind and weather
remained the same.   Poor Fanny had been half dead
with fright when they carried her on board, and I could
readily imagine how she must be suffering now.
Grandmother came often to my den, to say how thankful she was I did not go.   On the third morning she
rapped for me to come down to the storeroom.   The
poor old sufferer was breaking down under her weight
of trouble.   She was easily flurried now.   I found her
in a nervous, excited state, but I was not aware that
she had forgotten to lock the door behind her, as usual.
She was exceedingly worried about the detention of
the vessel.   She was afraid all would be discovered,
and then Fanny, and Peter, and I, would all be tortured to death, and Phillip would be utterly ruined,

and her house would be torn down. Poor Peter! If
he should die such a horrible death as the poor slave
James had lately done, and all for his kindness in trying to help me, how dreadful it would be for us all!
Alas, the thought was familiar to me, and had sent
many a sharp pang through my heart. I tried to suppress my own anxiety, and speak soothingly to her.
She brought in some allusion to aunt Nancy, the dear
daughter she had recently buried, and then she lost all
control of herself. As she stood there, trembling and
sobbing, a voice from the piazza called out, " Whar is
you, aunt Marthy ? " Grandmother was startled, and
in her agitation opened the door, without thinking of
me. In stepped Jenny, the mischievous housemaid,
who had tried to enter my room, when I was concealed
in the house of my white benefactress. " I's bin huntin
ebery whar for you, aunt Marthy," said she. " My
missis wants you to send her some crackers." I had
slunk down behind a barrel, which entirely screened
me, but I imagined that Jenny was looking directly at
the spot, and my heart beat violently. My grand
mother immediately thought what she had done, and
went out quickly with Jenny to count the crackers
locking the door after her. She returned to me, in a
few minutes, the perfect picture of despair. " Poor
child ! " she exclaimed, " my carelessness has ruined
you. The boat ain't gone yet. Get ready immedi
ately, and go with Fanny. I ain't got another word to
say against it now ; for there's no telling what may
happen this day."

Uncle Phillip was sent for, and he agreed with his
mother in thinking that Jenny would inform Dr. Flint

in less than twenty-four hours. He advised getting me on board the boat, if possible; if not, I had better keep very still in my den, where they could not find me without tearing the house down. He said it would not do for him to move in the matter, because suspicion would be immediately excited; but he promised to communicate with Peter. I felt reluctant to apply to him again, having implicated him too much already; but there seemed to be no alternative. Vexed as Peter had been by my indecision, he was true to his generous nature, and said at once that he would do his best to help me, trusting I should show myself a stronger woman this time.

He immediately proceeded to the wharf, and found that the wind had shifted, and the vessel was slowly beating down stream. On some pretext of urgent necessity, he offered two boatmen a dollar apiece to catch up with her. He was of lighter complexion than the boatmen he hired, and when the captain saw them coming so rapidly, he thought officers were pursuing his vessel in search of the runaway slave he had on board. They hoisted sails, but the boat gained upon them, and the indefatigable Peter sprang on board.

The captain at once recognized him. Peter asked him to go below, to speak about a bad bill he had given him. When he told his errand, the captain replied, "Why, the woman's here already; and I've put her where you or the devil would have a tough job to find her."

"But it is another woman I want to bring," said Peter. "*She* is in great distress, too, and you shall be paid any thing within reason, if you'll stop and take her."

" What's her name ? " inquired the captain.

" Linda," he replied.

" That's the name of the woman already here," rejoined the captain. " By George! I believe **you** mean to betray me."

" O! " exclaimed Peter, " God knows I wouldn't harm a hair of your head. I am too grateful to you. But there really *is* another woman in great danger. Do have the humanity to stop and take her ! "

After a while they came to an understanding. Fanny, not dreaming I was any where about in that region, had assumed my name, though she called herself Johnson. " Linda is a common name," said Peter, " and the woman I want to bring is Linda Brent."

The captain agreed to wait at a certain place till evening, being handsomely paid for his detention.

Of course, the day was an anxious one for us all. But we concluded that if Jenny had seen me, she would be too wise to let her mistress know of it; and that she probably would not get a chance to see Dr. Flint's family till evening, for I knew very well what were the rules in that household. I afterwards believed that she did not see me ; for nothing ever came of it, and she was one of those base characters that would have jumped to betray a suffering fellow being for the sake of thirty pieces of silver.

I made all my arrangements to go on board as soon as it was dusk. The intervening time I resolved to spend with my son. I had not spoken to him for seven years, though I had been under the same roof, and seen him every day, when I was well enough to sit at the loophole. I did not dare to venture beyond the storeroom; so they brought him there, and locked us up together, in a place concealed from the piazza door. It was an agitating interview for both of us. After we had talked and wept together for a little while, he said, "Mother, I'm glad you're going away. I wish I could go with you. I knew you was here; and I have been *so* afraid they would come and catch you!"

I was greatly surprised, and asked him how he had found it out.

He replied, "I was standing under the eaves, one day, before Ellen went away, and I heard somebody cough up over the wood shed. I don't know what made me think it was you, but I did think so. I missed Ellen, the night before she went away; and grandmother brought her back into the room in the night; and I thought maybe she'd been to see *you*, before she went, for I heard grandmother whisper to her, 'Now go to sleep; and remember never to tell.'"

I asked him if he ever mentioned his suspicions to his sister. He said he never did; but after he heard the cough, if he saw her playing with other children on that side of the house, he always tried to coax her round to the other side, for fear they would hear me cough, too. He said he had kept a close lookout for Dr. Flint, and if he saw him speak to a constable, or a patrol, he always told grandmother. I now recollected that I had seen him manifest uneasiness, when people were on that side of the house, and I had at the time been puzzled to conjecture a motive for his actions. Such prudence may seem extraordinary in a boy of twelve years, but slaves, being surrounded by mysteries, deceptions, and dangers, early learn to be suspicious and watchful, and prematurely cautious and cunning. He had never asked a question of grand-mother, or uncle Phillip, and I had often heard him chime in with other children, when they spoke of my being at the north.

I told him I was now really going to the Free States, and if he was a good, honest boy, and a loving child to his dear old grandmother, the Lord would bless him, and bring him to me, and we and Ellen would live together. He began to tell me that grandmother had not eaten any thing all day. While he was speaking, the door was unlocked, and she came in with a small bag of money, which she wanted me to take. I begged her to keep a part of it, at least, to pay for Benny's being sent to the north; but she insisted, while her tears were falling fast, that I should take the whole. "You may be sick among strangers," she said, "and they would send you to the poorhouse to die." Ah, that good grandmother!

For the last time I went up to my nook. Its deso-late appearance no longer chilled me, for the light of hope had risen in my soul. Yet, even with the blessed prospect of freedom before me, I felt very sad at leav-ing forever that old homestead, where I had been shel-tered so long by the dear old grandmother; where I had dreamed my first young dream of love; and where, after that had faded away, my children came to twine themselves so closely round my desolate heart. As the hour approached for me to leave, I again descended to the storeroom. My grandmother and Benny were there. She took me by the hand, and said, "Linda, let us pray." We knelt down together, with my child

pressed to my heart, and my other arm round the faithful, loving old friend I was about to leave forever.
On no other occasion has it ever been my lot to listen
to so fervent a supplication for mercy and protection.
It thrilled through my heart, and inspired me with trust
in God.

Peter was waiting for me in the street. I was soon
by his side, faint in body, but strong of purpose. I
did not look back upon the old place, though I felt
that I should never see it again.

XXX.

NORTHWARD BOUND.

I never could tell how we reached the wharf. My brain was all of a whirl, and my limbs tottered under me. At an appointed place we met my uncle Phillip, who had started before us on a different route, that he might reach the wharf first, and give us timely warning if there was any danger. A row-boat was in readiness. As I was about to step in, I felt something pull me gently, and turning round I saw Benny, looking pale and anxious. He whispered in my ear, " I've been peeping into the doctor's window, and he's at home. Good by, mother. Don't cry; I'll come." He hastened away. I clasped the hand of my good uncle, to whom I owed so much, and of Peter, the brave, generous friend who had volunteered to run such terrible risks to secure my safety. To this day I remember how his bright face beamed with joy, when he told me he had discovered a safe method for me to escape. Yet that intelligent, enterprising, noble-hearted man was a chattel! liable, by the laws of a country that calls itself civilized, to be sold with horses and pigs! We parted in silence. Our hearts were all too full for words!

Swiftly the boat glided over the water. After a while, one of the sailors said, " Don't be down-hearted, madam. We will take you safely to your husband, in ———." At first I could not imagine what he meant;

but I had presence of mind to think that it probably referred to something the captain had told him; so I thanked him, and said I hoped we should have pleasant weather.

When I entered the vessel the captain came forward to meet me. He was an elderly man, with a pleasant countenance. He showed me to a little box of a cabin, where sat my friend Fanny. She started as if she had seen a spectre. She gazed on me in utter astonishment, and exclaimed, " Linda, can this be *you ?* or is it your ghost?" When we were locked in each other's arms, my overwrought feelings could no longer be restrained. My sobs reached the ears of the captain, who came and very kindly reminded us, that for his safety, as well as our own, it would be prudent for us not to attract any attention. He said that when there was a sail in sight he wished us to keep below; but at other times, he had no objection to our being on deck. He assured us that he would keep a good lookout, and if we acted prudently, he thought we should be in no danger. He had represented us as women going to meet our husbands in ———. We thanked him, and promised to observe carefully all the directions he gave us.

Fanny and I now talked by ourselves, low and quietly, in our little cabin. She told me of the sufferings she had gone through in making her escape, and of her terrors while she was concealed in her mother's house. Above all, she dwelt on the agony of separation from all her children on that dreadful auction day. She could scarcely credit me, when I told her of the place where I had passed nearly seven years. " We have the same sorrows," said I. " No," replied she, " you are going to see your children soon, and there is no hope that I shall ever even hear from mine."

The vessel was soon under way, but we made slow progress. The wind was against us. I should not have cared for this, if we had been out of sight of the town; but until there were miles of water between us and our enemies, we were filled with constant apprehensions that the constables would come on board. Neither could I feel quite at ease with the captain and his men. I was an entire stranger to that class of people, and I had heard that sailors were rough, and sometimes cruel. We were so completely in their power, that if they were bad men, our situation would be dreadful. Now that the captain was paid for our passage, might he not be tempted to make more money by giving us up to those who claimed us as property? I was naturally of a confiding disposition, but slavery had made me suspicious of every body. Fanny did not share my distrust of the captain or his men. She said she was afraid at first, but she had been on board three days while the vessel lay in the dock, and nobody had betrayed her, or treated her otherwise than kindly.

The captain soon came to advise us to go on deck for fresh air. His friendly and respectful manner, combined with Fanny's testimony, reassured me, and we went with him. He placed us in a comfortable seat, and occasionally entered into conversation. He told us he was a Southerner by birth, and had spent the greater part of his life in the Slave States, and that he had recently lost a brother who traded in slaves. " But," said he, " it is a pitiable and degrading business, and I always felt ashamed to acknowledge my brother in con-

nection with it." As we passed Snaky Swamp, he
pointed to it, and said, " There is a slave territory that
defies all the laws." I thought of the terrible days I
had spent there, and though it was not called Dismal
Swamp, it made me feel very dismal as I looked at it.

I shall never forget that night. The balmy air of
spring was so refreshing! And how shall I describe
my sensations when we were fairly sailing on Chesa-
peake Bay ? O, the beautiful sunshine! the exhilarat-
ing breeze ! and I could enjoy them without fear or
restraint. I had never realized what grand things air
and sunlight are till I had been deprived of them.

Ten days after we left land we were approaching
Philadelphia. The captain said we should arrive there
in the night, but he thought we had better wait till
morning, and go on shore in broad daylight, as the best
way to avoid suspicion.

I replied, " You know best. But will you stay on
board and protect us ? "

He saw that I was suspicious, and he said he was
sorry, now that he had brought us to the end of our
voyage, to find I had so little confidence in him. Ah,
if he had ever been a slave he would have known how
difficult it was to trust a white man. He assured us
that we might sleep through the night without fear ;
that he would take care we were not left unprotected.
Be it said to the honor of this captain, Southerner as
he was, that if Fanny and I had been white ladies, and
our passage lawfully engaged, he could not have treated
us more respectfully. My intelligent friend, Peter, had
rightly estimated the character of the man to whose
honor he had intrusted us.

The next morning I was on deck as soon as the day dawned. I called Fanny to see the sun rise, for the first time in our lives, on free soil; for such I *then* believed it to be. We watched the reddening sky, and saw the great orb come up slowly out of the water, as it seemed. Soon the waves began to sparkle, and every thing caught the beautiful glow. Before us lay the city of strangers. We looked at each other, and the eyes of both were moistened with tears. We had escaped from slavery, and we supposed ourselves to be safe from the hunters. But we were alone in the world, and we had left dear ties behind us; ties cruelly sundered by the demon Slavery.

21

XXXI.

INCIDENTS IN PHILADELPHIA.

I HAD heard that the poor slave had many friends at the north. I trusted we should find some of them. Meantime, we would take it for granted that all were friends, till they proved to the contrary. I sought out the kind captain, thanked him for his attentions, and told him I should never cease to be grateful for the service he had rendered us. I gave him a message to the friends I had left at home, and he promised to deliver it. We were placed in a row-boat, and in about fifteen minutes were landed on a wood wharf in Philadelphia. As I stood looking round, the friendly captain touched me on the shoulder, and said, " There is a respectable-looking colored man behind you. I will speak to him about the New York trains, and tell him you wish to go directly on." I thanked him, and asked him to direct me to some shops where I could buy gloves and veils. He did so, and said he would talk with the colored man till I returned. I made what haste I could. Constant exercise on board the vessel, and frequent rubbing with salt water, had nearly restored the use of my limbs. The noise of the great city confused me, but I found the shops, and bought some double veils and gloves for Fanny and myself. The shopman told me they were so many levies. I had never heard the word before, but I did not tell him so. I thought if he knew I was a stranger he might ask me where I came from. I gave him a gold piece, and when he returned the change, I counted it, and found out how much a levy was. I made my way back to the wharf, where the captain introduced me to the colored man, as the Rev. Jeremiah Durham, minister of Bethel church. He took me by the hand, as if I had been an old friend. He told us we were too late for the morning cars to New York, and must wait until the evening, or the next morning. He invited me to go home with him, assuring me that his wife would give me a cordial welcome; and for my friend he would provide a home with one of his neighbors. I thanked him for so much kindness to strangers, and told him if I must be detained, I should like to hunt up some people who formerly went from our part of the country. Mr. Durham insisted that I should dine with him, and then he would assist me in finding my friends. The sailors came to bid us good by. I shook their hardy hands, with tears in my eyes. They had all been kind to us, and they had rendered us a greater service than they could possibly conceive of.

I had never seen so large a city, or been in contact with so many people in the streets. It seemed as if those who passed looked at us with an expression of curiosity. My face was so blistered and peeled, by sitting on deck, in wind and sunshine, that I thought they could not easily decide to what nation I belonged.

Mrs. Durham met me with a kindly welcome, without asking any questions. I was tired, and her friendly manner was a sweet refreshment. God bless her! I was sure that she had comforted other weary hearts, before I received her sympathy. She was surrounded

by her husband and children, in a home made sacred
by protecting laws. I thought of my own children,
and sighed.

After dinner Mr. Durham went with me in quest of
the friends I had spoken of. They went from my native town, and I anticipated much pleasure in looking
on familiar faces. They were not at home, and we
retraced our steps through streets delightfully clean.
On the way, Mr. Durham observed that I had spoken
to him of a daughter I expected to meet; that he was
surprised, for I looked so young he had taken me for
a single woman. He was approaching a subject on
which I was extremely sensitive. He would ask about
my husband next, I thought, and if I answered him
truly, what would he think of me? I told him I had
two children, one in New York the other at the south.
He asked some further questions, and I frankly told
him some of the most important events of my life. It
was painful for me to do it; but I would not deceive
him. If he was desirous of being my friend, I thought
he ought to know how far I was worthy of it. " Excuse me, if I have tried your feelings," said he. " I
did not question you from idle curiosity. I wanted to
understand your situation, in order to know whether
I could be of any service to you, or your little girl.
Your straight-forward answers do you credit; but
don't answer every body so openly. It might give
some heartless people a pretext for treating you with
contempt."

That word *contempt* burned me like coals of fire. I
replied, " God alone knows how I have suffered; and
He, I trust, will forgive me. If I am permitted to

have my children, I intend to be a good mother, and to live in such a manner that people cannot treat me with contempt."

"I respect your sentiments," said he. "Place your trust in God, and be governed by good principles, and you will not fail to find friends."

When we reached home, I went to my room, glad to shut out the world for a while. The words he had spoken made an indelible impression upon me. They brought up great shadows from the mournful past. In the midst of my meditations I was startled by a knock at the door. Mrs. Durham entered, her face all beaming with kindness, to say that there was an anti-slavery friend down stairs, who would like to see me. I overcame my dread of encountering strangers, and went with her. Many questions were asked concerning my experiences, and my escape from slavery; but I observed how careful they all were not to say any thing that might wound my feelings. How gratifying this was, can be fully understood only by those who have been accustomed to be treated as if they were not included within the pale of human beings. The anti-slavery friend had come to inquire into my plans, and to offer assistance, if needed. Fanny was comfortably established, for the present, with a friend of Mr. Durham. The Anti-Slavery Society agreed to pay her expenses to New York. The same was offered to me, but I declined to accept it; telling them that my grandmother had given me sufficient to pay my expenses to the end of my journey. We were urged to remain in Philadelphia a few days, until some suitable escort could be found for us. I gladly accepted the proposition, for I had a dread of meeting slaveholders, and some dread also of railroads. I had never entered a railroad car in my life, and it seemed to me quite an important event.

That night I sought my pillow with feelings I had never carried to it before. I verily believed myself to be a free woman. I was wakeful for a long time, and I had no sooner fallen asleep, than I was roused by fire-bells. I jumped up, and hurried on my clothes. Where I came from, every body hastened to dress themselves on such occasions. The white people thought a great fire might be used as a good opportunity for insurrection, and that it was best to be in readiness; and the colored people were ordered out to labor in extinguishing the flames. There was but one engine in our town, and colored women and children were often required to drag it to the river's edge and fill it. Mrs. Durham's daughter slept in the same room with me, and seeing that she slept through all the din, I thought it was my duty to wake her. "What's the matter?" said she, rubbing her eyes.

"They're screaming fire in the streets, and the bells are ringing," I replied.

"What of that?" said she, drowsily. "We are used to it. We never get up, without the fire is very near. What good would it do?"

I was quite surprised that it was not necessary for us to go and help fill the engine. I was an ignorant child, just beginning to learn how things went on in great cities.

At daylight, I heard women crying fresh fish, berries, radishes, and various other things. All this was

new to me. I dressed myself at an early hour, and
sat at the window to watch that unknown tide of life.
Philadelphia seemed to me a wonderfully great place.
At the breakfast table, my idea of going out to drag
the engine was laughed over, and I joined in the mirth.

I went to see Fanny, and found her so well contented among her new friends that she was in no haste
to leave. I was also very happy with my kind hostess.
She had had advantages for education, and was vastly
my superior. Every day, almost every hour, I was
adding to my little stock of knowledge. She took me
out to see the city as much as she deemed prudent.
One day she took me to an artist's room, and showed
me the portraits of some of her children. I had never
seen any paintings of colored people before, and they
seemed to me beautiful.

At the end of five days, one of Mrs. Durham's friends
offered to accompany us to New York the following
morning. As I held the hand of my good hostess in
a parting clasp, I longed to know whether her husband
had repeated to her what I had told him. I supposed
he had, but she never made any allusion to it. I presume it was the delicate silence of womanly sympathy.

When Mr. Durham handed us our tickets, he said,
" I am afraid you will have a disagreeable ride ; but I
could not procure tickets for the first class cars."

Supposing I had not given him money enough, I
offered more. " O, no," said he, " they could not be
had for any money. They don't allow colored people
to go in the first-class cars."

This was the first chill to my enthusiasm about the
Free States. Colored people were allowed to ride in a

filthy box, behind white people, at the south, but there they were not required to pay for the privilege. It made me sad to find how the north aped the customs of slavery.

We were stowed away in a large, rough car, with windows on each side, too high for us to look out without standing up. It was crowded with people, apparently of all nations. There were plenty of beds and cradles, containing screaming and kicking babies. Every other man had a cigar or pipe in his mouth, and jugs of whiskey were handed round freely. The fumes of the whiskey and the dense tobacco smoke were sickening to my senses, and my mind was equally nauseated by the coarse jokes and ribald songs around me. It was a very disagreeable ride. Since that time there has been some improvement in these matters.

XXXII.

THE MEETING OF MOTHER AND DAUGHTER.

When we arrived in New York, I was half crazed by the crowd of coachmen calling out, "Carriage, ma'am?" We bargained with one to take us to Sullivan Street for twelve shillings. A burly Irishman stepped up and said, "I'll tak' ye for sax shillings." The reduction of half the price was an object to us, and we asked if he could take us right away. "Troth an I will, ladies," he replied. I noticed that the hackmen smiled at each other, and I inquired whether his conveyance was decent. "Yes, it's dacent it is, marm. Devil a bit would I be after takin' ladies in a cab that was not dacent." We gave him our checks. He went for the baggage, and soon reappeared, saying, "This way, if you plase, ladies." We followed, and found our trunks on a truck, and we were invited to take our seats on them. We told him that was not what we bargained for, and he must take the trunks off. He swore they should not be touched till we had paid him six shillings. In our situation it was not prudent to attract attention, and I was about to pay him what he required, when a man near by shook his head for me not to do it. After a great ado we got rid of the Irishman, and had our trunks fastened on a hack. We had been recommended to a boarding-house in Sullivan Street, and thither we drove. There Fanny and I separated. The Anti-Slavery Society provided a home for her, and I afterwards heard of her in prosperous circumstances. I sent for an old friend from my part of the country, who had for some time been doing business in New York. He came immediately. I told him I wanted to go to my daughter, and asked him to aid me in procuring an interview.

I cautioned him not to let it be known to the family that I had just arrived from the south, because they supposed I had been at the north seven years. He told me there was a colored woman in Brooklyn who came from the same town I did, and I had better go to her house, and have my daughter meet me there. I accepted the proposition thankfully, and he agreed to escort me to Brooklyn. We crossed Fulton ferry, went up Myrtle Avenue, and stopped at the house he designated. I was just about to enter, when two girls passed. My friend called my attention to them. I turned, and recognized in the eldest, Sarah, the daughter of a woman who used to live with my grandmother, but who had left the south years ago. Surprised and rejoiced at this unexpected meeting, I threw my arms round her, and inquired concerning her mother.

"You take no notice of the other girl," said my friend. I turned, and there stood my Ellen! I pressed her to my heart, then held her away from me to take a look at her. She had changed a good deal in the two years since I parted from her. Signs of neglect could be discerned by eyes less observing than a mother's. My friend invited us all to go into the house; but Ellen said she had been sent of an errand, which she would do as quickly as possible, and go home and ask Mrs. Hobbs to let her come and see me. It was agreed that I should send for her the next day. Her companion, Sarah, hastened to tell her mother of my arrival. When I entered the house, I found the mistress of it absent, and I waited for her return. Before I saw her, I heard her saying, "Where is Linda Brent? I used to know her father and mother." Soon Sarah came with her mother. So there was quite a company of us, all from my grandmother's neighborhood. These friends gathered round me and questioned me eagerly. They laughed, they cried, and they shouted. They thanked God that I had got away from my persecutors and was safe on Long Island. It was a day of great excitement. How different from the silent days I had passed in my dreary den!

The next morning was Sunday. My first waking thoughts were occupied with the note I was to send to Mrs. Hobbs, the lady with whom Ellen lived. That I had recently come into that vicinity was evident; otherwise I should have sooner inquired for my daughter. It would not do to let them know I had just arrived from the south, for that would involve the suspicion of my having been harbored there, and might bring trouble, if not ruin, on several people.

I like a straightforward course, and am always reluctant to resort to subterfuges. So far as my ways have been crooked, I charge them all upon slavery. It was that system of violence and wrong which now left me no alternative but to enact a falsehood. I began my note by stating that I had recently arrived from Canada, and was very desirous to have my daughter come to see me. She came and brought a message from Mrs. Hobbs, inviting me to her house, and assuring me that I need not have any fears. The conversation I had with my child did not leave my mind at ease. When I asked if she was well treated, she answered yes; but there was no heartiness in the tone, and it seemed to me that she said it from an unwillingness to have me troubled on her account. Before she left me, she asked very earnestly, "Mother, when will you take me to live with you?" It made me sad to think that I could not give her a home till I went to work and earned the means; and that might take me a long time. When she was placed with Mrs. Hobbs, the agreement was that she should be sent to school. She had been there two years, and was now nine years old, and she scarcely knew her letters. There was no excuse for this, for there were good public schools in Brooklyn, to which she could have been sent without expense.

She staid with me till dark, and I went home with her. I was received in a friendly manner by the family, and all agreed in saying that Ellen was a useful, good girl. Mrs. Hobbs looked me coolly in the face, and said, " I suppose you know that my cousin, Mr. Sands, has *given* her to my eldest daughter. She will make a nice waiting-maid for her when she grows up." I did not answer a word. How *could* she, who knew by experience the strength of a mother's love, and who was perfectly aware of the relation Mr. Sands bore to my children, — how *could* she look me in the face, while she thrust such a dagger into my heart?

I was no longer surprised that they had kept her in such a state of ignorance. Mr. Hobbs had formerly heen wealthy, but he had failed, and afterwards obtained a subordinate situation in the Custom House. Perhaps they expected to return to the south some day; and Ellen's knowledge was quite sufficient for a slave's condition. I was impatient to go to work and earn money, that I might change the uncertain position of my children. Mr. Sands had not kept his promise to emancipate them. I had also been deceived about Ellen. What security had I with regard to Benjamin? I felt that I had none.

I returned to my friend's house in an uneasy state of mind. In order to protect my children, it was necessary that I should own myself. I called myself free, and sometimes felt so; but I knew I was insecure. I sat down that night and wrote a civil letter to Dr. Flint, asking him to state the lowest terms on which he would sell me; and as I belonged by law to his daughter, I wrote to her also, making a similar request.

Since my arrival at the north I had not been unmindful of my dear brother William. I had made diligent inquiries for him, and having heard of him in Boston, I went thither. When I arrived there, I found he had gone to New Bedford. I wrote to that place, and was informed he had gone on a whaling voyage, and would not return for some months. I went back to New York to get employment near Ellen. I received an answer from Dr. Flint, which gave me no encouragement. He advised me to return and submit myself to my rightful owners, and then any request I might make would be granted. I lent this letter to a friend, who lost it; otherwise I would present a copy to my readers.

XXXIII.

A HOME FOUND.

My greatest anxiety now was to obtain employment. My health was greatly improved, though my limbs continued to trouble me with swelling whenever I walked much. The greatest difficulty in my way was, that those who employed strangers required a recommendation; and in my peculiar position, I could, of course, obtain no certificates from the families I had so faithfully served.

One day an acquaintance told me of a lady who wanted a nurse for her babe, and I immediately applied for the situation. The lady told me she preferred to have one who had been a mother, and accustomed to the care of infants. I told her I had nursed two babes of my own. She asked me many questions, but, to my great relief, did not require a recommendation from my former employers. She told me she was an English woman, and that was a pleasant circumstance to me, because I had heard they had less prejudice against color than Americans entertained. It was agreed that we should try each other for a week. The trial proved satisfactory to both parties, and I was engaged for a month.

The heavenly Father had been most merciful to me in leading me to this place. Mrs. Bruce was a kind and gentle lady, and proved a true and sympathizing friend. Before the stipulated month expired, the necessity of passing up and down stairs frequently, caused my limbs to swell so painfully, that I became unable to perform my duties. Many ladies would have thoughtlessly discharged me; but Mrs. Bruce made arrangements to save me steps, and employed a physician to attend upon me. I had not yet told her that I was a fugitive slave. She noticed that I was often sad, and kindly inquired the cause. I spoke of being separated from my children, and from relatives who were dear to me; but I did not mention the constant feeling of insecurity which oppressed my spirits. I longed for some one to confide in; but I had been so deceived by white people, that I had lost all confidence in them. If they spoke kind words to me, I thought it was for some selfisn purpose. I had entered this family with the distrustful feelings I had brought with me out of slavery; but ere six months had passed, I found that the gentle deportment of Mrs. Bruce and the smiles of her lovely babe were thawing my chilled heart. My narrow mind also began to expand under the influences of her intelligent conversation, and the opportunities for reading, which were gladly allowed me whenever I had leisure from my duties. I gradually became more energetic and more cheerful.

The old feeling of insecurity, especially with regard to my children, often threw its dark shadow across my sunshine. Mrs. Bruce offered me a home for Ellen; but pleasant as it would have been, I did not dare to accept it, for fear of offending the Hobbs family. Their knowledge of my precarious situation placed me in their power; and I felt that it was important for me to keep on the right side of them, till, by dint of labor and economy, I could make a home for my children.

I was far from feeling satisfied with Ellen's situation. She was not well cared for. She sometimes came to New York to visit me; but she generally brought a request from Mrs. Hobbs that I would buy her a pair of shoes, or some article of clothing. This was accompanied by a promise of payment when Mr. Hobbs's salary at the Custom House became due; but some how or other the pay-day never came. Thus many dollars of my earnings were expended to keep my child comfortably clothed. That, however, was a slight trouble, compared with the fear that their pecuniary embarrassments might induce them to sell my precious young daughter. I knew they were in constant communication with Southerners, and had frequent opportunities to do it. I have stated that when Dr. Flint put Ellen in jail, at two years old, she had an inflammation of the eyes, occasioned by measles. This disease still troubled her; and kind Mrs. Bruce proposed that she should come to New York for a while, to be under the care of Dr. Elliott, a well known oculist. It did not occur to me that there was any thing improper in a mother's making such a request; but Mrs. Hobbs was very angry, and refused to let her go. Situated as I was, it was not politic to insist upon it. I made no complaint, but I longed to be entirely free to act a mother's part towards my children. The next time I went over to Brooklyn, Mrs. Hobbs, as if to apologize for her anger, told me she had employed her own physician to attend to Ellen's eyes, and that she had refused my request because she did not consider it safe to trust her in New York. I accepted the explanation in silence; but she had told me that my child *belonged* to her daughter, and I suspected that her real motive was a fear of my conveying her property away from her. Perhaps I did her injustice; but my knowledge of Southerners made it difficult for me to feel otherwise.

Sweet and bitter were mixed in the cup of my life, and I was thankful that it had ceased to be entirely bitter. I loved Mrs. Bruce's babe. When it laughed and crowed in my face, and twined its little tender arms confidingly about my neck, it made me think of the time when Benny and Ellen were babies, and my wounded heart was soothed. One bright morning, as I stood at the window, tossing baby in my arms, my attention was attracted by a young man in sailor's dress, who was closely observing every house as he passed. I looked at him earnestly. Could it be my brother William? It *must* be he — and yet, how changed! I placed the baby safely, flew down stairs, opened the front door, beckoned to the sailor, and in less than a minute I was clasped in my brother's arms. How much we had to tell each other! How we laughed, and how we cried, over each other's adventures! I took him to Brooklyn, and again saw him with Ellen, the dear child whom he had loved and tended so carefully, while I was shut up in my miserable den. He staid in New York a week. His old feelings of affection for me and Ellen were as lively as ever. There are no bonds so strong as those which are formed by suffering together.

22 *

XXXIV.

THE OLD ENEMY AGAIN.

My young mistress, Miss Emily Flint, did not return any answer to my letter requesting her to consent to my being sold.   But after a while, I received a reply, which purported to be written by her younger brother. In order rightly to enjoy the contents of this letter, the reader must bear in mind that the Flint family supposed I had been at the north many years.   They had no idea that I knew of the doctor's three excursions to New York in search of me; that I had heard his voice, when he came to borrow five hundred dollars for that purpose; and that I had seen him pass on his way to the steamboat.   Neither were they aware that all the particulars of aunt Nancy's death and burial were conveyed to me at the time they occurred.   I have kept the letter, of which I herewith subjoin a copy : —

"Your letter to sister was received a few days ago. I gather from it that you are desirous of returning to your native place, among your friends and relatives. We were all gratified with the contents of your letter; and let me assure you that if any members of the family have had any feeling of resentment towards you, they feel it no longer.   We all sympathize with you in your unfortunate condition, and are ready to do all in our power to make you contented and happy.   It is difficult for you to return home as a free person.   If you were purchased by your grandmother, it is doubtful whether you would be permitted to remain, although it would be lawful for you to do so. If a servant should be allowed to purchase herself, after absenting herself so long from her owners, and return free, it would have an injurious effect. From your letter, I think your situation must be hard and uncomfortable. Come home. You have it in your power to be reinstated in our affections. We would receive you with open arms and tears of joy. You need not apprehend any unkind treatment, as we have not put ourselves to any trouble or expense to get you. Had we done so, perhaps we should feel otherwise. You know my sister was always attached to you, and that you were never treated as a slave. You were never put to hard work, nor exposed to field labor. On the contrary, you were taken into the house, and treated as one of us, and almost as free; and we, at least, felt that you were above disgracing yourself by running away. Believing you may be induced to come home voluntarily has induced me to write for my sister. The family will be rejoiced to see you; and your poor old grandmother expressed a great desire to have you come, when she heard your letter read. In her old age she needs the consolation of having her children round her. Doubtless you have heard of the death of your aunt. She was a faithful servant, and a faithful member of the Episcopal church. In her Christian life she taught us how to live — and, O, too high the price of knowledge, she taught us how to die! Could you have seen us round her death bed, with her mother, all mingling our tears in one common stream, you would have

thought the same heartfelt tie existed between a master and his servant, as between a mother and her child.
But this subject is too painful to dwell upon. I must
bring my letter to a close. If you are contented to stay
away from your old grandmother, your child, and the
friends who love you, stay where you are. We shall
never trouble ourselves to apprehend you. But should
you prefer to come home, we will do all that we can to
make you happy. If you do not wish to remain in the
family, I know that father, by our persuasion, will be
induced to let you be purchased by any person you
may choose in our community. You will please answer this as soon as possible, and let us know your
decision. Sister sends much love to you. In the
mean time believe me your sincere friend and well
wisher."

This letter was signed by Emily's brother, who was
as yet a mere lad. I knew, by the style, that it was
not written by a person of his age, and though the
writing was disguised, I had been made too unhappy by
it, in former years, not to recognize at once the hand
of Dr. Flint. O, the hypocrisy of slaveholders ! Did
the old fox suppose I was goose enough to go into such
a trap ? Verily, he relied too much on " the stupidity
of the African race." I did not return the family of
Flints any thanks for their cordial invitation — a re-
missness for which I was, no doubt, charged with base
ingratitude.

Not long afterwards I received a letter from one of
my friends at the south, informing me that Dr. Flint
was about to visit the north. The letter had been
delayed, and I supposed he might be already on the

way. Mrs. Bruce did not know I was a fugitive. I told her that important business called me to Boston, where my brother then was, and asked permission to bring a friend to supply my place as nurse, for a fortnight. I started on my journey immediately; and as soon as I arrived, I wrote to my grandmother that if Benny came, he must be sent to Boston. I knew she was only waiting for a good chance to send him north, and, fortunately, she had the legal power to do so, without asking leave of any body. She was a free woman; and when my children were purchased, Mr. Sands preferred to have the bill of sale drawn up in her name. It was conjectured that he advanced the money, but it was not known. At the south, a gentleman may have a shoal of colored children without any disgrace; but if he is known to purchase them, with the view of setting them free, the example is thought to be dangerous to their "peculiar institution," and he becomes unpopular.

There was a good opportunity to send Benny in a vessel coming directly to New York. He was put on board with a letter to a friend, who was requested to see him off to Boston. Early one morning, there was a loud rap at my door, and in rushed Benjamin, all out of breath. "O mother!" he exclaimed, "here I am! I run all the way; and I come all alone. How d'you do?"

O reader, can you imagine my joy? No, you cannot, unless you have been a slave mother. Benjamin rattled away as fast as his tongue could go. "Mother, why don't you bring Ellen here? I went over to Brooklyn to see her, and she felt very bad when I bid her good by. She said, 'O Ben, I wish I was going too.' I thought she'd know ever so much; but she don't know so much as I do; for I can read, and she can't. And, mother, I lost all my clothes coming. What can I do to get some more? I 'spose free boys can get along here at the north as well as white boys."

I did not like to tell the sanguine, happy little fellow how much he was mistaken. I took him to a tailor, and procured a change of clothes. The rest of the day was spent in mutual asking and answering of questions, with the wish constantly repeated that the good old grandmother was with us, and frequent injunctions from Benny to write to her immediately, and be sure to tell her every thing about his voyage, and his journey to Boston.

Dr. Flint made his visit to New York, and made every exertion to call upon me, and invite me to return with him; but not being able to ascertain where I was, his hospitable intentions were frustrated, and the affectionate family, who were waiting for me with " open arms," were doomed to disappointment.

As soon as I knew he was safely at home, I placed Benjamin in the care of my brother William, and returned to Mrs. Bruce. There I remained through the winter and spring, endeavoring to perform my duties faithfully, and finding a good degree of happiness in the attractions of baby Mary, the considerate kindness of her excellent mother, and occasional interviews with my darling daughter.

But when summer came, the old feeling of insecurity haunted me. It was necessary for me to take little Mary out daily, for exercise and fresh air, and the city was swarming with Southerners, some of whom might recognize me. Hot weather brings out snakes and slaveholders, and I like one class of the venomous creatures as little as I do the other. What a comfort it is, to be free to *say* so!

XXXV.

PREJUDICE AGAINST COLOR.

It was a relief to my mind to see preparations for leaving the city. We went to Albany in the steamboat Knickerbocker. When the gong sounded for tea, Mrs. Bruce said, "Linda, it is late, and you and baby had better come to the table with me." I replied, "I know it is time baby had her supper, but I had rather not go with you, if you please. I am afraid of being insulted." "O no, not if you are with *me*," she said. I saw several white nurses go with their ladies, and I ventured to do the same. We were at the extreme end of the table. I was no sooner seated, than a gruff voice said, "Get up! You know you are not allowed to sit here." I looked up, and, to my astonishment and indignation, saw that the speaker was a colored man. If his office required him to enforce the by-laws of the boat, he might, at least, have done it politely. I replied, "I shall not get up, unless the captain comes and takes me up." No cup of tea was offered me, but Mrs. Bruce handed me hers and called for another. I looked to see whether the other nurses were treated in a similar manner. They were all properly waited on.

Next morning, when we stopped at Troy for breakfast, every body was making a rush for the table. Mrs. Bruce said, "Take my arm, Linda, and we'll go in together." The landlord heard her, and said, " Madam, will you allow your nurse and baby to take breakfast with my family?" I knew this was to be attributed to my complexion; but he spoke courteously, and therefore I did not mind it.

At Saratoga we found the United States Hotel crowded, and Mr. Bruce took one of the cottages belonging to the hotel. I had thought, with gladness, of going to the quiet of the country, where I should meet few people, but here I found myself in the midst of a swarm of Southerners. I looked round me with fear and trembling, dreading to see some one who would recognize me. I was rejoiced to find that we were to stay but a short time.

We soon returned to New York, to make arrangements for spending the remainder of the summer at Rockaway. While the laundress was putting the clothes in order, I took an opportunity to go over to Brooklyn to see Ellen. I met her going to a grocery store, and the first words she said, were, " O, mother, don't go to Mrs. Hobbs's. Her brother, Mr. Thorne, has come from the south, and may be he'll tell where you are." I accepted the warning. I told her I was going away with Mrs. Bruce the next day, and would try to see her when I came back.

Being in servitude to the Anglo-Saxon race, I was not put into a "Jim Crow car," on our way to Rockaway, neither was I invited to ride through the streets on the top of trunks in a truck; but every where I found the same manifestations of that cruel prejudice, which so discourages the feelings, and represses the energies of the colored people. We reached Rockaway before dark, and put up at the Pavilion—a large hotel, beautifully situated by the sea-side — a great resort of

the fashionable world.   Thirty or forty nurses were
there, of a great variety of nations.   Some of the ladies
had colored waiting-maids and coachmen, but I was
the only nurse tinged with the blood of Africa.   When
the tea bell rang, I took little Mary and followed the
other nurses.   Supper was served in a long hall.   A
young man, who had the ordering of things, took the
circuit of the table two or three times, and finally
pointed me to a seat at the lower end of it.   As there
was but one chair, I sat down and took the child in my
lap.   Whereupon the young man came to me and said,
in the blandest manner possible, " Will you please to
seat the little girl in the chair, and stand behind it and
feed her ?   After they have done, you will be shown to
the kitchen, where you will have a good supper."

This was the climax !   I found it hard to preserve
my self-control, when I looked round, and saw women
who were nurses, as I was, and only one shade lighter
in complexion, eyeing me with a defiant look, as if my
presence were a contamination.   However, I said
nothing.   I quietly took the child in my arms, went to
our room, and refused to go to the table again.   Mr.
Bruce ordered meals to be sent to the room for little
Mary and I.   This answered for a few days ; but the
waiters of the establishment were white, and they soon
began to complain, saying they were not hired to wait
on negroes.   The landlord requested Mr. Bruce to send
me down to my meals, because his servants rebelled
against bringing them up, and the colored servants of
other boarders were dissatisfied because all were not
treated alike.

My answer was that the colored servants ought to be

dissatisfied with *themselves*, for not having too much self-respect to submit to such treatment; that there was no difference in the price of board for colored and white servants, and there was no justification for difference of treatment. I staid a month after this, and finding I was resolved to stand up for my rights, they concluded to treat me well. Let every colored man and woman do this, and eventually we shall cease to be trampled under foot by our oppressors.

XXXVI.

THE HAIRBREADTH ESCAPE.

AFTER we returned to New York, I took the earliest opportunity to go and see Ellen. I asked to have her called down stairs; for I supposed Mrs. Hobbs's southern brother might still be there, and I was desirous to avoid seeing him, if possible. But Mrs. Hobbs came to the kitchen, and insisted on my going up stairs. "My brother wants to see you," said she, " and he is sorry you seem to shun him. He knows you are living in New York. He told me to say to you that he owes thanks to good old aunt Martha for too many little acts of kindness for him to be base enough to betray her grandchild."

This Mr. Thorne had become poor and reckless long before he left the south, and such persons had much rather go to one of the faithful old slaves to borrow a dollar, or get a good dinner, than to go to one whom they consider an equal. It was such acts of kindness as these for which he professed to feel grateful to my grandmother. I wished he had kept at a distance, but as he was here, and knew where I was, I concluded there was nothing to be gained by trying to avoid him; on the contrary, it might be the means of exciting his ill will. I followed his sister up stairs. He met me in a very friendly manner, congratulated me on my escape from slavery, and hoped I had a good place, where I felt happy.

I continued to visit Ellen as often as I could. She, good thoughtful child, never forgot my hazardous situation, but always kept a vigilant lookout for my safety. She never made any complaint about her own inconveniences and troubles; but a mother's observing eye easily perceived that she was not happy. On the occasion of one of my visits I found her unusually serious. When I asked her what was the matter, she said nothing was the matter. But I insisted upon knowing what made her look so very grave. Finally, I ascertained that she felt troubled about the dissipation that was continually going on in the house. Sho was sent to the store very often for rum and brandy, and she felt ashamed to ask for it so often; and Mr. Hobbs and Mr. Thorne drank a great deal, and their hands trembled so that they had to call her to pour out the liquor for them. "But for all that," said she, "Mr. Hobbs is good to me, and I can't help liking him. I feel sorry for him." I tried to comfort her, by telling her that I had laid up a hundred dollars, and that before long I hoped to be able to give her and Benjamin a home, and send them to school. She was always desirous not to add to my troubles more than she could help, and I did not discover till years afterwards that Mr. Thorne's intemperance was not the only annoyance she suffered from him. Though he professed too much gratitude to my grandmother to injure any of her descendants, he had poured vile language into the ears of her innocent great-grandchild.

I usually went to Brooklyn to spend Sunday afternoon. One Sunday, I found Ellen anxiously waiting for me near the house. "O, mother," said she, "I've been waiting for you this long time. I'm afraid Mr. Thorne has written to tell Dr. Flint where you are. Make haste and come in. Mrs. Hobbs will tell you all about it!"

The story was soon told. While the children were playing in the grape-vine arbor, the day before, Mr. Thorne came out with a letter in his hand, which he tore up and scattered about. Ellen was sweeping the yard at the time, and having her mind full of suspicions of him, she picked up the pieces and carried them to the children, saying, " I wonder who Mr. Thorne has been writing to."

" I'm sure I don't know, and don't care," replied the oldest of the children; " and I don't see how it concerns you."

" But it does concern me," replied Ellen; " for I'm afraid he's been writing to the south about my mother."

They laughed at her, and called her a silly thing, but good-naturedly put the fragments of writing together, in order to read them to her. They were no sooner arranged, than the little girl exclaimed, " I declare, Ellen, I believe you are right."

The contents of Mr. Thorne's letter, as nearly as I can remember, were as follows: " I have seen your slave, Linda, and conversed with her. She can be taken very easily, if you manage prudently. There are enough of us here to swear to her identity as your property. I am a patriot, a lover of my country, and I do this as an act of justice to the laws." He concluded by informing the doctor of the street and number where I lived. The children carried the pieces to Mrs. Hobbs, who immediately went to her brother's

room for an explanation. He was not to be found.
The servants said they saw him go out with a letter in
his hand, and they supposed he had gone to the post
office. The natural inference was, that he had sent
to Dr. Flint a copy of those fragments. When he
returned, his sister accused him of it, and he did not
deny the charge. He went immediately to his room,
and the next morning he was missing. He had gone
over to New York, before any of the family were astir.

It was evident that I had no time to lose; and I
hastened back to the city with a heavy heart. Again
I was to be torn from a comfortable home, and all my
plans for the welfare of my children were to be frustrated by that demon Slavery! I now regretted that
I never told Mrs. Bruce my story. I had not concealed it merely on account of being a fugitive; that
would have made her anxious, but it would have
excited sympathy in her kind heart. I valued her
good opinion, and I was afraid of losing it, if I told
her all the particulars of my sad story. But now I
felt that it was necessary for her to know how I was
situated. I had once left her abruptly, without explaining the reason, and it would not be proper to do
it again. I went home resolved to tell her in the
morning. But the sadness of my face attracted her
attention, and, in answer to her kind inquiries, I poured
out my full heart to her, before bed time. She listened
with true womanly sympathy, and told me she would do
all she could to protect me. How my heart blessed her!

Early the next morning, Judge Vanderpool and
Lawyer Hopper were consulted. They said I had better leave the city at once, as the risk would be great

if the case came to trial. Mrs. Bruce took me in a carriage to the house of one of her friends, where she assured me I should be safe until my brother could arrive, which would be in a few days. In the interval my thoughts were much occupied with Ellen. She was mine by birth, and she was also mine by Southern law, since my grandmother held the bill of sale that made her so. I did not feel that she was safe unless I had her with me. Mrs. Hobbs, who felt badly about her brother's treachery, yielded to my entreaties, on condition that she should return in ten days. I avoided making any promise. She came to me clad in very thin garments, all outgrown, and with a school satchel on her arm, containing a few articles. It was late in October, and I knew the child must suffer; and not daring to go out in the streets to purchase any thing, I took off my own flannel skirt and converted it into one for her. Kind Mrs. Bruce came to bid me good by, and when she saw that I had taken off my clothing for my child, the tears came to her eyes. She said, "Wait for me, Linda," and went out. She soon returned with a nice warm shawl and hood for Ellen. Truly, of such souls as hers are the kingdom of heaven.

My brother reached New York on Wednesday. Lawyer Hopper advised us to go to Boston by the Stonington route, as there was less Southern travel in that direction. Mrs. Bruce directed her servants to tell all inquirers that I formerly lived there, but had gone from the city.

We reached the steamboat Rhode Island in safety. That boat employed colored hands, but I knew that colored passengers were not admitted to the cabin. 1

was very desirous for the seclusion of the cabin, not
only on account of exposure to the night air, but also
to avoid observation.   Lawyer Hopper was waiting
on board for us.   He spoke to the stewardess, and
asked, as a particular favor, that she would treat us
well.   He said to me, " Go and speak to the captain
yourself by and by.   Take your little girl with you,
and I am sure that he will not let her sleep on deck."
With these kind words and a shake of the hand he
departed.

The boat was soon on her way, bearing me rapidly
from the friendly home where I had hoped to find
security and rest.   My brother had left me to purchase
the tickets, thinking that I might have better success
than he would.   When the stewardess came to me, I
paid what she asked, and she gave me three tickets
with clipped corners.   In the most unsophisticated
manner I said, " You have made a mistake ; I asked
you for cabin tickets.   I cannot possibly consent to sleep
on deck with my little daughter."   She assured me
there was no mistake.   She said on some of the routes
colored people were allowed to sleep in the cabin, but
not on this route, which was much travelled by the
wealthy.   I asked her to show me to the captain's
office, and she said she would after tea.   When the
time came, I took Ellen by the hand and went to the
captain, politely requesting him to change our tickets,
as we should be very uncomfortable on deck.   He said
it was contrary to their custom, but he would see that
we had berths below ; he would also try to obtain comfortable seats for us in the cars ; of that he was not
certain, but he would speak to the conductor about it,

when the boat arrived. I thanked him, and returned to the ladies' cabin. He came afterwards and told me that the conductor of the cars was on board, that he had spoken to him, and he had promised to take care of us. I was very much surprised at receiving so much kindness. I don't know whether the pleasing face of my little girl had won his heart, or whether the stewardess inferred from Lawyer Hopper's manner that I was a fugitive, and had pleaded with him in my behalf.

When the boat arrived at Stonington, the conductor kept his promise, and showed us to seats in the first car, nearest the engine. He asked us to take seats next the door, but as he passed through, we ventured to move on toward the other end of the car. No incivility was offered us, and we reached Boston in safety.

The day after my arrival was one of the happiest of my life. I felt as if I was beyond the reach of the bloodhounds; and, for the first time during many years, I had both my children together with me. They greatly enjoyed their reunion, and laughed and chatted merrily. I watched them with a swelling heart. Their every motion delighted me.

I could not feel safe in New York, and I accepted the offer of a friend, that we should share expenses and keep house together. I represented to Mrs. Hobbs that Ellen must have some schooling, and must remain with me for that purpose. She felt ashamed of being unable to read or spell at her age, so instead of sending her to school with Benny, I instructed her myself till she was fitted to enter an intermediate school. The winter passed pleasantly, while I was busy with my needle, and my children with their books.

XXXVII.

A VISIT TO ENGLAND.

In the spring, sad news came to me. Mrs. Bruce was dead. Never again, in this world, should I see her gentle face, or hear her sympathizing voice. I had lost an excellent friend, and little Mary had lost a tender mother. Mr. Bruce wished the child to visit some of her mother's relatives in England, and he was desirous that I should take charge of her. The little motherless one was accustomed to me, and attached to me, and I thought she would be happier in my care than in that of a stranger. I could also earn more in this way than I could by my needle. So I put Benny to a trade, and left Ellen to remain in the house with my friend and go to school.

We sailed from New York, and arrived in Liverpool after a pleasant voyage of twelve days. We proceeded directly to London, and took lodgings at the Adelaide Hotel. The supper seemed to me less luxurious than those I had seen in American hotels; but my situation was indescribably more pleasant. For the first time in my life I was in a place where I was treated according to my deportment, without reference to my complexion. I felt as if a great millstone had been lifted from my breast. Ensconced in a pleasant room, with my dear little charge, I laid my head on my pillow, for the first time, with the delightful consciousness of pure, unadulterated freedom.

As I had constant care of the child, I had little opportunity to see the wonders of that great city; but I watched the tide of life that flowed through the streets, and found it a strange contrast to the stagnation in our Southern towns. Mr. Bruce took his little daughter to spend some days with friends in Oxford Crescent, and of course it was necessary for me to accompany her. I had heard much of the systematic method of English education, and I was very desirous that my dear Mary should steer straight in the midst of so much propriety. I closely observed her little playmates and their nurses, being ready to take any lessons in the science of good management. The children were more rosy than American children, but I did not see that they differed materially in other respects. They were like all children — sometimes docile and sometimes wayward.

We next went to Steventon, in Berkshire. It was a small town, said to be the poorest in the county. I saw men working in the fields for six shillings, and seven shillings, a week, and women for sixpence, and sevenpence, a day, out of which they boarded themselves. Of course they lived in the most primitive manner; it could not be otherwise, where a woman's wages for an entire day were not sufficient to buy a pound of meat. They paid very low rents, and their clothes were made of the cheapest fabrics, though much better than could have been procured in the United States for the same money. I had heard much about the oppression of the poor in Europe. The people I saw around me were, many of them, among the poorest poor. But when I visited them in their little thatched cottages, I felt that

the condition of even the meanest and most ignorant
among them was vastly superior to the condition of the
most favored slaves in America. They labored hard;
but they were not ordered out to toil while the stars
were in the sky, and driven and slashed by an overseer, through heat and cold, till the stars shone out
again. Their homes were very humble; but they were
protected by law. No insolent patrols could come, in
the dead of night, and flog them at their pleasure.
The father, when he closed his cottage door, felt safe
with his family around him. No master or overseer
could come and take from him his wife, or his daughter. They must separate to earn their living; but the
parents knew where their children were going, and
could communicate with them by letters. The relations of husband and wife, parent and child, were too
sacred for the richest noble in the land to violate with
impunity. Much was being done to enlighten these
poor people. Schools were established among them,
and benevolent societies were active in efforts to amel-
iorate their condition. There was no law forbidding
them to learn to read and write; and if they helped
each other in spelling out the Bible, they were in no
danger of thirty-nine lashes, as was the case with myself and poor, pious, old uncle Fred. I repeat that the
most ignorant and the most destitute of these peasants
was a thousand fold better off than the most pampered
American slave.

I do not deny that the poor are oppressed in Europe.
I am not disposed to paint their condition so rose-
colored as the Hon. Miss Murray paints the condition
of the slaves in the United States. A small portion

of *my* experience would enable her to read her own pages with anointed eyes. If she were to lay aside her title, and, instead of visiting among the fashionable, become domesticated, as a poor governess, on some plantation in Louisiana or Alabama, she would see and hear things that would make her tell quite a different story.

My visit to England is a memorable event in my life, from the fact of my having there received strong religious impressions. The contemptuous manner in which the communion had been administered to colored people, in my native place; the church membership of Dr. Flint, and others like him; and the buying and selling of slaves, by professed ministers of the gospel, had given me a prejudice against the Episcopal church. The whole service seemed to me a mockery and a sham. But my home in Steventon was in the family of a clergyman, who was a true disciple of Jesus. The beauty of his daily life inspired me with faith in the genuineness of Christian professions. Grace entered my heart, and I knelt at the communion table, I trust, in true humility of soul.

I remained abroad ten months, which was much longer than I had anticipated. During all that time, I never saw the slightest symptom of prejudice against color. Indeed, I entirely forgot it, till the time came for us to return to America.

XXXVIII.

RENEWED INVITATIONS TO GO SOUTH.

We had a tedious winter passage, and from the distance spectres seemed to rise up on the shores of the United States. It is a sad feeling to be afraid of one's native country. We arrived in New York safely, and I hastened to Boston to look after my children. I found Ellen well, and improving at her school; but Benny was not there to welcome me. He had been left at a good place to learn a trade, and for several months every thing worked well. He was liked by the master, and was a favorite with his fellow-apprentices; but one day they accidentally discovered a fact they had never before suspected — that he was colored! This at once transformed him into a different being. Some of the apprentices were Americans, others American-born Irish; and it was offensive to their dignity to have a "nigger" among them, after they had been told that he *was* a "nigger." They began by treating him with silent scorn, and finding that he returned the same, they resorted to insults and abuse. He was too spirited a boy to stand that, and he went off. Being desirous to do something to support himself, and having no one to advise him, he shipped for a whaling voyage. When I received these tidings I shed many tears, and bitterly reproached myself for having left him so long. But I had done it for the best, and now all I could do was to pray to the heavenly Father to guide and protect him.

Not long after my return, I received the following letter from Miss Emily Flint, now Mrs. Dodge : —

" In this you will recognize the hand of your friend and mistress. Having heard that you had gone with a family to Europe, I have waited to hear of your return to write to you. I should have answered the letter you wrote to me long since, but as I could not then act independently of my father, I knew there could be nothing done satisfactory to you. There were persons here who were willing to buy you and run the risk of getting you. To this I would not consent. I have always been attached to you, and would not like to see you the slave of another, or have unkind treatment. I am married now, and can protect you. My husband expects to move to Virginia this spring, where we think of settling. I am very anxious that you should come and live with me. If you are not willing to come, you may purchase yourself; but I should prefer having you live with me. If you come, you may, if you like, spend a month with your grandmother and friends, then come to me in Norfolk, Virginia. Think this over, and write as soon as possible, and let me know the conclusion. Hoping that your children are well, I remain you friend and mistress."

Of course I did not write to return thanks for this cordial invitation. I felt insulted to be thought stupid enough to be caught by such professions.

" ' Come up into my parlor,' said the spider to the fly ;
' ' Tis the prettiest little parlor that ever you did spy.' "

It was plain that Dr. Flint's family were apprised of my movements, since they knew of my voyage to Europe. I expected to have further trouble from them; but having eluded them thus far, I hoped to be as successful in future. The money I had earned, I was desirous to devote to the education of my children, and to secure a home for them. It seemed not only hard, but unjust, to pay for myself. I could not possibly regard myself as a piece of property. Moreover, I had worked many years without wages, and during that time had been obliged to depend on my grandmother for many comforts in food and clothing. My children certainly belonged to me; but though Dr. Flint had incurred no expense for their support, he had received a large sum of money for them. I knew the law would decide that I was his property, and would probably still give his daughter a claim to my children; but I regarded such laws as the regulations of robbers, who had no rights that I was bound to respect.

The Fugitive Slave Law had not then passed. The judges of Massachusetts had not then stooped under chains to enter her courts of justice, so called. I knew my old master was rather skittish of Massachusetts. I relied on her love of freedom, and felt safe on her soil. I am now aware that I honored the old Commonwealth beyond her deserts.

24 *

XXXIX.

THE CONFESSION.

For two years my daughter and I supported ourselves comfortably in Boston.   At the end of that
time, my brother William offered to send Ellen to a
boarding school.   It required a great effort for me to
consent to part with her, for I had few near ties, and
it was her presence that made my two little rooms seem
home-like.   But my judgment prevailed over my selfish feelings.   I made preparations for her departure.
During the two years we had lived together I had
often resolved to tell her something about her father ;
but I had never been able to muster sufficient courage.
I had a shrinking dread of diminishing my child's
love.   I knew she must have curiosity on the subject,
but she had never asked a question.   She was always
very careful not to say any thing to remind me, of my
troubles.   Now that she was going from me, I thought
if I should die before she returned, she might hear
my story from some one who did not understand the
palliating circumstances ; and that if she were entirely
ignorant on the subject, her sensitive nature might
receive a rude shock.

When we retired for the night, she said, " Mother,
it is very hard to leave you alone.   I am almost sorry
I am going, though I do want to improve myself.
But you will write to me often ; won't you, mother ? "

I did not throw my arms round her.   I did not answer her. But in a calm, solemn way, for it cost me great effort, I said, " Listen to me, Ellen ; I have something to tell you ! " I recounted my early sufferings in slavery, and told her how nearly they had crushed me. I began to tell her how they had driven me into a great sin, when she clasped me in her arms, and exclaimed, " O, don't, mother ! Please don't tell me any more."

I said, " But, my child, I want you to know about your father."

" I know all about it, mother," she replied; " I am nothing to my father, and he is nothing to me. All my love is for you. I was with him five months in Washington, and he never cared for me. He never spoke to me as he did to his little Fanny. I knew all the time he was my father, for Fanny's nurse told me so ; but she said I must never tell any body, and I never did. I used to wish he would take me in his arms and kiss me, as he did Fanny ; or that he would sometimes smile at me, as he did at her. I thought if he was my own father, he ought to love me. I was a little girl then, and didn't know any better. But now I never think any thing about my father. All my love is for you." She hugged me closer as she spoke, and I thanked God that the knowledge I had so much dreaded to impart had not diminished the affection of my child. I had not the slightest idea she knew that portion of my history. If I had, I should have spoken to her long before ; for my pent-up feelings had often longed to pour themselves out to some one I could trust. But I loved the dear girl better for the delicacy she had manifested towards her unfortunate mother.

The next morning, she and her uncle started on their journey to the village in New York, where she was to be placed at school. It seemed as if all the sunshine had gone away. My little room was dreadfully lonely. I was thankful when a message came from a lady, accustomed to employ me, requesting me to come and sew in her family for several weeks. On my return, I found a letter from brother William. He thought of opening an anti-slavery reading room in Rochester, and combining with it the sale of some books and stationery ; and he wanted me to unite with him. We tried it, but it was not successful. We found warm anti-slavery friends there, but the feeling was not general enough to support such an establishment. I passed nearly a year in the family of Isaac and Amy Post, practical believers in the Christian doctrine of human brotherhood. They measured a man's worth by his character, not by his complexion. The memory of those beloved and honored friends will remain with me to my latest hour.

and as for the system of slavery, she had a most hearty
dislike of it. No sophistry of Southerners could blind
her to its enormity. She was a person of excellent
principles and a noble heart. To me, from that hour
to the present, she has been a true and sympathizing
friend. Blessings be with her and hers!

About the time that I reëntered the Bruce family,
an event occurred of disastrous import to the colored
people. The slave Hamlin, the first fugitive that came
under the new law, was given up by the bloodhounds
of the north to the bloodhounds of the south. It was
the beginning of a reign of terror to the colored popu-
lation. The great city rushed on in its whirl of excitement, taking no note of the "short and simple
annals of the poor." But while fashionables were
listening to the thrilling voice of Jenny Lind in Met-
ropolitan Hall, the thrilling voices of poor hunted
colored people went up, in an agony of supplication, to
the Lord, from Zion's church. Many families, who had
lived in the city for twenty years, fled from it now.
Many a poor washerwoman, who, by hard labor, had
made herself a comfortable home, was obliged to sacrifice her furniture, bid a hurried farewell to friends,
and seek her fortune among strangers in Canada.
Many a wife discovered a secret she had never known
before — that her husband was a fugitive, and must
leave her to insure his own safety. Worse still, many
a husband discovered that his wife had fled from slavery years ago, and as " the child follows the condition
of its mother," the children of his love were liable to
be seized and carried into slavery. Every where, in
those humble homes, there was consternation and

anguish. But what cared the legislators of the "dominant race" for the blood they were crushing out of trampled hearts?

When my brother William spent his last evening with me, before he went to California, we talked nearly all the time of the distress brought on our oppressed people by the passage of this iniquitous law; and never had I seen him manifest such bitterness of spirit, such stern hostility to our oppressors. He was himself free from the operation of the law; for he did not run from any Slaveholding State, being brought into the Free States by his master. But I was subject to it; and so were hundreds of intelligent and industrious people all around us. I seldom ventured into the streets; and when it was necessary to do an errand for Mrs. Bruce, or any of the family, I went as much as possible through back streets and by-ways. What a disgrace to a city calling itself free, that inhabitants, guiltless of offence, and seeking to perform their duties conscientiously, should be condemned to live in such incessant fear, and have nowhere to turn for protection! This state of things, of course, gave rise to many impromptu vigilance committees. Every colored person, and every friend of their persecuted race, kept their eyes wide open. Every evening I examined the newspapers carefully, to see what Southerners had put up at the hotels. I did this for my own sake, thinking my young mistress and her husband might be among the list; I wished also to give information to others, if necessary; for if many were "running to and fro," I resolved that "knowledge should be increased."

This brings up one of my Southern reminiscences,

which I will here briefly relate. I was somewhat acquainted with a slave named Luke, who belonged to a
wealthy man in our vicinity. His master died, leaving
a son and daughter heirs to his large fortune. In the
division of the slaves, Luke was included in the son's
portion. This young man became a prey to the vices
growing out of the "patriarchal institution," and when
he went to the north, to complete his education, he
carried his vices with him. He was brought home, deprived of the use of his limbs, by excessive dissipation.
Luke was appointed to wait upon his bed-ridden master, whose despotic habits were greatly increased by
exasperation at his own helplessness. He kept a cowhide beside him, and, for the most trivial occurrence,
he would order his attendant to bare his back, and
kneel beside the couch, while he whipped him till his
strength was exhausted. Some days he was not allowed to wear any thing but his shirt, in order to be
in readiness to be flogged. A day seldom passed without his receiving more or less blows. If the slightest
resistance was offered, the town constable was sent for
to execute the punishment, and Luke learned from
experience how much more the constable's strong arm
was to be dreaded than the comparatively feeble one
of his master. The arm of his tyrant grew weaker,
and was finally palsied ; and then the constable's services were in constant requisition. The fact that he
was entirely dependent on Luke's care, and was obliged
to be tended like an infant, instead of inspiring any
gratitude or compassion towards his poor slave, seemed
only to increase his irritability and cruelty. As he
lay there on his bed, a mere degraded wreck of man-

hood, he took into his head the strangest freaks of despotism; and if Luke hesitated to submit to his orders, the constable was immediately sent for. Some of these freaks were of a nature too filthy to be repeated. When I fled from the house of bondage, I left poor Luke still chained to the bedside of this cruel and disgusting wretch.

One day, when I had been requested to do an errand for Mrs. Bruce, I was hurrying through back streets, as usual, when I saw a young man approaching, whose face was familiar to me. As he came nearer, I recognized Luke. I always rejoiced to see or hear of any one who had escaped from the black pit; but, remembering this poor fellow's extreme hardships, I was peculiarly glad to see him on Northern soil, though I no longer called it *free* soil. I well remembered what a desolate feeling it was to be alone among strangers, and I went up to him and greeted him cordially. At first, he did not know me; but when I mentioned my name, he remembered all about me. I told him of the Fugitive Slave Law, and asked him if he did not know that New York was a city of kidnappers.

He replied, "De risk ain't so bad for me, as 'tis fur you. 'Cause I runned away from de speculator, and you runned away from de massa. Dem speculators vont spen dar money to come here fur a runaway, if dey ain't sartin sure to put dar hans right on him. An I tell you I's tuk good car 'bout dat. I had too hard times down dar, to let 'em ketch dis nigger."

He then told me of the advice he had received, and the plans he had laid. I asked if he had money enough to take him to Canada. "'Pend upon it, I

25

hab," he replied. "I tuk car fur dat. I'd bin workin all my days fur dem cussed whites, an got no pay but kicks and cuffs. So I tought dis nigger had a right to money nuff to bring him to de Free States. Massa Henry he lib till ebery body vish him dead; an ven he did die, I knowed de debbil would hab him, an vouldn't vant him to bring his money 'long too. So I tuk some of his bills, and put 'em in de pocket of his ole trousers. An ven he was buried, dis nigger ask fur dem ole trousers, an dey gub 'em to me." With a low, chuckling laugh, he added, "You see I didn't *steal* it; dey *gub* it to me. I tell you, I had mighty hard time to keep de speculator from findin it; but he didn't git it."

This is a fair specimen of how the moral sense is educated by slavery. When a man has his wages stolen from him, year after year, and the laws sanction and enforce the theft, how can he be expected to have more regard to honesty than has the man who robs him? I have become somewhat enlightened, but I confess that I agree with poor, ignorant, much-abused Luke, in thinking he had a *right* to that money, as a portion of his unpaid wages. He went to Canada forthwith, and I have not since heard from him.

All that winter I lived in a state of anxiety. When I took the children out to breathe the air, I closely observed the countenances of all I met. I dreaded the approach of summer, when snakes and slaveholders make their appearance. I was, in fact, a slave in New York, as subject to slave laws as I had been in a Slave State. Strange incongruity in a State called free!

Spring returned, and I received warning from the

south that Dr. Flint knew of my return to my old place, and was making preparations to have me caught. I learned afterwards that my dress, and that of Mrs. Bruce's children, had been described to him by some of the Northern tools, which slaveholders employ for their base purposes, and then indulge in sneers at their cupidity and mean servility.

I immediately informed Mrs. Bruce of my danger, and she took prompt measures for my safety. My place as nurse could not be supplied immediately, and this generous, sympathizing lady proposed that I should carry her baby away. It was a comfort to me to have the child with me; for the heart is reluctant to be torn away from every object it loves. But how few mothers would have consented to have one of their own babes become a fugitive, for the sake of a poor, hunted nurse, on whom the legislators of the country had let loose the bloodhounds! When I spoke of the sacrifice she was making, in depriving herself of her dear baby, she replied, "It is better for you to have baby with you, Linda; for if they get on your track, they will be obliged to bring the child to me; and then, if there is a possibility of saving you, you shall be saved."

This lady had a very wealthy relative, a benevolent gentleman in many respects, but aristocratic and pro-slavery. He remonstrated with her for harboring a fugitive slave; told her she was violating the laws of her country; and asked her if she was aware of the penalty. She replied, "I am very well aware of it. It is imprisonment and one thousand dollars fine. Shame on my country that it *is* so! I am ready to incur the penalty. I will go to the state's prison, rather than have any poor victim torn from *my* house, to be carried back to slavery."

The noble heart! The brave heart! The tears are in my eyes while I write of her. May the God of the helpless reward her for her sympathy with my persecuted people!

I was sent into New England, where I was sheltered by the wife of a senator, whom I shall always hold in grateful remembrance. This honorable gentleman would not have voted for the Fugitive Slave Law, as did the senator in "Uncle Tom's Cabin;" on the contrary, he was strongly opposed to it; but he was enough under its influence to be afraid of having me remain in his house many hours. So I was sent into the country, where I remained a month with the baby. When it was supposed that Dr. Flint's emissaries had lost track of me, and given up the pursuit for the present, I returned to New York.

XLI.

FREE AT LAST.

Mrs. Bruce, and every member of her family, were exceedingly kind to me. I was thankful for the blessings of my lot, yet I could not always wear a cheerful countenance. I was doing harm to no one; on the contrary, I was doing all the good I could in my small way; yet I could never go out to breathe God's free air without trepidation at my heart. This seemed hard; and I could not think it was a right state of things in any civilized country.

From time to time I received news from my good old grandmother. She could not write; but she employed others to write for her. The following is an extract from one of her last letters: —

"Dear Daughter: I cannot hope to see you again on earth; but I pray to God to unite us above, where pain will no more rack this feeble body of mine; where sorrow and parting from my children will be no more. God has promised these things if we are faithful unto the end. My age and feeble health deprive me of going to church now; but God is with me here at home. Thank your brother for his kindness. Give much love to him, and tell him to remember the Creator in the days of his youth, and strive to meet me in the Father's kingdom. Love to Ellen and Benjamin. Don't neglect him. Tell him for me, to be a good boy. Strive, my child; to train them for God's

25 *

children. May he protect and provide for you, is the
prayer of your loving old mother."

These letters both cheered and saddened me. I was
always glad to have tidings from the kind, faithful old
friend of my unhappy youth; but her messages of
love made my heart yearn to see her before she died,
and I mourned over the fact that it was impossible.
Some months after I returned from my flight to New
England, I received a letter from her, in which she
wrote, " Dr. Flint is dead. He has left a distressed
family. Poor old man ! I hope he made his peace
with God."

I remembered how he had defrauded my grandmother of the hard earnings she had loaned; how he
had tried to cheat her out of the freedom her mistress
had promised her, and how he had persecuted her children; and I thought to myself that she was a better
Christian than I was, if she could entirely forgive him.
I cannot say, with truth, that the news of my old
master's death softened my feelings towards him.
There are wrongs which even the grave does not bury.
The man was odious to me while he lived, and his
memory is odious now.

His departure from this world did not diminish my
danger. He had threatened my grandmother that his
heirs should hold me in slavery after he was gone;
that I never should be free so long as a child of his
survived. As for Mrs. Flint, I had seen her in deeper
afflictions than I supposed the loss of her husband
would be, for she had buried several children; yet I
never saw any signs of softening in her heart. The
doctor had died in embarrassed circumstances, and had

little to will to his heirs, except such property as he was unable to grasp. I was well aware what I had to expect from the family of Flints; and my fears were confirmed by a letter from the south, warning me to be on my guard, because Mrs. Flint openly declared that her daughter could not afford to lose so valuable a slave as I was.

I kept close watch of the newspapers for arrivals; but one Saturday night, being much occupied, I forgot to examine the Evening Express as usual. I went down into the parlor for it, early in the morning, and found the boy about to kindle a fire with it. I took it from him and examined the list of arrivals. Reader, if you have never been a slave, you cannot imagine the acute sensation of suffering at my heart, when I read the names of Mr. and Mrs. Dodge, at a hotel in Courtland Street. It was a third-rate hotel, and that circumstance convinced me of the truth of what I had heard, that they were short of funds and had need of my value, as *they* valued me; and that was by dollars and cents. I hastened with the paper to Mrs. Bruce. Her heart and hand were always open to every one in distress, and she always warmly sympathized with mine. It was impossible to tell how near the enemy was. He might have passed and repassed the house while we were sleeping. He might at that moment be waiting to pounce upon me if I ventured out of doors. I had never seen the husband of my young mistress, and therefore I could not distinguish him from any other stranger. A carriage was hastily ordered; and, closely veiled, I followed Mrs. Bruce, taking the baby again with me into exile. After various turnings and cross-ings, and returnings, the carriage stopped at the house of one of Mrs. Bruce's friends, where I was kindly received. Mrs. Bruce returned immediately, to instruct the domestics what to say if any one came to inquire for me.

It was lucky for me that the evening paper was not burned up before I had a chance to examine the list of arrivals. It was not long after Mrs. Bruce's return to her house, before several people came to inquire for me. One inquired for me, another asked for my daughter Ellen, and another said he had a letter from my grandmother, which he was requested to deliver in person.

They were told, " She *has* lived here, but she has left."

" How long ago ? "

" I don't know, sir."

" Do you know where she went ? "

" I do not, sir." And the door was closed.

This Mr. Dodge, who claimed me as his property, was originally a Yankee pedler in the south ; then he became a merchant, and finally a slaveholder. He managed to get introduced into what was called the first society, and married Miss Emily Flint. A quarrel arose between him and her brother, and the brother cowhided him. This led to a family feud, and he proposed to remove to Virginia. Dr. Flint left him no property, and his own means had become circumscribed, while a wife and children depended upon him for support. Under these circumstances, it was very natural that he should make an effort to put me into his pocket.

I had a colored friend, a man from my native place, in whom I had the most implicit confidence. I sent for him, and told him that Mr. and Mrs. Dodge had arrived in New York. I proposed that he should call upon them to make inquiries about his friends at the south, with whom Dr. Flint's family were well acquainted. He thought there was no impropriety in his doing so, and he consented. He went to the hotel, and knocked at the door of Mr. Dodge's room, which was opened by the gentleman himself, who gruffly inquired, "What brought you here? How came you to know I was in the city?"

"Your arrival was published in the evening papers, sir; and I called to ask Mrs. Dodge about my friends at home. I didn't suppose it would give any offence."

"Where's that negro girl, that belongs to my wife?"

"What girl, sir?"

"You know well enough. I mean Linda, that ran away from Dr. Flint's plantation, some years ago. I dare say you've seen her, and know where she is."

"Yes, sir, I've seen her, and know where she is. She is out of your reach, sir."

"Tell me where she is, or bring her to me, and I will give her a chance to buy her freedom."

"I don't think it would be of any use, sir. I have heard her say she would go to the ends of the earth, rather than pay any man or woman for her freedom, because she thinks she has a right to it. Besides, she couldn't do it, if she would, for she has spent her earnings to educate her children."

This made Mr. Dodge very angry, and some high words passed between them. My friend was afraid to come where I was; but in the course of the day I received a note from him. I supposed they had not come from the south, in the winter, for a pleasure excursion; and now the nature of their business was very plain.

Mrs. Bruce came to me and entreated me to leave the city the next morning. She said her house was watched, and it was possible that some clew to me might be obtained. I refused to take her advice. She pleaded with an earnest tenderness, that ought to have moved me; but I was in a bitter, disheartened mood. I was weary of flying from pillar to post. I had been chased during half my life, and it seemed as if the chase was never to end. There I sat, in that great city, guiltless of crime, yet not daring to worship God in any of the churches. I heard the bells ringing for afternoon service, and, with contemptuous sarcasm, I said, " Will the preachers take for their text, ' Proclaim liberty to the captive, and the opening of prison doors to them that are bound ' ? or will they preach from the text, ' Do unto others as ye would they should do to you ' ? " Oppressed Poles and Hungarians could find a safe refuge in that city; John Mitchell was free to proclaim in the City Hall his desire for " a plantation well stocked with slaves ;" but there I sat, an oppressed American, not daring to show my face. God forgive the black and bitter thoughts I indulged on that Sabbath day! The Scripture says, " Oppression makes even a wise man mad ;" and I was not wise.

I had been told that Mr. Dodge said his wife had never signed away her right to my children, and if he could not get me, he would take them. This it was, more

than any thing else, that roused such a tempest in my
soul. Benjamin was with his uncle William in California, but my innocent young daughter had come to
spend a vacation with me. I thought of what I had
suffered in slavery at her age, and my heart was like a
tiger's when a hunter tries to seize her young.

Dear Mrs. Bruce! I seem to see the expression of
her face, as she turned away discouraged by my obstinate mood. Finding her expostulations unavailing, she
sent Ellen to entreat me. When ten o'clock in the
evening arrived and Ellen had not returned, this watchful and unwearied friend became anxious. She came
to us in a carriage, bringing a well-filled trunk for my
journey — trusting that by this time I would listen to
reason. I yielded to her, as I ought to have done
before.

The next day, baby and I set out in a heavy snow
storm, bound for New England again. I received letters from the City of Iniquity, addressed to me under
an assumed name. In a few days one came from Mrs.
Bruce, informing me that my new master was still
searching for me, and that she intended to put an end
to this persecution by buying my freedom. I felt grateful for the kindness that prompted this offer, but the
idea was not so pleasant to me as might have been
expected. The more my mind had become enlightened,
the more difficult it was for me to consider myself an
article of property; and to pay money to those who
had so grievously oppressed me seemed like taking
from my sufferings the glory of triumph. I wrote to
Mrs. Bruce, thanking her, but saying that being sold
from one owner to another seemed too much like

slavery; that such a great obligation could not be easily cancelled; and that I preferred to go to my brother in California.

Without my knowledge, Mrs. Bruce employed a gentleman in New York to enter into negotiations with Mr. Dodge. He proposed to pay three hundred dollars down, if Mr. Dodge would sell me, and enter into obligations to relinquish all claim to me or my children forever after. He who called himself my master said he scorned so small an offer for such a valuable servant. The gentleman replied, " You can do as you choose, sir. If you reject this offer you will never get any thing; for the woman has friends who will convey her and her children out of the country."

Mr. Dodge concluded that "half a loaf was better than no bread," and he agreed to the proffered terms. By the next mail I received this brief letter from Mrs. Bruce : " I am rejoiced to tell you that the money for your freedom has been paid to Mr. Dodge. Come home to-morrow. I long to see you and my sweet babe."

My brain reeled as I read these lines. A gentleman near me said, " It's true ; I have seen the bill of sale." " The bill of sale ! " Those words struck me like a blow. So I was *sold* at last ! A human being *sold* in the free city of New York ! The bill of sale is on record, and future generations will learn from it that women were articles of traffic in New York, late in the nineteenth century of the Christian religion. It may hereafter prove a useful document to antiquaries, who are seeking to measure the progress of civilization in the United States. I well know the value of that bit of paper; but much as I love freedom, I do not like to look upon it. I am deeply grateful to the generous friend who procured it, but I despise the miscreant who demanded payment for what never rightfully belonged to him or his.

I had objected to having my freedom bought, yet I must confess that when it was done I felt as if a heavy load had been lifted from my weary shoulders. When I rode home in the cars I was no longer afraid to unveil my face and look at people as they passed. I should have been glad to have met Daniel Dodge himself; to have had him seen me and known me, that he might have mourned over the untoward circumstances which compelled him to sell me for three hundred dollars.

When I reached home, the arms of my benefactress were thrown round me, and our tears mingled. As soon as she could speak, she said, "O Linda, I'm *so* glad it's all over! You wrote to me as if you thought you were going to be transferred from one owner to another. But I did not buy you for your services. I should have done just the same, if you had been going to sail for California to-morrow. I should, at least, have the satisfaction of knowing that you left me a free woman."

My heart was exceedingly full. I remembered how my poor father had tried to buy me, when I was a small child, and how he had been disappointed. I hoped his spirit was rejoicing over me now. I remembered how my good old grandmother had laid up her earnings to purchase me in later years, and how often her plans had been frustrated. How that faithful, loving old heart would leap for joy, if she could look on me and

26

my children now that we were free !   My relatives had been foiled in all their efforts, but God had raised me up a friend among strangers, who had bestowed on me the precious, long-desired boon.   Friend !   It is a common word, often lightly used.   Like other good and beautiful things, it may be tarnished by careless handling ; but when I speak of Mrs. Bruce as my friend, the word is sacred.

My grandmother lived to rejoice in my freedom ; but not long after, a letter came with a black seal.   She had gone " where the wicked cease from troubling, and the weary are at rest."

Time passed on, and a paper came to me from the south, containing an obituary notice of my uncle Phillip.   It was the only case I ever knew of such an honor conferred upon a colored person.   It was written by one of his friends, and contained these words : " Now that death has laid him low, they call him a good man and a useful citizen ; but what are eulogies to the black man, when the world has faded from his vision ?   It does not require man's praise to obtain rest in God's kingdom."   So they called a colored man a *citizen !*   Strange words to be uttered in that region !

Reader, my story ends with freedom ; not in the usual way, with marriage.   I and my children are now free !   We are as free from the power of slaveholders as are the white people of the north ; and though that, according to my ideas, is not saying a great deal, it is a vast improvement in *my* condition.   The dream of my life is not yet realized.   I do not sit with my children in a home of my own.   I still long for a hearthstone of my own, however humble.   I wish it for my children's sake far more than for my own. But God so orders circumstances as to keep me with my friend Mrs. Bruce. Love, duty, gratitude, also bind me to her side. It is a privilege to serve her who pities my oppressed people, and who has bestowed the inestimable boon of freedom on me and my children.

It has been painful to me, in many ways, to recall the dreary years I passed in bondage. I would gladly forget them if I could. Yet the retrospection is not altogether without solace; for with those gloomy recollections come tender memories of my good old grandmother, like light, fleecy clouds floating over a dark and troubled sea.

Appendix.

THE following statement is from Amy Post, a member of the Society of Friends in the State of New York, well known and highly respected by friends of the poor and the oppressed. As has been already stated, in the preceding pages, the author of this volume spent some time under her hospitable roof.   L. M. C.

"The author of this book is my highly-esteemed friend. If its readers knew her as I know her, they could not fail to be deeply interested in her story. She was a beloved inmate of our family nearly the whole of the year 1849. She was introduced to us by her affectionate and conscientious brother, who had previously related to us some of the almost incredible events in his sister's life. I immediately became much interested in Linda; for her appearance was prepossessing, and her deportment indicated remarkable delicacy of feeling and purity of thought.

"As we became acquainted, she related to me, from time to time some of the incidents in her bitter experiences as a slave-woman. Though impelled by a natural craving for human sympathy, she passed through a baptism of suffering, even in recounting her trials to me, in private confidential conversations. The burden of these memories lay heavily upon her spirit — naturally virtuous and refined. I repeatedly urged her to consent to the publication of her narrative; for I felt that it would arouse people to a more earnest work for the disinthralment of millions still remaining in that soul-crushing condition, which was so unendurable to her. But her sensitive spirit shrank from publicity. She said, 'You

(304)

know a woman can whisper her cruel wrongs in the ear of a dear friend much easier than she can record them for the world to read.' Even in talking with me, she wept so much, and seemed to suffer such mental agony, that I felt her story was too sacred to be drawn from her by inquisitive questions, and I left her free to tell as much, or as little, as she chose. Still, I urged upon her the duty of publishing her experience, for the sake of the good it might do; and, at last, she undertook the task.

"Having been a slave so large a portion of her life, she is unlearned; she is obliged to earn her living by her own labor, and she has worked untiringly to procure education for her children; several times she has been obliged to leave her employments, in order to fly from the man-hunters and woman-hunters of our land; but she pressed through all these obstacles and overcame them. After the labors of the day were over, she traced secretly and wearily, by the midnight lamp, a truthful record of her eventful life.

"This Empire State is a shabby place of refuge for the oppressed; but here, through anxiety, turmoil, and despair, the freedom of Linda and her children was finally secured, by the exertions of a generous friend. She was grateful for the boon; but the idea of having been *bought* was always galling to a spirit that could never acknowledge itself to be a chattel. She wrote to us thus, soon after the event: 'I thank you for your kind expressions in regard to my freedom; but the freedom I had before the money was paid was dearer to me. God gave me *that* freedom; but man put God's image in the scales with the paltry sum of three hundred dollars. I served for my liberty as faithfully as Jacob served for Rachel. At the end, he had large possessions; but I was robbed of my victory; I was obliged to resign my crown, to rid myself of a tyrant.'

"Her story, as written by herself, cannot fail to interest the reader. It is a sad illustration of the condition of this country, which boasts of its civilization, while it sanctions laws and customs which make the experiences of the present more strange than any fictions of the past.

AMY POST.

"ROCHESTER, N. Y., Oct. 30th, 1859."

26 *

The following testimonial is from a man who is now a highly respectable colored citizen of Boston.   L. M. C.

"This narrative contains some incidents so extraordinary, that, doubtless, many persons, under whose eyes it may chance to fall, will be ready to believe that it is colored highly, to serve a special purpose. But, however it may be regarded by the incredulous, I know that it is full of living truths. I have been well acquainted with the author from my boyhood. The circumstances recounted in her history are perfectly familiar to me. I knew of her treatment from her master; of the imprisonment of her children; of their sale and redemption; of her seven years' concealment; and of her subsequent escape to the North. I am now a resident of Boston, and am a living witness to the truth of this interesting narrative.

GEORGE W. LOWTHER."